In this book, Jeanette Malkin considers a broad spectrum of postwar plays in which characters are created, coerced, and destroyed by language. The playwrights examined are diverse and include Handke, Pinter, Bond, Albee, Mamet, and Shepard, as well as Václav Havel and two of his plays: *The Garden Party* and *The Memorandum*. These playwrights portray language's power over our political, social, and interpersonal worlds. The violence that language does, the "tyranny of words," grabs center stage in these plays. Characters are manipulated and defined through language; their actions and identity limited by verbal options. Writing in a variety of idioms and styles, the playwrights all adduce, and reveal, the link between language and power.

The book will be of interest to students and scholars of drama, theater history, American and European literature, and comparative literature.

VERBAL VIOLENCE IN CONTEMPORARY DRAMA

VERBAL VIOLENCE IN CONTEMPORARY DRAMA

From Handke to Shepard

JEANETTE R. MALKIN

*Department of Theatre History,
Hebrew University, Jerusalem*

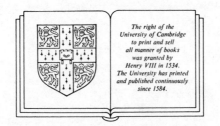

The right of the
University of Cambridge
to print and sell
all manner of books
was granted by
Henry VIII in 1534.
The University has printed
and published continuously
since 1584.

CAMBRIDGE UNIVERSITY PRESS

Cambridge
New York   Port Chester
Melbourne   Sydney

Published by the Press Syndicate of the University of Cambridge
The Pitt Building, Trumpington Street, Cambridge CB2 1RP
40 West 20th Street, New York, NY 10011-4211, USA
10 Stamford Road, Oakleigh, Victoria 3166, Australia

First published 1992

Printed in Great Britain at the University Press, Cambridge

*A cataloguing in publication record for this book is
available from the British Library*

Library of Congress cataloguing in publication data

Malkin, Jeanette, R.
Verbal violence in contemporary drama: from Handke to Shepard/
Jeanette R. Malkin.
p.   cm.
Includes bibliographical references and index.
ISBN 0 521 38335 8
1. Drama – 20th century – History and criticism.   2. Dialogue.
3. Violence in literature.   I. Title.
PN1861.M28   1992
809.2′045 – dc20   91-19764   CIP

ISBN 0 521 38335 8 hardback

Dedicated to the memory of my dear Father
Samuel Rosenzweig

Contents

CHAPTER I

Introduction

Dramatic inquiry into the relationship between man and his language is hardly a uniquely contemporary (post-World War II) phenomenon. Jarry's *King Ubu* (1896), Shaw's *Pygmalion* (1913), Hofmannsthal's *The Difficult Man* (*Der Schwierige*, 1921), some Dada theater evenings, the *Volksstücke* of Ödön von Horváth and Marieluise Fleisser all suggest, in varying ways, a concern with this issue. The group of postwar plays studied here differ, however, in their elevation of language to the central action, and actor; in their pessimistic vision of man's ability to remain free and humane in the face of verbal coercion; and in their warning that man has become a prisoner of his speech. The violent action of language is directed both against the audience and against the characters. In either case language is on trial: it stands accused of usurping and molding reality, of replacing critical thought with fossilized and automatic verbiage, of violating man's autonomy, of destroying his individuality.

The plays that animate these views are varied; they vary in genre, in idiom, and in subject matter. However, they all answer to the double criterion according to which I chose my texts; *thematically*, they are all concerned with man's subjugation or victimization through imposed or inherited verbal structures; *dramatically*, they all demonstrate concrete actions of language which are violent, coercive, and domineering. Language is either metamorphosed into a dramatic antagonist which destroys the characters or forces them into conformity with its pre-given structures and precepts; or it is portrayed as an inescapable prison which determines the characters' fate and defines the limits of their world – conceptual and moral. This double axis, thematic concern and dramatic demonstration, is translated into a multiplicity of dramatic forms in the more than a dozen postwar plays studied here. There is, for example, the abstract thesis drama of Handke's *Kaspar* (alternate title "Sprachfolterung": language torture) – in which language is demonstrated to be the antagonist, the force which shapes and reduces man into mindless obedience; the absurdity of Ionesco's *The Lesson* – in which language is a tyrannical weapon of dominance and destruction; the hyperrealism of Mamet's *American Buffalo* or Kroetz's *Farmyard* – in which a painfully limited, obscene and cliché-ridden language imprisons and brutalizes. There is the menacing torture/interrogation of Pinter's *The Birthday Party* – in which clichés of speech and thought brainwash a social outcast into cleanshaven conformity; the exposure of dogma and jargon in Havel's *The Garden Party* – in which language is shown to embody and control political power; the unceasing vituperation and reality-replacement of Albee's *Who's Afraid of Virginia Woolf?* – in which verbal cruelty defines human relationships; the postmodern language-battles of Shepard's *The Tooth of Crime* – in which power and identity depend on the possession of the more potent verbal style. The reason that these and other related plays need to be studied together is that each focuses on the relationship between man and his language, and all contain a distinctive usage of language as a form of aggression. Moreover, they illuminate a new connection between dramatic language and dramatic violence.

Thus, the plays discussed here focus on the action of language. Language is either the explicit subject, or it is implicit to a degree which makes it impossible to analyze the play's thematics without dealing explicitly with its language. In this sense I am dealing with a theater of language.

In 1956 Jean Vannier published an article in *Théâtre populaire* titled "Langages de l'avant-garde." It was translated and printed in 1963 in the *Tulane Drama Review* as "A Theatre of Language."[1] In this influential article Vannier distinguishes three different types of dramatic languages: "traditional" dramatic language which represents the passions and thoughts of its characters, their "'psychological' relationships which language only translates." This language is always close to that of the public for whom it was written and therefore does not call unusual attention to itself. The second type of dramatic language is one that acts physically upon its audience, "disturbing (its) rapport with the world" by provoking it and forcing it to enter the exaggerated world of the theater. Vannier places this language within the "poetic avant-garde" of the period between the wars, under the aegis of Artaud, through whom language becomes "a vocal form of gesture." This language, Vannier claims, revolutionized the *nature* of dramatic language but not its function, for "this language always remains absorbed in its theatrical finality." That is: the language functions as an element of the theatrical event, not as the focal subject at which the drama is aimed. The third type of dramatic language emerged after the second World War and is what Vannier terms "a theatre of language," in which the *function* of language is radically altered, effecting a "revolution in the *relationship* between theatre and language" (my emphasis). Language which till now had functioned to translate psychological states, or as theatrical gesture, here becomes "the very content of the drama itself" existing before us "as a dramatic reality." Language is thus moved to the forefront of the stage, reflecting not the world of the drama, but itself. For the first time language finds itself "literally *exposed* upon the stage, promoted to the dignity of a theatrical object" (Vannier's emphasis). Language has become the very subject and object of the drama and with it comes "a dramaturgy of human relations at the level of language itself."

Vannier limits his study of this new function of language to the plays of Beckett, Adamov, and Ionesco and thus claims that this language creates a "drama of absurdity," an anti-theater. Most of the plays which I will show to partake of this dramaturgy "at the level of language itself" were written after Vannier's article; thus, his limited scope becomes understandable. While I accept this analysis of a postwar drama in which language reflects back upon itself, becomes the central action of the play and the focus of its content, I will expand this idea to demonstrate that critical language-consciousness functions far beyond mere dramatic absurdity. The problem with such a limited definition is its implicit claim to an equally limited philosophical conclusion. Martin Esslin, whose analysis of language in *The Theatre of the Absurd* (1961) concurs with many of Vannier's insights, draws our attention to the fact that the nonsensical, devalued language of the Absurd assumes and reveals an experienced "insufficiency" of speech, a metaphysical gap between man's need to *mean* and the incapacity of inauthentic, mechanical language to bear or convey the anguish of reality. Alienation from language and its "failure to communicate" is depicted in much of Absurdist drama, according to Esslin, as an expression of both social and existential isolation.[2] As Ionesco paradigmatically shows in his *The Bald Soprano* (*La Cantatrice chauve*, 1948), we stand outside of the words we speak, words which have a life and logic of their own and which inhibit integrity or authentic communication. For Ionesco: "Words are only noise stripped of all meaning. These houses, the sky are only facades of nothingness; people seem to evaporate, everything is threatened, including myself by an imminent, silent sinking into I know not what abyss."[3] This Absurdist perspective develops the intuitions of a turn-of-the-century language *malaise* which was especially strong in central Europe. From Kafka through Hofmannsthal, Broch, Kraus, and up to Ionesco a sense of verbal despair, of "a crisis experienced by many a serious writer of the period," according to Erich Heller,[4] is apparent. In 1904 Yeats wondered whether it was any longer possible to create a play that would live, "out of a dying, or at any rate a very ailing language."[5] Hofmannsthal gave this crisis especially cogent expression in his famous "Lord Chandos Letter" (*Ein Brief*, 1902). Not unlike Sartre's Roquentin, Lord Chandos suffers nausea when faced with words which once had flowed "as through never-congested conduits" with "deep, true, inner form," and had now turned into "whirlpools which gave me vertigo and...led into the void."[6] Sickened by the fluid abstraction of words and their slippery inadequacy, Lord Chandos chooses silence. Hofmannsthal later translated this pessimistic view of language into dramatic form in his play *The Difficult Man*. The "difficult man" of the title is Hans Karl Bühl who, momentarily buried alive in the trenches of World War I, realizes the impossibility of describing experience – that "essentially inexpressible" – through "wohlgesetzte Wörter."

It's rather ridiculous, I admit, for a man to imagine that by stringing words together skilfully he can exert God knows how great an influence in this life of ours, where in the long run everything depends on what is essentially inexpressible. Speech is based on an indecent excess of self-esteem.[7]

Surrounded by the trivial social banter of his friends and servants, watching meaning recede with each attempt to put it into words – Bühl concludes that speech is an *indecency*, a profanation of the final "inexpressible" truth of Experience. Like Lord Chandos, he rejects language. This separation from meaning, the gap felt between language and experience, is one of the essential themes of Absurdist drama (and will be discussed in the context of chapter 3). It is however *not* the theme of this book. Alienation has, in the plays I will discuss, transmuted into aggression. Language is no longer depicted as absurd or isolated; rather it is shown to be actively domineering and dangerous, a force which controls and manipulates man, becoming the essence of his being and the limit of his world. Thus my focus will be rather different from Vannier's; the verbal activity which I will identify functions not only to elevate language into focal attention, but also as a comment on its nature: language as an aggression. This aggression which, in many of the plays under consideration, culminates in acts of language-motivated violence, signals a disturbed and threatening relationship between contemporary man and his language. One of the questions which these plays implicitly pose is: do we control language, or does it control us? Does language speak *for* us – or *through* us.

    The Difficult Man was published in book form in 1921. That same year another Viennese, Ludwig Wittgenstein, published his *Tractatus Logico-philosophicus*, a work which confronted

similar questions in a rather different form. Wittgenstein was
concerned with the logical limits of the "sayable," the boundaries of philosophically legitimate and thus logically truth-
bearing utterances. Through a strict, almost mathematical
procedure Wittgenstein attempted to combat "the bewitchment of our intelligence by means of language."[8] Seeking the relationship between the word and the fact, Wittgenstein in the
Tractatus finds reality eternally clouded by the infinite regression
of words. Language, he claims, can only truthfully picture a
narrow portion of reality: for the rest, its validity is questionable. Wittgenstein believed that if we could only learn to
use language correctly and not burden words with "meanings"
– metaphysical, aesthetic, ethical – which they cannot support,
then clarity would replace chaos. Wittgenstein (who will be
discussed in chapter 2) was fighting "word superstition," as
had a fellow Viennese, Fritz Mauthner, twenty years earlier.
Mauthner's epistemological scepticism was born of a deep
distrust of words which, he argued (and Hans Karl Bühl would
agree), are always at a remove from experience and thus can
never really speak about reality – but only about themselves.
In his *Contributions toward a Critique of Language* (*Beiträge zu einer
Kritik der Sprache*, 1902), Mauthner argues that language
cannot convey truth but only emotive equivalencies, imprecisions, and ambiguities. Like Leibnitz, Herder, or Humboldt
before him, Sapir or Whorf after him, Mauthner makes a case
for the inevitable relativity and deterministic power of language
which traps us each within our individual linguistic skin,
determining our view of the world and of ourselves (this will be
discussed in chapter 4). Both Mauthner and Wittgenstein were
practicing *Sprachkritik* – a critique of language. Motivated by
the same awareness of a "crisis" of language which had
paralyzed Hofmannsthal, they hoped to make us more critical
in our attitude toward language and more aware of the danger
which uncontrolled and unconscious use posed. They thus join
a long row of philosophers, linguists, and critics who through
language scepticism sought to escape the threatening spiral of
language, and to encourage a critical reassessment of our means
of speech. Thus, from Leibnitz to Whorf there runs a common
theme of the "tyranny" of words and man's subjugation

through that which is supposed to be the crowning achievement of his humanity: language.

The "subjugation" of man through language and language-systems is also an implicit element in the influential contemporary linguistic/philosophic movement, Structuralism; although here this subjugation is not necessarily critiqued. Centered in linguistic theory, Structuralism studies the internal functioning of systems by divorcing them from their historical context, and by "bracketing off" both the real (historical) object of its analysis and the human subject through whom the systems operate.[9] Inverting the humanist perspective which finds the source of meaning in the individual, structural analysis focuses on systems of conventions, generative rules which function *through* the individual but neither originate in, nor are controlled by him. As Jonathan Culler puts it in his study of *Structuralist Poetics*:

...once the conscious subject is deprived of its role as source of meaning – once meaning is explained in terms of conventional systems which may escape the grasp of the conscious subject – the self can no longer be identified with consciousness. It is "dissolved" as its functions are taken up by a variety of interpersonal systems that operate through it. The human sciences, which begin by making man an object of knowledge, find, as their work advances, that "man" disappears under structural analysis.[10]

Whatever its philosophic value, or its importance as a tool for cultural analysis, Structuralism in its various forms has certainly deprived the functioning self of free will and thus reaffirmed the deterministic hold of sign-systems – foremost among which is language – over man. This point of view and cultural context are reflected, or questioned, in some of the plays under discussion.

The "aggression" which this study addresses centers to a great extent on the dramatization of man's loss of autonomy and selfhood through the normative pressures, reductive tendencies, or pre-determination of language. Thus, the above mentioned philosophers and linguists, among others, often underlie, and sometimes directly inform, the substance of the following plays.

This study consists of four central chapters, each of which examines one play or a group of plays. The axis of each chapter is different, suggesting four general contexts within which the various devices and implications of verbal aggression can be focused. The division is as follows:

In "Language torture" (chapter 2), Peter Handke's *Kaspar* provides a theoretical or formal context, and a model, for the study of man's *Versprachlichung*; his "speechification" or being rendered a speech object. Kaspar, who begins the play as a virtual *tabula rasa*, a puppet figure, is created and destroyed through disembodied "voices" which force him to assimilate an abstraction of public language – "model" sentences which induce "model" behavior – and thus become, like language itself, well-formed and orderly. Kaspar unfolds less as a person than as a process, the process of man's forced incorporation into Procrustean language systems. These systems become the scaffolding of his consciousness, determine his thoughts and values, and thus the limits of his humanity. It is against this that Kaspar, and Handke, rebel.

"Gagged by language" (chapter 3) views language through a political, or power context. The plays which I discuss by Ionesco, Pinter, and Havel all demonstrate forms of man's domination and subjugation through language. In them, characters are "overtaken" by language and are either destroyed (as in *The Lesson*), or "converted" (as in *The Birthday Party* or *The Garden Party*) – forced into pre-existing verbal molds which, implicitly or explicitly, implicate a ruling ideology. Coercion to conformity and uniformity operates through a number of recurring devices: verbal automatism; the ritualization of language into magical formulae; the use of extended clichés and jargon which control meaning and preclude its development. In each case, to control language is to control, and manipulate, power.

"Language as a prison" (chapter 4) centers on the social implications of verbal deprivation. Kroetz, Bond, and

Mamet all recreate the fragmented and radically restricted language of fringe or debased social groups. Rooted in three different nationalities, their plays nevertheless share in uncommunicative banalities, "unowned" language, excessive obscenity; and demonstrate the relationship between inarticulacy and brutality. Deprived of free verbal options, their characters show an alarming lack of compassion and all seem pre-determined by the verbal poverty which shapes their limited desires, and informs their violent behavior. The seven plays discussed demonstrate and indict the deterministic relationship between verbal poverty and social immorality.

"Wrestling with language" (chapter 5) focuses on the inter-personal context of verbal aggression. Albee's self-consciously obscene *Who's Afraid of Virginia Woolf?* and Shepard's postmodern verbal style-battles in *The Tooth of Crime* provide models for the connection between language, identity, and relationship-struggles. Aggressive and subversive, language functions here both as a dangerous weapon and as a form of rebellion against deadening conformity. The abundant use of self-conscious and self-referential language alerts us to the centrality of language in the formation of personal identity and inter-personal responsibility.

CHAPTER 2

Language torture: on Peter Handke's Kaspar

Die Sprache spricht, nicht der Mensch. Der Mensch
spricht nur, indem er geschicklich der Sprache entspricht.
(Language speaks, not man. Man speaks only in so far as
he skilfully conforms to language.)[1]

This quote from Martin Heidegger might have been written by
Peter Handke about his play *Kaspar*. It concisely sums up
Handke's view, or rather critique, of language, and in a voice
– controlled, aphoristic, sensitive to the texture and cadence of
a well-formed sentence – which is an echo of Handke's own.
Kaspar (1968), Handke's first full-length play, is about language
and the ways in which the form of language shapes the lives of
man. The "story" of the play is that of one speechless man –
Kaspar – and how he is created and destroyed through his
forced acquisition of language. "The play could also be called
speech torture," Handke writes,[2] thereby making explicit his view
of the relationship between language and man: a relationship
of torture, pain, and coercion. The play shows, Handke
explains, "how someone can be made to speak through
speaking."[3] This is, then, the central "action" of the play:
Speech (represented by three disembodied voices, *Einsager*, i.e.
Prompters) creating the Speechless (Kaspar) in its own image.
These are also the two main "characters" of the play: Kaspar,
a clown figure, a human abstraction whom Handke ironically
calls "the HERO"[4]; and Speech, voices heard over loudspeakers,
voices to which Kaspar reacts and with which he is in conflict,
voices which teach and finally coerce Kaspar into becoming
like speech itself: well-formed and orderly.

It is, of course, a misuse of dramatic terminology to speak, as
I have, of "story," "action," and "character" in connection

with *Kaspar*. These are, after all, the terms of an illusionist theatre which Handke rejects. Handke doesn't tell a story through the action of characters – he shows the action of words on a stage: a theatrical event.

The audience...should recognize at once that they will witness an event that plays only on stage and not in some other reality. They will not experience a story but watch a theatrical event...because no story will take place, the audience will not be in a position to imagine that there is a sequel to the story, other than their own...[5]

Not unlike Brecht, Handke takes pains to alienate the audience from the stage event, to confront the audience with the stage event, and ultimately hopes to "make us aware," more sensitive, more conscious, *through* the stage event.[6] In his earlier audience-provoking *Sprechstück* (Speech-play), *Offending the Audience* (*Publikumsbeschimpfung*, 1966), the audience is turned into the "action." It is frontally addressed, and attacked, and becomes the subject of the play. *Kaspar* contains elements of this, but the verbal aggression is more sophisticated, attacking not only the audience (especially through the irritating insistence of the "intermission text"), but also destroying the character Kaspar and, most importantly, exposing the viciousness of language itself. "The only thing that preoccupies me as a writer...is nausea at stupid speechification (*Versprachlichung*) and the resulting brutalization of people," Handke told an interviewer.[7] This connection between speech and brutality, the claim that speech *is* a brutality, is the theme of most of Handke's early plays, but is most forcefully and coherently demonstrated in *Kaspar*.

Thematically Handke's plays have two major thrusts: they attack the conventions of the illusionist theatre tradition and its complacent audience, and thus continue a theatrical "rejectionist" tradition which runs from Jarry through Dada, Artaud, Pirandello, Brecht, and includes contemporary experimental theatre in most of its forms. This theme is particularly pronounced in Handke's "speech-plays," but also occurs in *Kaspar*, *Quodlibet* (1970), and *The Ride Across Lake Constance* (1971). In the last, the "characters" (in the printed text) are named for prominent German actors, thus signifying that there are no characters, only actors on a stage who play themselves. Handke's second theme recurs even more obsessively in his plays: the dramatization of the nature of language. As Richard Gilman put it, Handke's plays "demonstrate how we operate with words and are operated upon by them... Handke's dramaturgy comes directly out of his 'nausea', the sickness induced by the sight of language escaped from our control, the feeling of helplessness in the face of its perverse and independent life."[8] This nausea is both the result of "stupid speechification" and the beginning of its cure. "One should learn to be nauseated by language, as the hero of Sartre's *Nausea* is by things," Handke has said; "At least that would be a beginning of consciousness."[9] This nausea is akin to the sickness and vertigo which Ionesco experienced while writing *The Bald Soprano* (*La Cantatrice chauve*). Language, he felt, "had gone mad"; rather than serve, it had become master of the speaker.[10] For Handke – as for Ionesco, Pinter, Havel, Albee, and other postwar dramatists – language seems to have taken on a life of its own, and with this life a power, a demonic and threatening usurpation of reality.

Handke's stated aim of "encircling" his audience with words[11] is a dramatization of how language functions upon us: closing us in within its own laws and restrictions, coercing our obedience to its forms, rules, limitations. Handke has repeatedly said that the goal of his plays is not "to revolutionize, but to make aware,"[12] and believes that his literature "can effect changes in others."[13] What we are to be made aware of is precisely the danger of our subservience to inherited verbal forms which condition our consciousness and determine our thoughts, feelings, and actions. Handke is, then, actually involved in what Fritz Mauthner termed a "Critique of Language," and like Mauthner he would make us critical in our attitude toward language and direct us away from "word superstition." In this concern for language and its abuses Handke becomes part of a tradition with a peculiarly strong hold in his homeland, Austria. Language scepticism and a crisis of faith in language's potency and benevolence has been voiced in this century by many Austrian writers and philosophers.

Hugo von Hofmannsthal's despairing "Lord Chandos Letter"
(1902) expresses the same nausea at the sight of words as
Handke experiences. Words, cut off from humanly felt
meaning, become threatening objects: "everything disintegrated into parts...words floated round me; they congealed into
eyes which stared at me and into which I was forced to stare
back...led into the void."[14] Lord Chandos is overtaken by a
verbal paralysis which will later characterize Hofmannsthal's
Count Bühl of *The Difficult Man* (*Der Schwierige*, 1921) who,
having been buried alive in the trenches of World War I, loses
faith in the efficacy and integrity of the slippery words which
try to define him. Karl Kraus's mistrust of language and his
concern with the abuse of language by cliché and rhetoric is a
recurring theme in his essays. He warned that we must "learn
to see an abyss where platitudes abound"[15] and demonstrated
the danger of mindless language in his enormous "drama" –
it does not quite fit into any one genre – *The Last Days of
Mankind* (1922). Ödön von Horváth's *Bildungsjargon*, his critical
recreation of the clichés, platitudes, and sentimental idioms
which characterized the post-Hapsburgian Austrian middle
class, condemns a society by exposing it through its language.
Hermann Broch's *The Death of Virgil* (1945) contains some of
the longest sentences in literature, sentences which struggle for
a precision of expression which escapes him, and obsesses
Handke. From Ingeborg Bachmann to Thomas Bernhard to
Handke, this obsessive "Critique of language" is carried over
into post-World War II Austrian literature.

Echoes of this century's inquiry into the nature of language
abound in *Kaspar*, and foremost among them are the
reverberations of the work of another Austrian: Ludwig
Wittgenstein. Both Wittgenstein's *Tractatus Logico-philosophicus*
(1920) and his *Philosophical Investigations* (1951) suggest that all
philosophical problems are created by linguistic confusion.
Hanke seems to believe, with Wittgenstein, that our problems
can only be solved by:

looking into the workings of our language, and that in such a way as
to make us recognize those workings: in despite of an urge to
misunderstand them. The problems are solved not by giving new

information, but by arranging what we have always known. Philosophy is a battle against the bewitchment of our intelligence by means of language.[16]

Handke seems to adopt Wittgenstein's proposed method of not giving new information but only "arranging what we have always known." As Handke has said, "my words are not descriptions, only quotations,"[17] i.e. rearrangements of common coins of speech, quotes from a variety of sources, "found language," not verbal invention. As with Wittgenstein, language itself is used to alert us to the danger of language: it is not only the subject but also the strategy. Although *Kaspar* is certainly not a philosophic treatise, it does share "a common ground and atmosphere" with Wittgenstein. As Richard Gilman has claimed: Handke's play constitutes "the aesthetic counterpart of Wittgenstein's thought"[18] and draws on some of the same premises. In his *Tractatus*, Wittgenstein attempts an inference from the logical structure of language to the world, and assumes that a definite relation must exist between the two. Language is a mirror that reflects the world in its logical form; the world comes to be for us only through and within language:[19] "The limits of my language mean the limits of my world."[20] Similarly, Handke seems to imply that through language, which both forms and limits us, existential as well as social issues can be exposed and affected.

The play *Kaspar* begins in visual chaos: we see a stage strewn with random domestic objects. The back curtain then begins to move, as someone seeks the slit through which to enter. After a few futile attempts, Kaspar finally succeeds and is "born" on the stage. Kaspar's face is a mask which expresses astonishment and confusion; he is "the incarnation of astonishment" (2).[21] His clothes – large hat, wide pants, untied clumsy shoes – are those of a clown. One connotation of his name becomes immediately obvious: Kasper (Kasperl) is the name of a German clown figure, similar to the English Punch. Kaspar is at first barely capable of walking. Like an infant, he is a stranger to his body and to the objects which surround him. His mind too is unformed: he is a virtual *tabula rasa*. The object of the play, as in many a German *Bildungsroman*, is to demonstrate the "education" of an innocent. Only here the education is achieved through the imprinting of the forms of language on a blank mind.

From the start Kaspar possesses one grammatically correct though pre-conscious sentence which he repeats over and over, without comprehension: "I want to be a person like somebody else was once." This sentence is abstracted from the historical Kaspar Hauser, that strange sixteen-year-old youth who, one day in 1828, appeared in Nuremberg, emaciated and terrified, with a letter in his hand and one cryptic sentence in his possession – "Ich möcht a sochener Reiter warn, wie mei Voter aner gween is" (i.e. "I want to be a Horseman (or Rider) like my father was").[22] He had apparently lived in almost total isolation until his appearance, and was subsequently taken in and educated by a guardian. Some years later he was mysteriously attacked and died of stab wounds. The image of a grown man with the innocent and blank mind of a child, suddenly thrust into the world and confronted with the need to learn the speech and ways of society, sparked the imagination of many writers before Handke. Verlaine, Hofmannsthal, and Trakl used Kaspar as a symbol of the Poet or the Stranger "without country and without king" who, as Verlaine saw it, "does not know what he is to do in this world." Other writers – Hans Arp, Jakob Wasserman, Ernst Jandl – were also intrigued by the reverberations of this strange figure.[23] Handke, of course, does not write about the historical Kaspar Hauser, but rather finds in the life of that man "the model of a sort of linguistic myth" which came to represent for him the isolation and estrangement of men "at odds with themselves and their environment."[24] Handke abstracts from Kaspar Hauser the essence of that estrangement, and of the process of social integration through linguistic assimilation. In a sense, *Kaspar* is the study of an attempted – and failed – socialization process.

The text of *Kaspar* is divided into sixty-five numbered units or "scenes." This division is, however, not apparent in production and the viewing audience would experience the play as consisting of two acts or parts, separated by an intermission (to which I will return). Within each act, moments of sudden darkness further divide up the action. Only in section

8 do the Prompters begin to speak. With their first sentence the process of Kaspar's education, his "reconstruction" through language, as Handke put it,[25] begins. Handke is very precise in describing the voices (he suggests three) of the unseen Prompters. These voices, which emanate "from all sides" of the stage, must be devoid of all warmth, humor, or irony; must harbor neither overtones nor undertones. Since they speak without nuance the Prompters remain formal – never personal – teachers: they embody a *principle*, not a personality. The voices must sound as though they were speaking over a telephone, a megaphone, a radio or TV set, some technical medium which sets the voices at an even further remove and also implicates the instruments of mass language transportation. The voices are to sound automatic, conventionalized, like – Handke suggests – the voices of sports commentators, or the telephone voice which gives the time, or the precise voices on language-course records. They are *corporate* voices: "they speak comprehensibly"(8). These instructions are included in the rather long opening stage directions which Handke stipulates should be read over a loudspeaker, over and over, as the audience enters the theater and waits for the play to begin. Thus Handke's intentions are meant to be explicitly understood by the audience from the start. In the stage directions of section 8 Handke comments that the text which the Prompters speak "is not theirs." This is a clear indication that what we are about to read is *not* spontaneous dialogue, thoughts which emerge from the psyche and personality of some unseen individuals. Rather, we will read a text which is taken, borrowed, "quoted" from the stock of public language, a language which – like the Prompters' voices – surrounds *us* "from all sides," no longer belonging to anyone but directed "from above" against everyone.

In the first phase of Kaspar's education he is commended on the possession of a sentence with which he can make himself noticeable in the dark; a sentence is the beginning of comfort, shelter, belonging. It is self-awareness and self-assertion. But more importantly for the Prompters: a sentence is the beginning of order; "You have a sentence to bring order into every disorder" (12). The Prompters begin by trying to teach Kaspar to master objects. An object without a name is a threat, a source of chaos and pain, he is told. By naming it, Kaspar can gain mastery, he can protect himself against the arbitrariness of the phenomenal world. But, to achieve this, one sentence is not enough. Kaspar must learn many sentences and the relation between sentences: he must acquire language. The Prompters' first task is, therefore, to rid Kaspar of his one automatic, pre-conscious sentence – to which he stubbornly clings – and to replace it with their sentences. They do this through an unrelenting barrage of words which confuse and torture Kaspar, depriving him of his verbal innocence. The Prompters first speak in chopped up, rhythmic lines: "You begin, with yourself, you, are a, sentence you, could form, of yourself, innumerable, sentences..." Kaspar tries to defend himself against this onslaught with his one already fading possession: his sentence. Although the meaning of the Prompters' words is at this stage subordinated to the sound pattern of an almost ritual exorcism, it is significant that Kaspar is being told that he *is* a sentence, but that he could (if his education succeeds, that is) spin out of himself innumerable sentences. Kaspar grows more confused. His sentence twists into disorder and, despite his efforts, even the single words finally disintegrate under the Prompters' will. He can only utter letters and then sputter sounds. In the end he is silenced, his resistance broken: "His sentence has been exorcised"(17). The first phase of Kaspar's reconstruction has ended in success.

It has been suggested that Kaspar's meager original sentence contains his potential for individuality and autonomy. With its loss Kaspar is defenceless and open to the pressures of social conformity, which is the goal of his education.[26] Only at the very end of the play will Kaspar again display resistance to the process of acquiring orderly speech, and with it an ordered existence. The paradox of Kaspar's desire to cling to his one sentence is that his sentence can only acquire meaning through its relation to other sentences. Yet, in learning that relation, Kaspar must also learn other sentences (and thus the formal order and logic of speech) which consequently rob his one sentence of its uniqueness and place it within the accepted order, and meaning, of public speech. Sentences are of great

importance to Handke. All of his early plays are collections,
almost litanies, of (usually) well-formed sentences, grammatical
specimens. Handke goes so far as to claim that "in *Kaspar*,
history is conceived as a story of sentences."[27] Kaspar is never
taught words, only sentences, verbal structures which become
the scaffolding of his consciousness. "Only with a sentence, not
with a word, can you ask leave to speak," the Prompters tell
him (9). A sentence is a unit of order, and the progression from
"right-speaking" to right-thinking and right-acting is assumed
by the Prompters to be inevitable. "We are delivered to the
Sentence," claims Roland Barthes. "The Sentence is hier-
archical: it implies subjections, subordinations, internal
reactions…The Sentence is complete: it is precisely that
language which is complete…it is the power of completion
which defines sentence mastery and marks…the agents of the
Sentence."[28] "Sentences, not words, are the essence of speech,"
wrote the linguist Benjamin Lee Whorf.[29] A language, he
claims, "is a *system*, not just an assemblage of norms,"[30] and the
basic unit of that system, its building block, is the sentence.
Handke shows that this system, this hierarchy, is self-generating
and selfhood-annihilating. "…a sentence is a monster,"
Kaspar will later realize; "…with each new sentence I become
nauseous…I am in someone's hand" (65). The "monstrosity"
of sentences is that to speak one is to be already integrated,
subsumed, subordinated within the larger system of language.
Kaspar will finally speak in the same voice as the Prompters, he
will become like them and realize that: "Already with my first
sentence I was trapped" (64). He will learn that to accept any
pre-given system is to be controlled by that system.

After losing his original sentence Kaspar begins to acquire
speech. He begins by uttering individual, disconnected words,
words which will recur and echo throughout the play: words
which conjure up visions of coercion, torture, terror.

How dark…
Pronounced dead…
Boiled. From behind…
Never stood. Screams.
Faster. Pus. Thrashing.

Whimpers. The knee.
Back. Crawls. (18)

Finally Kaspar utters his first complete, and telling sentence:
"At that time, while I was still away, my head never ached as
much, and I was not tortured the way I am now that I am
here" (18).
The stage goes dark, Kaspar has been taught to speak.

With Kaspar's first gropings for speech and his first conscious
sentence, the thematic center of the play is established: order
= torture. The images of brutal torture, of beatings and
screams, of pus and fear, grow more graphic and insistent as the
play progresses and Kaspar's coercion into speech mold
becomes firmer. The root image is that of the interrogation
room where the reluctant victim is "brought to speech," where
the desired answers and confessions are tortured out of the
interrogated. This image appears in other of Handke's works.
Hörspiel (*Radioplay*) no. 1, for example, is a nightmarish
transcription of an interrogation in which the questions and
responses are not synchronized, and the terror of manipulation,
all verbal, becomes physically painful.

They persecuted me with words to such an extent, that even in sleep
I did not belong to myself, but to the words: they pursued me into
sleep itself with their words.[31]

The interrogated is overtaken by the words, as is Kaspar.
Kaspar is taught that he lives within sentences, inhabits
them; and a man of good taste, of order and responsibility, will
surround himself with sentences which – like furniture – make
him feel at home.

What matters is that you form sentences that you can at least feel at
ease with...You need homely sentences: sentences as furnishings:
sentences which you could actually save: sentences which are a
luxury. (22)

Handke often compares language to housekeeping since both
are processes which maintain order and contain the individual.
Moreover, it is only through the order of the one that the other
can be achieved, since both – an orderly sentence and an

orderly house – are determined and demanded by social norms. The order which the Prompters demand, which is their one guiding and consistent ideology, is all-encompassing. The order of language, of objects, of morals, of thought, of desires: this is a middle-class, sound, structured order within which one set of reality implicates all others. A sentence, therefore, is more than just a collection of words: it is a model structure, a paradigm with which everything else must be compared. "Ever since you can speak a normal sentence you are beginning to compare everything that you perceive with this normal sentence, so that the sentence becomes a model" (20).

In section 25, a high point of Kaspar's education, Kaspar begins to assimilate the Prompters' order. This section consists entirely of a row of aphorisms which the Prompters speak at Kaspar while he, gradually adjusting his movements to the rhythm of their sentences, organizes the stage. The aphorisms begin with dictums of order:

Each new order creates disorder...
Good order is the foundation of all things...
The room informs you about its inhabitant...
Disorder outrages all right-thinking men.
One of the most beautiful things in life is a well-set table...
A place for everything and everything in its place.

These platitudes of middle-class order are presented as the basic norms of "right-thinking men." Cleanliness, neatness, politeness, submissiveness, the clichés of the right-thinking and right-living are Kaspar's models of speech and axioms of thought. The truth of these sententious statements, and a certain emotional power, are implied as the aphorisms become rhythmic poems which promise a happiness that only order can bring:

The order
of the objects
creates
all
prerequisites
for
happiness.

While the Prompters have been reciting their truisms of order, Kaspar has been transforming the stage – which until now had contained a haphazard jumble of domestic objects – into a perfectly arranged room, a home, the "picture" of the dictums of housely order he is being taught. The stage becomes a meticulously tidy bourgeois salon, almost a parody, with the requisite vase of flowers and bowl of fruit, even a painting which matches the decor. And Kaspar exchanges his motley clothes for a suit which fits in with the setting. "Everything on stage goes with everything else."

During Kaspar's transformation from clown to conformity, to the "picture" of a right-thinking member of society, echoes of the philosophical vocabulary of Wittgenstein are heard. The core of Wittgenstein's widely influential *Tractatus* is his "picture theory" of language. Wittgenstein suggests that propositions – sentences – are logical "pictures" of reality. "The proposition is a picture of reality. The proposition is a model of the reality as we think it is."[32] A sentence shows the form of a possible "fact" (i.e. element of reality) through its structure and the relation of its parts. "The elements of the picture stand, in the picture, for the objects... In order to be a picture, a fact must have something in common with what it pictures."[33] The sentence *corresponds* to reality (the world) and mirrors it; and we may infer from the image in the mirror to that which it reflects. Wittgenstein's picture theory aims to clarify the way in which language functions and what we can empirically know and say through it. It attempts to demarcate the limits of language and thus to prevent our speaking non-sense. "Everything that can be thought at all can be thought clearly. Everything that can be said can be said clearly."[34] The Prompters use, and abuse, Wittgenstein by borrowing his vocabulary of thought and perverting it to their own ends. At the height of Kaspar's indoctrination he is told:

Every object must be the *picture* of an object: every proper table is the *picture* of a table. Every house must be the *picture* of a house... (23, my emphasis)

Moreover:

A table is a true table when the picture of the table coincides with the table... If the table is already a picture of a table, you cannot change it: if you can't change the table, you must change yourself: you must become a picture of yourself just as you must make the table into a picture of a table and every possible sentence into a picture of a possible sentence. (24)

For the Prompters, the "picture" of an object is not its correspondence to reality, but rather its *ideal* form. Almost like a Platonic Idea, the picture is said to exist before the object: language *creates* reality. Thus, language ceases to be a mirror, a logical model of the world in Wittgenstein's sense, rather it becomes its determining factor.[35] "Every object can be what you designate it to be," Kaspar is told (28). For Wittgenstein a proposition can only meaningfully picture empirical reality; i.e. it can share its logical form. The Prompters, on the contrary, insist that Kaspar reject empirical reality and the evidence of sense experience in favor of the dictates of language: "...if you see the object differently from the way you *speak* of it, you must be mistaken" (28). Not only must objects fit their "picture," their verbal form, but Kaspar too must change *himself* in order to become a "picture" of himself; i.e. in order to fit the inherited forms of language, the verbal mold into which he is being forced.

Kaspar, who in the beginning was overcome by the strangeness of the phenomenal world, has learned to master objects by subjecting them to verbal order. But while learning to create order, Kaspar, too, has *been* ordered. He has become one more object, the object of language. The proof of his subjugation is in his movements which perfectly reproduce not only the contents of the Prompters' dictums of order, but also the form of their sentences: he begins to move in perfect rhythm to their speech. Quite contrary to Wittgenstein's aims, Kaspar has been "bewitched" by means of language. "People act about situations in ways which are like the ways they talk about them," wrote the relativist Whorf.[36] The phenomenal world is only an extension of our linguistic world; and we experience objects and nature through the conceptual grid imposed upon us by our language. According to Whorf:

We dissect nature along lines laid down by our native languages... We cut nature up, organize it into concepts, and ascribe significances as we do, largely because we are parties to an agreement to organize it in this way – an agreement that holds throughout our speech community and is codified in the patterns of our language. The agreement is, of course, an implicit and unstated one, *but its terms are absolutely obligatory*; we cannot talk at all except by subscribing to the organization and classification of data which the agreement decrees.[37]

We tend to hold on to the illusion that through speech we "express" ourselves spontaneously, but in fact "this illusory appearance results from the fact that the obligatory phenomena within the apparently free flow of talk are so completely *autocratic* that speaker and listener are bound unconsciously as though in the grip of a law of nature."[38] Whorf's use of "autocratic" to describe the power of language is very much in accord with Handke's depiction of language. Autocratic means absolute rule and literally, self-might: i.e. language has an independent power which, as Whorf claims, *determines* the framework of the thought and behavior of the speaker. It is this independence of language which Handke demonstrates in the floating voices of the Prompters, voices which have a life of their own and which fulfill the role of a dramatic character. In Handke's extension of Whorf, language not only determines the limits of thought, it victimizes the speaker by robbing him of his autonomy and compelling him to pre-formed speech. Barthes, in his "Inaugural Lecture" at the Collège de France, addressed precisely this point:

Language is legislation, speech is its code. We do not see the power which is in speech because we forget that all speech is a classification, and that all classifications are oppressive: *ordo* means both distribution and commination. Jakobson has shown that a speech-system is defined less by what it permits us to say than by what it compels us to say... To speak, and, with even greater reason, to utter a discourse is not, as is too often repeated, to communicate; it is to subjugate... In speech, then, servility and power are inescapably intermingled. If we call freedom not only the capacity to escape power but also and especially the capacity to subjugate no one, then freedom can exist only outside language. Unfortunately, human language has no exterior: there is not exit.[39]

This subjugation through language now becomes even more explicit as the Prompters, not yet satisfied with Kaspar's achievements, proceed to drive out any remains of individuality.

After Kaspar's transformation into the picture of a right-thinking, orderly citizen of the speech-world, a double process of higher education ensues. Kaspar is taught model sentences "with which an orderly person struggles through life" (27), while also being subjected to verbal torture and threats of terror. These are, perhaps, meant to ensure his compliance with his new reality, while also exposing the nature of that reality. In the following sections (26-7) the relationship between order (language) and terror (subjugation) becomes ever more deeply entwined. The Prompters' model sentences evoke images of fear and violent pain; and the orderly form of speech is shown to correspond to this terror, to shape it. While Kaspar recites a semi-logical sequence which leads him to the conclusion that "everything that is orderly is beautiful," and "everything that is in order is in order because I say to myself that it is in order" (26), the Prompters whisper repetitious images which conjure up the, torture chamber or the interrogation room.

... Slammed the door. Rolled up sleeves. Struck the chairs. Beaten to a pulp. Struck the table... Struck between the eyes. Broke the china... Knocked out. Beat down the request... Struck a low blow. Exterminated from head to toe. Smashed the floor... Struck down the heckler. Stayed tough. Smashed all prejudices. (26)

These are "model" sentences in that they are (especially in the original German) idiomatic expressions, correct forms of speech, common conjugations of common verbs. The expression "beaten to a pulp" is a good example of what Handke is doing here. Its German equivalent is the rather picturesque and quite common phrase: "windelweich geprügelt," whose connotations are rather different from its English translation. "Windelweich" literally means: soft as a baby's diaper. This positive image of infancy and great softness, security, care, is combined with "geprügelt," beaten, to form a horrifying if incongruous image. It implies that the victim is beaten into the soft compliance of a baby's diaper. This is an idiom and, of course, we rarely think of the literal implications of our idiomatic speech. It is precisely the automatic combination of words, of verbal forms and formulae, which is here equated with terror. The terror is not merely in the meaning of the words, but in the form, the fact of their grammatical correctness, their idiomatic expressiveness. The physical domination which they express is equated with the verbal domination which their common, unthinking usage implies. The horror of these sentences of physical abuse is, perhaps, that the terror which they express is *well* expressed.

Now Kaspar is finally taught the crucial lesson of speech, the lesson which will rid him of any last traces of individuality: speech – which is always public, pre-formed, and inherited – is *prior* to thought. When you have begun to speak: you will *think what you are saying*:

Say what you think. Say what you don't think. When you have begun to speak you will think what you are saying. You think what you are saying, that means you can think what you are saying, that means it is good that you think what you are saying, that means you ought to think what you are saying, that means, on the one hand, that you may think what you are saying, and on the other hand, that you must think what you are saying, because you are not allowed to think anything *different* from what you are saying. Think what you are saying. (27)

Language, as Whorf wrote, "is not merely a reproducing instrument for voicing ideas but rather is itself the *shaper* of ideas, the program and guide for the individual's mental activity..."[40] Taken to an extreme, this indeed implies that we cannot help but think that which we speak. In a poem titled "Einige Alternativen in der indirekten Rede" ("A Few Alternatives in Indirect Speech"), Handke wrote: "But then again words, they say, are the alternative to THINKING," and the only choices which words allow us are: "PARIER oder KREPIER!".[41] The ironic battle-cry which ends the poem – OBEY or DIE! – is precisely Kaspar's situation. Until now he has obeyed the dictates of language; but forced completely to adjust thought to speech and thus robbed both of individuality and of the potential for creativity, he finally breaks down and sputters a long and incoherent list of variations on the verb "to be," ending with the thrice repeated statement (echoing the biblical God's definition of himself): "I am who I am." This breakdown under the strain of verbal torture is not so much a mental collapse (*Kaspar* has no real psychological dimension) as a disintegration of selfhood. His existence has been displaced and replaced by his *Versprachlichung*, i.e. the reduction of his being to words. Kaspar's last sentence as an individual is one of bewildered and very human pain: "Why are there so many black worms flying about?" (27).[42] With this inward-looking cry, the stage blackens.

The first part of *Kaspar* ends with a cowed and brainwashed Kaspar reciting a self-descriptive list of attributes which perfectly fit the nondescript though well-adjusted personality which the Prompters have been trying to create. He goes so far as to declare, in rhymed verse, his acceptance of sentences/ order and the rationality they require.

Früher war mir jeder vernünftige Satz eine Last
und jede vernünftige Ordnung verhasst
doch künftig
bin ich vernünftig. (58)
(Once every reasonable sentence was a burden/ and to all reasonable order I felt aversion / but since / I've become sensible. (my translation))

Kaspar has become the master of objects and the servant of language. The world no longer frightens him, for it is now an orderly world: the orderly world of language.

Following an intermission, the play resumes with two Kaspars on stage. Their masks are now no longer the incarnation of astonishment; rather, they portray contentment. With the breakdown of Kaspar's individuality, newly acquired through speech and simultaneously lost to language's constraints of form and order, other Kaspars begin to appear. They are exact duplicates, mirror-images of the original Kaspar: but they don't speak, they only perform actions prescribed by the

Prompters. As the Kaspars multiply on stage, the Prompters give a long and detailed lecture on the methods of torture used "in the process of putting-into-order" (61). This is not the first time that physical torture is described as the logical extension of verbal order, but here, in the opening words of Act II, torture takes on a new, sinister significance.

Water dripping regularly
down on one's head
is no reason
to complain about a lack of order
a sip of acid in one's mouth
or a kick in the guts
or two sticks
in the nostrils being wriggled
about
or something on that order
only more pointed
introduced
into the ears...
is no reason
to lose any words over the lack
of order:
for
in the process
of putting-into-order
for better or worse
one makes others sing...
(denn
beim In-Ordnung-Bringen
bringt man wohl oder übel
andre zum Singen...) (61)

This poem, which in the original German consists of soft rhymes and a lilting rhythm, is another almost grotesque example of the contrast between the well-formedness of language, its smooth, correct surface, and the terror it harbors. Handke has chosen to give the most repulsive, graphic descriptions of torture poetic form. Like the "regelmässiger Wassertropfen" (water dripping regularly) which the Prompters invoke, their words drip and poison Kaspar's mind. The torture which they propose is presented as a rational and

justifiable process, a guard to order. Force, as Kaspar was
previously told, "is indeed a dubious method, but it can be
useful" (27). And the usefulness of torture is that "those who
have been brought into order" through the torture (of
language) can best implement "sentences valid for all" ("[die]
für alle gültigen Sätzen") (61). Torture, like the Prompters'
language, is reductive: it reduces the individual to a common
level of compliance with order. This is precisely the process
which Kaspar is undergoing: he is being tortured into
embracing, and endorsing, "sentences valid for all."

While the Prompters describe torture in rhythmic, seductive
language, their words *act* as torture on Kaspar, and the result
is as predicted: total integration. Now, when Kaspar speaks, his
voice resembles the voices of the Prompters. Using verse, as
they had, Kaspar recounts his own history from uncon-
sciousness to speech, advocating order and speech-order. It is
now Kaspar who recites the dictums of social integration,
obedience, cleanliness, firmness, compliance, which the Prompters had previously taught him.

Everyone must wash his hands
before eating
everyone must empty his pockets
before a beating...
everyone must clean his nose
everyone should smell like a rose... (62)

During this recital a strange thing occurs; the five duplicate
Kaspars sitting on the couch begin to make unusual noises:
sounds of sobbing and giggling, of croaking, lamenting, hissing,
sounds of nature – wind, leaves, sea – screams, groans. The
noise becomes overwhelming and Kaspar is forced to shout his
mechanical and unending litany of order. Thus, while the
ultimate rules of order are expounded by Kaspar himself, the
elemental sounds of disorder – both in man and in nature –
puncture and drown him out.

Kaspar persists, he sings a hymn to order, joined by the
Prompters to create a canon of faith listing table manners and
rules of personal hygiene. All the while, the duplicate Kaspars

create an ever growing din with grating, filing, snorting, clapping, churning noises like those, perhaps, of madness. If there is any psychological dimension to this play, it is in these externalized reactions of the duplicate Kaspars to the mental and physical conformity of the original Kaspar. It is unclear whether these duplicate Kaspars represent "others," i.e. society, of which Kaspar has become an undifferentiated part; or splinters of the inner original Kaspar. Both suggestions have been put forward and both possibilities are probably equally obvious precisely because they are equally valid. Visually, the appearance on stage of precise copies of Kaspar cannot help but evoke the equation – already fairly explicit in the spoken text itself – that verbal conformity *is* social conformity and purports the loss of individuality. On the other hand, the multiple Kaspars do not act merely as reflections of the original Kaspar but also – increasingly as Kaspar becomes more like the Prompters – as rejections of the conformity which Kaspar has accepted. And indeed, Kaspar's second mental collapse, following his declaration of faith in the strictures of order, results from the reactions of the duplicate Kaspars. Kaspar must strain against a growing tide of non-verbal, chaotic, elemental noise. This noise – which is actually parallel to the "noise" of the truisms which he sputters forth – is also the noise of consciousness or, more basically, of a subconscious self in rebellion against the imposed restrictions of social regimentation. As containers of multiple connotations – society and splinter selves – the duplicate Kaspars thus function as symbolic correlatives for the process which Kaspar undergoes. It is significant that the duplicates appear after Kaspar's first breakdown (27) in which he questions his very mode of being through the wild combinations of the verb "to be." They will remain on stage until the end of the play and are destroyed together with the original Kaspar.

The cacophony of sound – Kaspar's recitation of norms, the Prompters' accompanying singing, and the squeaking, barking, blowing, grating noises of the duplicate Kaspars – suddenly comes to a halt; and a disoriented Kaspar asks, in eight slight variations:

What was it
that
I said
just now? (64)

Kaspar has lost his train of thought; his barrage of banalities
seems to have been wiped out by the duplicate Kaspars' chaotic
noises. All of the Kaspars now begin to giggle and laugh, and
Kaspar, in final rebellion against what he has become, says –
in rhyme – :

Jeder Satz
ist für die Katz
jeder Satz ist für
die Katz
jeder Satz ist für die Katz. (64)
(Nicely rendered by N. Hern as "All words are for the birds.")[43]

After this rejection of the logic of language, and before his
final destruction, two further sections of speech occur. Both are
recapitulations and confessions by Kaspar. The first (64) begins
calmly and in coherent sentences, although the tone is now
personal, subjective, an autobiography. It differs from the
previous self-history (62) in that prose rather than verse is
spoken; and Kaspar uses his own, rather than the Prompters',
voice. Further, whereas the previous self-history follows the
Prompters' torture sentences and leads to Kaspar's acceptance
of order, this confession follows Kaspar's rejection of orderly
language and leads to his realization that "Already with my
first sentence I was trapped."

The last section of the play shows the final rebellion of
Kaspar and his destruction by the stage curtain, thus returning
the "story" to the theatre reality to which it belongs. That
scene is totally chaotic. Kaspar speaks a nonsensical text which
Handke has called "deranged,"[44] interspersed with tortured
insights into what he now perceives to be the true nature of
language:

...a sentence is a monster...with each new sentence I become
nauseous: figuratively: I have been turned topsy-turvy: I am in
someone's hand...I cannot rid myself of myself any more... (65)

The play ends with Kaspar repeating, five times, the words "goats and monkeys." These words are taken directly from Shakespeare's Othello who, having been called back to Venice and maddened by the world's hypocrisy, calls out in contempt "Goats and monkeys!" (*Othello*, IV, i, 274). But against whom is Kaspar's cry directed? The Prompters? The audience? All of those who with the docility of "goats and monkeys," of the "herd," conform to language uncritically and have thus contributed to his destruction? With these words the curtain jolts forward, each time moving closer to the screeching, wriggling Kaspars until it knocks them down behind the curtain. "The play is over."

In the original version of the text one significant sentence follows "goats and monkeys."[45] It reads:

I:
am:
me:
only:
by:
chance:

Handke later cut this out, probably because of its too great clarity. That sentence confirms the deterministic power of language which has, after all, been apparent throughout. It is against this determinism and arbitrariness of individual existence that Kaspar rebels. If perception and expression do not emerge from a personality but from socially imposed linguistic structures and norms, then the Kaspar created by the Prompters is interchangeable with all other products of that system.

Yet it is difficult, or at least problematic, to speak of Kaspar as of an individual. Kaspar is conceived and presented not as a "character" but as a contrivance. While not quite as seamlessly artificial as Ionesco's Smiths and Martins, he is equally unreal. The theatre for Handke is always an "artifact," a contrived and artificial space; and within this space Kaspar is placed as an invention, a theatrical device. Kaspar is never allowed to appear quite human. He is from the start distanced from the audience through his mask-face and the mechanical movements of his puppet-like body. Kaspar unfolds less as a person than as a process, the process of man's construction and destruction through language. This process brings Kaspar closer to the audience when moments of personality and struggle break through the speech-object he is becoming; it however also distances Kaspar, for as speech systems displace him he becomes increasingly inhuman. Kaspar is in many ways like the Subject in Structuralist analysis who is rejected and dissolved by systems which operate through him. Kaspar too is subjected to systems, viewed through generative rules of speech and thought. He is, as Jonathan Culler puts it, "displaced from [his] function as center or source," and thus "the self comes to appear more and more as a construct, the result of systems of convention." These systems – and foremost among them is the system of language – generate rules, constantly expand as autonomous entities, and make "even the creation of *new* sentences a process governed by rules which escape the subject."[46] The Structuralists endorse this process of the "decentering" of the Subject (to use Foucault's term) and see the individual as assimilating the rules of his culture, as incorporating them, but not as originating or controlling them. Meaning resides in systems of convention which are prior to the individual and escape his conscious grasp. "The goal of the human sciences," writes Lévi-Strauss, "is not to constitute but to dissolve [man]."[47] Man is "dissolved" into the systems which constitute him and operate through him. *Kaspar* fits well into this Structuralist perspective, but with an essential difference: Handke is not writing from the point of view of the interpersonal systems of convention (as are the Structuralists), but from the point of view of *man* who is subjugated through these systems and victimized through the repression – or disavowal – of his individual "self." The conflict in *Kaspar* is between language – perversely presented though it is by the Prompters – as the ultimate system of order, and Kaspar who, although a product of this order, rebels against his absolute displacement by it. By the end of the play, Handke claims,

Kaspar's language "is suddenly deranged – until complete schizophrenia sets in."[48] This psychological terminology does not necessarily refer to Kaspar's "mind" which, like himself, is only a construct. It refers to a possible course of revenge available to the individual who through "derangement" rebels against the system by refusing to allow it to operate through him.[49] Thus, when Kaspar finally rejects the ideas of his Prompters, he also rejects their grammar (and vice versa) and speaks deranged nonsense as a rebellion.

The "model" nature of Kaspar's story is underlined by Handke through an additional strategic section of the play. "Because no story will take place, the audience will not be in a position to imagine that there is a sequel to the story, other than their own," Handke writes in the opening directions to the play.[50] There is no continuation of Kaspar the "character" although there is a continuation of the theme of *Kaspar* outside of the theatre. At the end of the *Tractatus* Wittgenstein makes this comment about his philosophical work:

he who understands me finally recognizes...he must, so to speak, throw away the ladder, after he has climbed up on it...he must surmount these propositions; then he sees the world rightly.[51]

Handke seems to be suggesting a similar task for his audience, *Kaspar* is almost a heuristic device, a "ladder" to that awareness which Handke constantly stresses is the goal of all of his writing. Within *Kaspar*, one short although very important section acts as the link between the play and its sequel in reality. This is the "Intermission Text," spoken during the intermission between the two acts of the play.[52] This text is to be piped through loudspeakers into the auditorium, lobby, cafeteria, even out onto the street if possible: wherever the audience may have gathered to take a break from the play. The text is to be pre-recorded and consist of fragments of the Prompters' speeches, a variety of sounds, actual taped speeches by real political leaders, Presidents, Popes, commentators, writers, poets who lecture on public occasions – any public figure who seeks to influence us through his or her words. The voices sound familiar, the phrases are recognizable although we hear only fragments of speeches which tumble over each other in an acoustic barrage. All of the words are delivered in formal, persuasive voices: corporate voices, like those of the Prompters. Cheers and boos respond and blend with electric drills, waterfalls, elemental and industrial sounds. Sirens and laughter interrupt sentences about war and life. The final section of this ongoing text returns us directly to the play: in coherent sentences we hear the description of a dinner party, with an exquisitely set table of perfect decorum. But the description includes "off" sentences, like warps in a record.

The soup is handed from the right. The drinks are handed from the right. Everything that you serve yourself is handed from the left. *The stab comes from the right*... The spoon is lying on the outside to the right of the knife. The spoon lies bottom up. *The grip that chokes comes from both sides*... You drink in small sips. *The blow is more effective when it comes from below*... You always look for friendly words. *The victim of an assassination lies in the middle of each setting*... (59, my emphases)

Again, as so often in the play, housely order and the order of terror are equated. The well-set table becomes the bier for assassinated corpses. The table, that epitome of social culture, of bourgeois order, is for Handke the direct counterpart of verbal order. Handke's text ends with the sounds of bombs falling, of houses (and probably dinner tables) crumbling, of chimes, bells, gongs, and finally the buzzer calling the audience back for the second act of the play.

This text is undoubtedly a source of irritation for the audience. The verbal torrent is a continuation of the grating, endless words of the play itself: only now the text is drawn from the realm of words and noises which surround us in life, not in the theatre. Thus the audience finds *itself* subjected to "language torture," not unlike Kaspar's. The *Versprachlichung* of existence – the reduction of reality to words – confronts the audience precisely when they have left the suspended time of the theatre for the "real" time of intermission. This torture is, however, not meant to educate or to bring the audience "into order," but rather to expose the sources of language which have *already* formed the audience in Kaspar's image. This section combines the character Kaspar and the audience into one: the audience is drawn directly into the play. But not only is the audience shown to suffer the same fate as Kaspar, it is also accused of participating in Kaspar's destruction: "goats and monkeys." The words which destroy Kaspar are their words, our words; and the value of order which necessitates Kaspar's torture is lifted from the world of the audience, not invented by Handke.

Language is conceived by Handke is *Kaspar* as a system for creating, and maintaining, order. Kaspar's progress from creation to destruction through language is, in a sense, a parable of the nature, not only of language, but of *power*.[53] To again quote Barthes: "Once uttered...speech enters the service of power...in each sign sleeps that monster: a stereotype. I can speak only by picking up what *loiters* around in speech. Once I speak...I am both master and slave."[54] The Prompters too are not only representatives of language, but of "what *loiters* around in speech." The language they speak, and teach Kaspar, is both an abstraction of linguistic norms, and grounded in a concrete and particular social reality. This is the reality of a middle-class well-formedness: the smooth language of the TV newsreel, the radio speech, the fully grammatical, persuasively structured verbal patterns of the ruling organization, patterns which contain and perpetuate a system of beliefs. To speak is to "enter the service of power," to surrender subjectivity to order. Ultimately, the clash between the individual need for freedom from abstraction and systems, and the inability of rigid verbal structures to bend to that need, will lead to Kaspar's destruction.

Without structures there could be no language, no state, no morality. But when the structures become an end in themselves, when they grow autonomous, gain a life of their own, then man no longer creates order: he only serves it. For Handke, "Questions of form are actually moral questions,"[55] and his goal is to expose those forms by allowing language to reveal its despotic character. Whorf, too, was troubled by the relationship between language and society. How do they interact? Which precedes and forms the other? He concluded that they co-exist in an uneasy partnership:

But in this partnership the nature of language is the factor that limits free plasticity and rigidifies channels of development in the more autocratic way. This is because a language is a system, not just an assemblage of norms. Large systematic outlines can change only very slowly, while many other cultural innovations are made with comparative quickness.[56]

Thus language represents the "mass mind" which has a rigid and inhibiting influence on development. Handke goes further than Whorf. He sees in language not only rigidity and autocratic tendencies but the potential for the manipulation of the individual. Handke rejects the humanist concept of language as the apex of culture, the mark of man's humanity. He insists that we need to rethink our very means of thought, to penetrate into "insidious language... and show how things can be warped through language. This stylistic exercise would be completed by pointing to a social one."[57] Others have sounded the same warning. Mauthner believed that language is an instrument of the "herd"[58] which, like Whorf's "mass mind," traps the individual and twists him into conformity and depersonalization. The prophet of this bleak vision is of course George Orwell who in *Nineteen Eighty-Four* demonstrates all too vividly the inextricable connection between power structures, verbal manipulation, and the herd mentality. The horror of *Nineteen Eighty-Four* is, above all, the meticulous and gapless order that the state has imposed, an order which is perfected through its language – Newspeak – and reflected in every detail of personal and communal life. Newspeak has two principles: cutting language down to a bare and basic minimum; and imposing on words forms which can only express linear and unambiguous concepts. Language thus restricted awakens no connotations, no emotional response; and thought too becomes unambiguously structured and easy to manipulate.

Don't you see that the whole aim of Newspeak is to narrow the range of thought? In the end we shall make thought-crime literally impossible, because there will be no words in which to express it.[59]

This is precisely what the Prompters are doing through their "model" sentences and axioms of thought which are reductive, simplistic, and force an unambiguous acceptance of the norms of order. "When you begin to speak you will begin to think what you speak even when you want to think something different" (27). Orwell's point, precisely.

Kaspar's originality lies not only in its pointed thematization of the inherent dangers of language, but in its elevation of language itself to the status of a *character*. Language is imbued with the traits of a dramatic antagonist. Represented through the disembodied voices of the Prompters, language both develops and acts: its nature unfolds and grows more ominous as it engages in a struggle for dominion with Kaspar. It is only in postwar drama that language actually becomes the active antagonist, the dramatic locus of social coercion and conformity. Language is presented as possessing a will of its own, outside of the control of the individual, to which the unaware individual can only bend or break—"PARIER oder KREPIER!". We are thus called to awareness, warned of the potential danger to autonomy and meaning which lurks in an uncritical subservience to language. The following chapters will expand on Handke's insights and will study a variety of plays by other postwar dramatists which expose, often in more overtly political and less theoretical terms, this postwar dramatic concern with the dangers of language aggression and language domination.

CHAPTER 3

Gagged by language: verbal domination and subjugation

The elevation of language to the status of a dramatic antagonist can be achieved through a number of techniques, Handke's solution in *Kaspar* is in keeping with the abstract minimalism of that play: language is returned to its purely aural source. Disembodied voices surround Kaspar with a language which actively functions as a character. Since language in *Kaspar* is not represented through a physical figure, and since Handke takes pains to strip even those voices of any personality traits, we are directed toward the reductive forms of language itself, as used in a reductive social context. Handke's achievement is to assert a total identification between the Prompters' "model" sentences, i.e. correct grammatical forms, and the forms of "model" behavior which they induce and coerce – solely through the use of language.

The plays to which we turn here are written in the Absurdist idiom. They present a variety of characters who struggle against language domination: and lose. Like Handke, these playwrights assign to language the role of dramatic antagonist and, as in *Kaspar*, language is identified with power, aggression, and victimization. The techniques, however, differ. In each of these plays language is embodied in a physical character who becomes a "medium" for language's aggression. All of the plays are clearly concerned with this verbal aggression and with its power to destroy personality, eradicate individuality, maim and even kill. Moreover, verbal assault is identified, at least implicitly and sometimes explicitly, with ideological and political power structures. The major plays I will examine are: Eugène Ionesco's *The Lesson*; Harold Pinter's *The Birthday Party*

38

and *The Dwarfs*; and Václav Havel's *The Garden Party* and *The Memorandum*.

Ionesco, Pinter, and Havel write in three different languages and, despite certain similarities, their plays are independent personal statements. They were first studied together by Martin Esslin in his revised edition of *The Theatre of the Absurd* (1968).[1] Since the term "Absurdist" is often invoked in discussions of these playwrights, it may be useful to begin by asking to what extent Esslin's analysis of the language of Absurd theater is relevant to the plays to be discussed, and to the theme of this study.

A few basic concepts – by now themselves platitudes – characterize language in Esslin's discussion. First, as a theater of "concrete imagery of the stage", Absurd theater, according to Esslin, subordinates logic, discursive thought, and language to visual imagery, movement, light, and so on. Thus, language is merely one component of a "multidimensional poetic imagery."[2] Language, when used, emerges as devalued, dissolved, disintegrated, nonsensical, insufficient, and ultimately "fails to communicate."[3] Devalued language implies a lack of efficacy and an alienation from meaning, the source of which is the experienced insufficiency of words to encompass existential bewilderment. The dramatic product of this verbal deterioration takes the form of inarticulate noises, empty clichés, verbal inversions, distortions, non sequiturs.[4] Esslin uses these as generally descriptive terms, but they form the basis for his analysis of Absurdist language.

We can distinguish between the devices: devalued, nonsensical language, and their philosophical implications: language is "insufficient" and thus there exists a failure of communication. *The Lesson*, *The Birthday Party*, *The Garden Party*, and *The Memorandum* all employ the devices of Absurdity to one degree or another: verbal inversions, mechanical clichés, extensive banality, meaningless sound patterns, are all common to these plays. But the *implications*, I will contend, are different. As we shall see, language in these plays does not fail to communicate; in fact, it communicates all too well its aggressive, leveling tendencies. The relationships stressed by the authors is precisely the one *between* man and language. Language is shown to be not insufficient but rather ominously powerful, wielding the characters rather than being wielded by them. In this context of the danger and power of language, the above mentioned verbal devices take on a different significance: they become the forms through which language gains dominance over the characters. Esslin is not unaware of the struggle which exists between man and language, but for him its source is existential and resides in man's absurd separation from linguistic communion. I will attempt to show, on the contrary, that the power which language displays in these plays is concrete and part of the potential nature of language itself. These playwrights are leveling accusations *against* language, against its capacity to manipulate and dominate, to control man's life and destroy his individuality. Ionesco, Pinter, and Havel all employ a number of recurring verbal devices through which language domination operates. The three broadest and most significant are: the ritualization of language and a resultant verbal hypnotism; the use of extended clichés and jargon as forms of coercion; and verbal mechanization in which language speaks through man without recourse to the speaker's intent or control. Most importantly: while Esslin views language in Absurdist drama as subordinate to images and visual stage effects, these plays elevate language to a central position. Language is the theme, target, and dominant threat in them all.

EUGÈNE IONESCO: *THE LESSON*

We discover not without dismay that, for thought, words are not simply a frame of reference or a support, but the whole of reality. *A prisoner of his speech*, man thinks himself protected by his own psittacism ... [Ionesco's] accumulation of puns, spoonerisms, equivocations, misunderstandings and a thousand and one other nonsensical drolleries, down to outright disintegration of articulate language into onomatopoeias, brayings and belchings ... is a perpetually renewed act of *accusation against language* ... Instead of men using language to think, we have language thinking for men.

J. S. Doubrovsky (my emphases)[5]

This passage from Doubrovsky's article pinpoints a few of the essential themes of Ionesco's early plays: the accusation – and warning – that language is the jailhouse of reality; the claim that man has lost control of language; and the conclusion that robbed of verbal autonomy, independent thought has been usurped *by* language. To this we can add that the usurping language is not only absurdly comical, as Doubrovsky's list of "nonsensical drolleries" implies, but also dangerous, even deadly. Language has an almost magical power to wound and destroy; and the victims of this language are not only those against whom it is directed, but also those through whom it is uttered.

Ionesco's first play, *The Bald Soprano* (*La Cantatrice chauve,* 1948) was mainly concerned with the mechanical, fossilized nature of social speech. It is an aggressive spoof and ends in an explosion of verbal anarchy which was intended to spill over into the audience. Its circular structure reflects the mechanical nature it attacks, and tends toward the comic. *The Lesson* (*La Leçon,* 1950), Ionesco's second one-act play, is also circular in structure, but here the circularity harbors menace and tends toward the grotesque. The language of these two plays shares certain characteristics, but with essential differences. In *The Bald Soprano* language is single-faceted and parodic. Clichés, formulae, mechanical trivia, and mindless inanities are sustained on one plane throughout; all of the characters speak the same interchangeable language, and are thus all leveled to one-dimensional insignificance. There is no protagonist, no antagonist, the characters lack self-consciousness: language alone is on heightened display. *The Lesson* is a more muted play; it probes deeper into the relationship between man and language, and is multi-faceted. Language here also eventually explodes, but it explodes into real violence, not only into chaos. *The Lesson* is more than a parody: it is a parable, with personal and political implications, regarding the dangers of language domination.

Power is the central theme of *The Lesson.* The play's three characters – the Student, the Professor, and Marie, the maid – relate to each other in terms of dominance/weakness. Only one character is at any given time in a position of dominance, and that character then also possesses verbal superiority. The

Student, who has come to prepare for her "Total Doctorate," begins in the superior position: she is confident, lively, and fluent. The Professor, by contrast, is weak and stammering: "I don't know quite how to apologize to you for having kept you waiting....I was just finishing...you understand, I was just...er...I do beg your pardon...I hope you will forgive me....⁶ The action of the play charts a gradual power shift; it shows the Student's loss of vigor, her reduction to verbal parrotry and repetitive cries of pain, and the Professor's rise to verbal and physical dominance. Ionesco explains in a long opening stage direction that the Student, who is at first gay and dynamic, will grow depressed, numbed and near paralysis by the end. She goes from determined and "almost aggressive," to passive, "nothing more than an object, limp and inert, lifeless, in the hands of the Professor" (p. 182). We are told from the start that by the time the Professor stabs her she can no longer react, she is already deadened. This total domination of one person by another is achieved through strictly verbal means. *The Lesson* shows a Strindbergian battle of wills stripped of any psychological dimension. The image which best describes this domination is verbal vampirism: the Student is drained through the Professor's mass of hypnotic, self-perpetuating language and sound. Her weakness is his strength. Vampirism is a theme which, like the struggle of opposed wills, obsessed the Expressionist Strindberg. But whereas Strindberg's "vampires" – in *To Damascus* or *The Ghost Sonata* – drain the heroes' vitality through a mystical, subjective dominance of the spirit, in *The Lesson* vampirism is objectified and comes to define the play's true antagonist: language.

The lesson begins with banal banter about geography and mathematics. The Professor is diffident and the Student retains her position of strength until they begin subtraction, for which she has no talent. The Professor's explanation includes technical terms – elements, figures, units, numbers – which confuse the Student, and with these terms the Professor's shift from weakness to power begins.

The central and dominant subject of the lesson concerns "the essentials of linguistics and comparative philology." Marie, the maid, warns the Professor against teaching philology, begging him to stop before it is too late: "No, Monsieur, no!... I shouldn't do that if I were you!... [...] Of all things, not philology, Monsieur, philology is the worst of all..." (p. 198). The Professor, however, rejects her warning and in his opening lecture on the philology of the "neo-Spanish languages" speaks for the first time "with authority."

With the introduction of language as a subject within the plot – and not only a dramatic device – the complexities and implications multiply. Had Ionesco merely depicted the verbal aggressions of the Professor without using the discussion of language itself as the direct impetus for accelerating violence, the connection between language and power would have been apparent enough. But the injection of linguistics as an overt subject – it is indeed the major portion of the lesson, taking up half the length of the play – gives Ionesco the opportunity to *comment* on the verbal domination which he is demonstrating. Thus a double process ensues: the Professor's use of language gathers momentum and grows increasingly vicious in a linear progression; while his *discussion* of language both partakes of that progression and comments on its mechanism.

From the moment the Professor begins his lecture on linguistics the Student's energy begins to wane. Her voice grows dull and her responses are either an acquiescent "Yes, Sir!" or a mechanical repetition of his words. A marked contrast between her originally vital personality and her subsequent loss of individuality is indicated. This loss of energy and her weakening resistance are directly related to the two controlling devices of the Professor's speech: a barrage of academic jargon leading to opaque, senseless abstractions; and a rhythmic, incantatory repetition of sounds. The jargon constantly slips into hypnotic, almost mechanical chains of words and sounds which undermine its "professional" function, and stress its manipulative effect. Words thus denuded of sense tend to function "magically" rather than rationally. In speaking of the differences between the various neo-Spanish languages, for example, the Professor begins with the details and syntax of an academic lecture, but soon slips into a nonsensical, circular argument with (especially in the original French) a recurrent "dis" sound:

PROFESSOR: What distinguishes the neo-Spanish languages one from the other and separates them from other linguistic groups [...] what distinguishes them, I say, is their striking resemblance to one another [...] their distinctive characteristics [are] unquestionable and indisputable evidence of that remarkable resemblance that renders their common origin indisputable and, at the same time, clearly differentiates them – through the conservation of those distinctive characteristics I have just mentioned. (pp. 199–200)

The Student's answer is "Ooooh! Oooooh, Sir!" She is "regretful, fascinated." The accelerating "dis" sound and the growing meaninglessness of the jargon are not mere parodies but a form of verbal hypnotism. Sense disintegrates into aural patterning, seductive sound. The technical/academic jargon of the Professor-figure alternates with the ritual/incantatory chants of the verbal vampire; and as the Professor gains in strength, incantation escalates:

PROFESSOR: Summing up, then; learning to pronounce takes years and years. [...] air has to be pitilessly forced out of the lungs [...] so that harps or leaves beneath the wind, they suddenly start quivering, trembling, vibrating, vibrating, vibrating or hissing, or rustling, or bristling, or whistling, and with a whistle set everything in motion... (p. 201–2)

The words now cluster almost mechanically around an "ent" sound: "...sous le vent, frémissent, s'agitent, vibrent, vibrent, vibrent ou grasseyent, ou chuintent ou se froissent, ou sifflent, sifflent mettant tout en mouvement..." The seductive sound, rhythmic, senseless, functions hypnotically, silencing the student. Ionesco expressly notes that the Student grows more and more "bewitched." She develops a toothache, a pain which the maid declares is "the final symptom" (p. 211), and which increases in intensity in direct proportion to her subjugation by the Professor. Her cries of pain – "I've got toothache!" – are a mechanical refrain which punctuate his lecture: it is the one form of resistance of which she becomes capable. The Professor "possesses" the Student through words which she cannot comprehend, sounds which entice and numb the mind, ideas which are forced upon her without the option of discussion –

"Be quiet. Sit where you are. Don't interrupt," she is warned whenever she speaks. His is a magical form of rhetoric which, as I will later show, bullies and seduces in a totalitarian fashion.

The Professor's domination of the Student climaxes in her murder/rape which culminates with the knife stab, but is in fact a *verbal* murder, a rape through language. This is doubly underlined by Ionesco's repeated stage direction in the original edition of the play, that the knife be "imaginary" and "invisible"; thus, the threat it poses, the wounds it inflicts can only be heard, not seen. The long ritual murder passage has the aural rhythm of sexual intercourse and the brutality of physical assault. Ostensibly teaching the Student to say "knife" in each of the neo-Spanish languages, the Professor performs a ritual "scalp dance" around her, brandishing his invisible knife and openly chanting. He forces her to repeat the word "knife" after him and with each repetition the pain in her teeth spreads to another part of her body. The invaded part is wounded by the *word* which has so completely absorbed the concept that its pronouncement suffices to wound and kill. As the bodily organs named by the Student grow more intimate – thighs, hips, breast, stomach – so the violation takes on an additional sexual connotation.

PROFESSOR: Ah! (*He goes quickly to the drawer and finds a big imaginary knife; he takes hold of it and brandishes it exultantly.*) [...] Knife...Watch it...Knife...Watch it...Knife...Watch it...

PUPIL: You make my ears ache, too. What a voice you've got! How piercing it is! [...] I'm aching all over...my throat, neck... ah...my shoulders...my breasts...knife...

PROFESSOR: Knife...Knife...Knife...

PUPIL: My hips...Knife...My thighs...Kni...[...] Knife...my shoulders...my arms, my breasts, my hips...knife...knife... (pp. 212–14)

Language is concretized into action. The final knife plunge only serves to dramatize the violation; language has already defiled her. The Student falls in an obscene position while the Professor, shaking with a spasm of relief, "mutters something unintelligible" (p. 214).

Ionesco writes that the Professor utters the word "knife" –

"like a cuckoo." He is "almost beside himself" (p. 213), overtaken by the hypnotic spell no less than is the Student. This explosion of language in *The Lesson* shares with the final sequence of *The Bald Soprano* a sense of language taking over; but the differences between the two passages are important. In *The Bald Soprano* the rhyming rhythmic nonsense of Mr. and Mrs. Smith demonstrates the disintegration of language into letters, sounds, and pure noise. Language is committing suicide, dissolving: the characters, however, remain untouched. The sight of mechanically sputtering characters tends to produce a comic effect which Henri Bergson described as "laughable in exact proportion as that body reminds us of a mere machine."[7] In *The Lesson*, language does not destroy *itself*, it destroys its utterer. Language remains intact and in control: it is the Student who is killed, the Professor who is beside himself, "breathing with difficulty [...] panic-stricken" (p. 214). The effect produced is not comic but grotesque; language is not to be laughed at, but feared.

The Student is destroyed through her submission; the Professor, however, is also transformed. He loses complete control of himself, becomes sub-human "like a cuckoo"; language has taken over. As Richard Coe writes: "...in the absence of meaning, the words themselves take absolute control, and drive their unfortunate victim whithersoever their blind and dangerous energies may choose to direct." It is a case of words "destroying their own utterer."[8] The Professor becomes both victim and victimizer. He falls into a trance and after the violent murder/rape rises in a panic "as though he were waking up" (p. 214), awakening from the spell of his own incantations. Marie, the wise maid, hints a number of times that the Professor will fall prey to his own deranged rhetoric. When she begs the Professor to "please be careful" (p. 188), protests that "philology is the worst of all" (p. 198), and warns that "it'll take you further than you want to go, you'll go too far" (p. 211), she is implying that the danger in the language is beyond his control: that he too will fall victim to it. The oppressive tyranny of the Professor's words, once unshackled, feeds on itself. As Ionesco has remarked, words "proliferate in

The Lesson. Words and murder."[9] Not only does the Professor use words as a weapon, but the words, as they proliferate, take over the Professor – and use him as an instrument. There is a growing strain between the Professor and his language; he seems to lose control of it the more he gains control of the Student. This mechanism of growth has both a comic and a tragic aspect, begins in the comic but leads to the tragic – as is well described by Claude Bonnefoy, in conversation with Ionesco:

In most of your plays the mechanical aspect is very important... there's the mechanical nature of language, the automatism of behavior, the proliferation of objects, the acceleration and chaotic disintegration of the action... In the classical theatre there are two basic dramatic mechanisms: a tragic mechanism which corresponds to the fate that leads the hero to his death; and a comic mechanism which involves the repetition of phrases or situations, the tangling up of the plot... In your work, on the other hand, the mechanical aspect starts out as something comic and ludicrous that appears to derive from the actual behavior of the characters; it gradually increases, until suddenly, because of its very excessiveness, of the fact that it's quite out of control, it becomes tragic.[10]

Such, precisely, is the Professor's situation. He loses control of his behavior, his actions, and his language; and what had begun as a comical, or at least ludicrous use of nonsense and jargon, degenerates into frenzied abdication, and real brutality.

The murder/rape is not the end of the play; one further shift of power follows. Marie, who until now had only appeared in order to give warning and comment, and to predict the consequences of the Professor's lecture, almost like a dramatic *raisonneur*, now enters to find the whimpering Professor and the defiled corpse. She begins to take charge, scolding the Professor as a mother would a naughty child. The Professor is horrified by what he has done, Marie is merely disgusted. As she explains: it is the fortieth time that day that a Student has fallen victim to his aggression; "And every day it's the same story! Every day!" (p. 215). The Professor tries to stab her too, but she is the stronger, striking him to the floor as he begs for forgiveness. Marie's strength is directly connected to her imperviousness to his rhetoric. The Professor is reduced to childish whimpering but Marie speaks, by turns, sarcastically, harshly, or with critical acumen:

> MAID (*sarcastically*): So you're pleased with your pupil, then? She learnt a lot from her lesson? [...] You little murderer! Revolting little swine! [...] And I gave you proper warning, too, only a little while ago! Arithmetic leads to Philology, and Philology leads to Crime...
> PROFESSOR: You said Philology was the worst of all!
> MAID: It all comes to the same in the end.
> PROFESSOR: I didn't quite understand. I thought when you said Philology was the worst of all, you just meant it was the hardest to learn...
> MAID: Liar! Old fox, you! A clever man like you doesn't go making mistakes about what words mean. (pp. 215–16)

Marie knows the meanings of words and is thus safe from the Professor. But this last line is also an ironic wink and overt comment by Ionesco, which ties in with the final feature of the play. Marie, to allay the Professor's fears, takes out an armband imprinted with an insignia, "perhaps the Nazi swastika," and puts it on his arm.

> MAID: Here you are! Put this on if you're frightened, then you won't have anything to be afraid of. (*She puts it round his arm.*)...It's political.
> PROFESSOR: Thank you, thank you, kind Marie; I feel much safer like that... (p. 217)

The play ends as it began, with the doorbell ringing and a new student entering for her lesson.

The Lesson is marred by its ending: the donning of the armband emblazoned with a Nazi swastika, overt symbol of repression and totalitarian power. This final gesture seems out of place; but my objection to it is not the same as that of Ronald Hayman, for example, who claims:

> So suddenly, gratuitously, perversely, an anti-didactic play is given a didactic twist and the invisible knife, which was already under severe strain, being partly phallic and partly a symbol of language made solid, is made to bear the weight of extra associations with fascism. Ionesco may have been wanting to make the point that fascism

distorted the language and made it into a weapon but this idea is not organically integrated and there is too much logic in the illogic of the play's structure for a new idea to be introduced so late.[11]

A distinction needs to be made: injecting a concrete political symbol of repression into this unrealistic and abstract attack against authoritarianism is clumsy, even embarrassing. The solution is too strident: but the idea it represents is neither "gratuitous" nor "unorganic" to the play. Nor is it a "new" idea. The relation between verbal and political domination which it concretizes is elemental to the play's thematics. *The Lesson* is not really concerned with the student–teacher relationship: that relationship, even at its worst, is certainly too trivial to support the violence with which Ionesco invests it. There is, however, in the student–teacher relationship a kernel of authority and acquiescence, of dominance and submission. In short, there is an element of power relations. It is this kernel which is abstracted and exaggerated, expanded into a broader exposure of power and domination which has clearly political and ideological implications.

An audience viewing the play in 1951, when it was first performed, might easily have identified the ranting, tyrannical Professor with the Nazi rhetorics and regime, so recently overcome. It is not so much the content of the Professor's speech which acts as victimizer, as the authority of its tone, its prescriptive tendency, and its manic, manipulative energy. The Student is brutally restrained from asking questions or interrupting. She is continuously silenced and threatened, told to listen and take note without being allowed to think or respond. In short: she is being indoctrinated. The Professor, as Esslin puts it, "derives his progressive increase of power from his role as giver, a very arbitrary prescriber of meanings."[12] His language from the start is in the totalitarian mold. He is the creator of language and meaning, and the Student's verbal world shrinks to the imposed confines of his will. Words and meanings are invented and forced on the Student, and in this lies the Professor's strength. He rejects completely the possibility of true objective communication, which for him is an illusion stemming from "the vulgar empiricism of the plebs [...] one of

the little oddities of human nature" (p. 210). He inverts
Wittgenstein's theory that meaning in language can only be
derived from empirical situations and usurps language to fit his
own definitions. Since he controls the shifting meaning of the
words, he also controls the Student and reality. This process can
be seen as parallel to the degeneration of the German language
under the Nazi regime, and shows the intimate connection
between language control and political domination.

A number of dictionaries of Nazi word usage have been
compiled, demonstrating precisely this point. Cornelia Berning's *Vom "Abstammungsnachweis" zum "Zuchtwart"* shows how
within the space of a dozen years words were removed from the
German language and, more frightening still, others were given
totally new meanings which replaced earlier donations and
created a new realm of connotations. For example: the 1924
edition of the popular dictionary *Meyers Lexicon* explained the
term "Abstammungsnachweis" ("proof of origin or descent")
with the note "s. Viehzucht" (see: "cattle-breeding"). The
Nazi-endorsed 1936 edition of that dictionary defined that same
word as "Genealogical proof of German or related origin...
today required of every German citizen."[13] A word that had
previously connoted animal stock control now became a term
for racial purity. Meanings were often completely reversed.
Words like "barbarisch" ("barbarian") and "rücksichtslos"
("ruthless"), which had previously contained negative connotations of degenerate, unsocial behavior, now connoted
positive values. Consider, for example, this quote from Hitler's
"government program" printed in the *Völkischer Beobachter* in
1933: "Landes und Volksverrat soll künftig mit barbarischer
Rücksichtslosigkeit verfolgt werden" ("State and national
treason should in the future be persecuted with barbarian
ruthlessness").[14] Such shifts in meaning may be consciously
inaugurated; Ionesco has indeed claimed that "it is quite
possible – deliberately – to deflect language from its normal
course."[15] But as Dolf Sternberger and Victor Klemperer have
shown, once set loose, the words take on a life of their own
which expands and inflates, much like the corpse in *Amédée*,
finally not only expressing an attitude, but creating one.

"Words are not innocent," wrote Sternberger in the introduction to his study of Nazi language, *Aus dem Wörterbuch des Unmenschen*, "rather, the guilt of the speaker grows into the language itself, becomes part of its flesh."[16] The Professor deflects language from its original meaning in a similarly authoritarian manner. Language ceases to function through commonly accepted denotative meaning, nor is language allowed to awaken new connotations within the Student. Its only function is to stifle, to bully the Student into silence and then hypnotize her into obedience to the Professor's will.

For Ionesco the true tragedy of communication resides in the inevitable systemization of thought through language: the public system defeats private creativity and originality. As the Professor explains to the Student, all of the neo-Spanish languages are identical, they all use "always and invariably the same word, with the same root, same suffix, same prefix, [...] the same meaning, the same composition, the same structure of sound, not only in this word, but in all the words you can conceive, in every language" (p. 204). This vision of total identity in all languages is a pessimistic statement of the coercive conformism of public speech, and individual thought, to the forms of language. It is to this danger that Ionesco is referring when Jack says: "Oh words, what crimes are committed in your name!"[17] Like *The Lesson, Jack, or The Submission* (*Jacques, ou la soumission*, 1950) shows the submission and conformity of a lively, spirited person, to the will and language of others. Language is again on trial and is shown as a reductive and dangerous threat to personal autonomy. The initial problem of the play concerns the rebellion of Jack who stubbornly refuses to recite the family creed: "I adore hashed brown potatoes." This ridiculous slogan epitomizes the totally clichéd mode of speech and thought which characterizes the Jack family, and to which he will have to succumb if he accepts the slogan. This is apparent in his mother's plea that he give up his individualism and conform:

MOTHER JACK: Son! Son! Listen to me. I beg you, do not reply to my brave mother's heart, but speak to me, without reflecting on what you say. It is the best way to think correctly, as an intellectual and as a good son. (*She waits in vain for a reply; Jack obstinately remains silent.*) But you are not a good son. Come, Jacqueline, you alone have sense enough to come in out of the rain.

JACQUELINE: Oh! Mother, all roads led to Rome.[18]

Jack's resistance is eventually overcome by his sister Jacqueline who attacks him with the word "chronometrable." This verbal invention, implying that he too is subject to the working of "chronos" – time – fills him with anguish. Defeated, he declares in a mechanical voice, "like an automaton," the slogan he had rejected. This submission to verbal parrotry, this pledge of verbal allegiance, subjects him to the control of his family and their concept of life. He has conformed to their language and thus will have to accept the values it represents.

Although the Professor insists that all languages are identical, and thus equally coercive, he concedes that differences do exist, subtle differences which reside in a certain vague experience: "It is an intangible thing. An intangible thing you can only grasp after much time, with much difficulty and long experience…" (p. 207). The difference is *subjective* and not given to formulation in language. This personal experience cannot carry over into the schematic generality of conceptual language; it finds expression only in non-public forms of language such as poetry. Thus, Ionesco claims, language tends toward two poles: platitude and cliché, or literature. Both themes appear in his plays. Conformity is the overriding concern and underlies *The Bald Soprano*, *The Lesson*, and *Jack*. Its political consequences are demonstrated in *Rhinoceros* (1958). But literary language is shown to be equally barren, at least in the face of existential absolutes. Bérenger's fifteen-page monologue at the end of *The Killer* (*Tueur sans gages*, 1957), uses every rhetorical device, verbal ploy, literary and philosophical formulation to convince the killer – death – to refrain; but words are of no avail. "I'm dying," cries the King in *Exit the King* (*Le Roi se meurt*, 1961), "you hear, I'm trying to tell you that I'm dying, but I can't express it, all I can do is make literature of it." To which the doctor replies: "And that's what we do until the bitter end. As long as we live we turn everything into literature."[19] Living experience, that "intangible thing," is lost in language. Words become either literary structures or, worse, slogans and ideologies which manipulate and endanger the individual by trying, according to Ionesco, "to make an objective reality out of subjectivity... In logic, in dialectics, in systematologies, all the mechanisms come into play, [and] all types of madness are possible."[20]

HAROLD PINTER: *THE BIRTHDAY PARTY* AND *THE DWARFS*

Pinter's *The Birthday Party*, like Ionesco's *The Lesson*, shows the destruction of an apparently innocent character through violent verbal assault; a destruction which, however, results not in death, but rather in an implied rebirth, a "conversion." *The Birthday Party* is a complex and mystifying play containing two parallel plots and two verbal torture scenes of unusual density and power. It was Pinter's first full-length play (first version: 1958), and has received much and varied critical attention. It has been diversely interpreted as expressing nostalgia for the loss of childhood security; as an externalized study of anxiety and the fear of death; as showing social pressures brought to bear on the wayward artist; and, more generally, as exposing how society coerces us all into a relentless mold of conformity. All of these interpretations are possible for this complex, ambiguous play; but only the last ties the diverse elements of the play together and allows for a reading which explains not only the plot of the play, but also Pinter's central dramatic device: the extensive use of verbal violence. Despite the centrality of verbal violence in *The Birthday Party*, the question of its significance, and of the role which language itself plays in this parable of forced social conformity, has been largely skirted by the critics. I will focus on these questions and try to correlate the action of the play and its unusual, almost aberrant language, in order to show how the theme and the meaning of the play are directly contained in the function of its language.

The Birthday Party centers around Stanley Webber, a slovenly, unemployed pianist, "a bit of a washout," as Lulu puts it, who for some years has been living in idle seclusion as lodger and substitute-son at the seaside boarding-house of Meg and Peter Boles. We know little about him, and what we do learn is ambiguous. He claims to have once been a concert pianist whose career ended due to bad reviews; "They carved me up. Carved me up. It was all arranged, it was all worked out."[21] Apparently he had at one time lived a very different type of life, but we cannot be certain of the details. What *is* certain is Stanley's current idleness and indifferent squalor. Unshaven, unwashed, perpetually dressed in his pajama jacket, he no longer even bothers leaving the house.

Stanley's relationship with the Boles is one of easy familiarity. Act one begins at the family breakfast table where cornflakes and weather are discussed, and Petey reads "nice bits" from the morning newspaper. Meg and Petey are caricatures of domestic banality. They are cast in the familiar comic roles of the lower-class couple, silly and innocent, and they never break out of that mold.

The cosy domesticity is shattered by the arrival of two new lodgers, well-dressed men on a visit from the city. Their arrival fills Stanley with unexplained fear; they are intruders, emissaries from an outside world with which Stanley has for years had no contact. From the first it is clear that the visitors, Goldberg and McCann, are not innocent transients. They have been sent to the Boles' house to do a "job": "This job," McCann asks his boss Goldberg, "...is it going to be like anything we've ever done before?" (p. 29). The nature of the job, its goal, and the previous relationship between Stanley and the intruders, remain purposely obscure.

With the entrance of Goldberg and McCann a switch in idiom is immediately apparent. Their language differs greatly from the childish banality of the Boles: it is a sophisticated mixture of corporate jargon, gangster slang, and social pieties. Goldberg, the more verbose of the two, tends toward long, evasive speeches. When McCann asks him, for example, about the nature of their "job", his reply is a tissue of evasive bureaucratic terminology:

GOLDBERG: The main issue is a singular issue and quite distinct from your previous work. Certain elements, however, might well approximate in points of procedure to some of your other activities. All is dependent on the attitude of our subject. At all events, McCann, I can assure you that the assignment will be carried out and the mission accomplished with no excessive aggravation to you or myself. (p. 30)

Pinter draws the two intruders with careful detail, and much depends on their characterization. Goldberg is a self-satisfied, successful businessman of dangerous charm who speaks abundantly and with devious facility in Jewish intonations, uses Yiddish idioms, and dwells at length on various – contradictory – stories of his youth and family. He is a man of authority and "position";

GOLDBERG: Well, I've got a position, I won't deny it.
McCANN: You certainly have.
GOLDBERG: I would never deny that I had a position.
McCANN: And what a position!
GOLDBERG: It's not a thing I would deny. (p. 30)

His conversation is fraught with paternalistic advice delivered in a highly clichéd style. As he advises McCann:

GOLDBERG: [...] Learn to relax McCann, or you'll never get anywhere. [...] The secret is breathing. Take my tip. It's a well-known fact. Breathe in, breathe out, take a chance, let yourself go, what can you lose? Look at me [...] Pull yourself together. Everywhere you go these days it's like a funeral.
McCANN: That's true.
GOLDBERG: True? Of course it's true. It's more than true. It's a fact. (pp. 27–8)

I will return below to the significance of Goldberg's style of speech. McCann, Goldberg's strongman, is a stage Irishman, a Catholic – (Goldberg claims he is a defrocked priest) – who drinks only Irish whisky (never Scotch), sings sentimental ballads, and talks little. Although the two men are quite different they must be viewed as a team, and they rarely appear separately.

By the end of the first act we can clearly discern two groups of characters who comprise the two plot lines: Meg, Petey, and their silly neighbor Lulu, on the one hand; and Goldberg and McCann, on the other. Stanley stands poised between the two, and the play charts his transition from the hub of the family

into the complete control of the intruders. Richard Schechner
has suggested that in *The Birthday Party* Pinter merges two
actions, two levels of reality, and represents them in varying,
disparate rhythms.[22] The "outer" action is a naturalistic
family comedy exploiting a cast of familiar types: Petey, a deck-
chair attendant, and Meg, a landlady; their lodger, Stanley;
and Lulu, a tart. Into this group intrude two additional
comic types, the stage-Jew and stage-Irishman, Goldberg and
McCann, who, however, reverse the mood and comprise a
threatening "inner" action.[23]

This "inner" action comes to the fore in Act II, and with it
the play's interpretative problems begin. Act II opens with a
meeting between Stanley and McCann during which Stanley
tries to convince the unresponsive McCann of his "innocence."
His references to his past are, typically for Pinter, elliptic, and
do more to mystify than to clarify. Stanley speaks of his home
town, of the quiet life he had led, and of his plans to return
there: "I'll stay there too, this time. No place like home" (p.
40). McCann makes no accusations and we are never told of
what crime Stanley thinks himself accused; but obviously he
feels endangered. "I mean, you wouldn't think, to look at me,
really ... I mean, not really, that I was the sort of bloke to – to
cause any trouble, would you?" (p. 40). McCann's indifference
enrages him and he grows more aggressive.

STANLEY: It's a mistake! Do you understand?
MCCANN: You're in a bad state, man.
STANLEY (*whispering, advancing*): Has he told you anything? Do you
    know what you're here for? Tell me. You needn't be frightened
    of me. Or hasn't he told you?
MCCANN: Told me what?
STANLEY (*hissing*): I've explained to you, damn you, that all those
    years I lived in Basingstoke I never stepped outside the door.
MCCANN: You know, I'm flabbergasted with you. (p. 42)

The tone and mysterious hints belong to the genre of the
detective or mystery story. An expectation is built that soon we
will discover both the nature of Stanley's "crime" and the
goal of Goldberg and McCann's mission. John Russell Brown
attributes this expectation to Pinter's "two-pronged tactic of
awakening the audience's desire for verification and repeatedly

disappointing this desire."[24] And indeed we are disappointed. Instead of clarification, the mystification deepens. Goldberg enters; he and McCann surround Stanley and using gangster tactics force Stanley to sit down, taking up positions on either side of his chair. What ensues is six pages of massive, totally unrealistic verbal assault.

The switch from conversation to interrogation is abrupt. Again there is a shift in genre: we are now in a Kafkaesque world of secret, incomprehensible mental torture. Goldberg and McCann speak in a quick, gapless rhythm, a totalitarian style which allows no space for response and no option for self-defence.

GOLDBERG: Webber, what were you doing yesterday?
STANLEY: Yesterday?
GOLDBERG: And the day before. What did you do the day before that?
STANLEY: What do you mean?
GOLDBERG: Why are you wasting everybody's time, Webber? Why are you getting in everybody's way?
STANLEY: Me? What are you –
GOLDBERG: I'm telling you, Webber. You're a washout. (p. 47)

The questions sound familiar: they are the opening ploys of an almost stereotyped police interrogation of the where-were-you-on-the-night-of-the-crime sort. As the assault continues, the questions retain their familiar note, so that despite their absurdity and contradictory quality we have a sense of having heard all of this before.

MCCANN: Why did you leave the organization?
GOLDBERG: What would your old mum say, Webber?
MCCANN: Why did you betray us?
GOLDBERG: You hurt me, Webber. You're playing a dirty game.
MCCANN: That's a Black and Tan fact. [...]
GOLDBERG: You stink of sin.
MCCANN: I can smell it.
GOLDBERG: Do you recognize an external force?
MCCANN: That's the question! [...]
MCCANN: You contaminate womankind.
GOLDBERG: Why don't you pay the rent?
MCCANN: Mother defiler! [...]
GOLDBERG: You verminate the sheet of your birth.

MCCANN: What about the Albigensenist heresy?
GOLDBERG: Who watered the wicket in Melbourne?
MCCANN: What about the blessed Oliver Plunkett? (pp. 48–51)

The torrent of irrational, contradictory accusations grows in intensity and viciousness, climaxing in outright threats of violence as Stanley's very existence is put in question.

GOLDBERG: Why did the chicken cross the road?
STANLEY: He wanted to – he wanted to…
GOLDBERG: Why did the chicken cross the road?
STANLEY: He wanted…
MCCANN: He doesn't know. He doesn't know which came first!
GOLDBERG: Which came first?
MCCANN: Chicken? Egg? Which came first?
   (*Stanley screams.*) […]
MCCANN: Wake him up. Stick a needle in his eye.
GOLDBERG: You're a plague, Webber. You're an overthrow. […]
MCCANN: You betrayed our land.
GOLDBERG: You betray our breed.
MCCANN: Who are you, Webber?
GOLDBERG: What makes you think you exist?
MCCANN: You're dead.
GOLDBERG: You're dead. You can't live, you can't think, you can't love. You're dead. You're a plague gone bad. There's no juice in you. You're nothing but an odour! (pp. 51–2)

Stanley ends up screaming and striking out in horror.

A number of things need to be noted about this torture/ interrogation. The accusations themselves are too diverse and contradictory to comprise a sustained argument; but I do not agree that their power resides merely in their mass or their "weirdness," as some critics have claimed. Martin Esslin, describing the torture scene of Act II, writes, almost in passing: "Stanley…had been subjected to a weird surrealist cross-examination by his tormentors before the party got under way…"[25] Austin E. Quigley, in his book *The Pinter Problem*, writes: "In *The Birthday Party* conflict is waged not in terms of quality of usage but by the sheer weight, variety, and quantity of usage. Stanley is confronted by two visitors, who…verbally bludgeon him into submission and silence by the sheer number and variety of their accusations."[26] Both of these glosses seem to discount the centrality of the torture scene – through which Stanley is rendered dumb and seemingly deranged for the rest of the play. It seems to me that something more, and more significant, is at work here. Stanley is accused, among other things, of betraying the "organization," of murdering his wife, of never having married, of not recognizing an external force, of being unable to distinguish the possible from the necessary. Philosophical and theological jargon are massed together and thrown at him in a gapless confusion. The seemingly absurd mixture of jargon ("What about the Albigensenist heresy?"), cliché cuts ("Mother defiler!"), pathos ("You betrayed our land"), and trivialities ("Which came first? Chicken? Egg?") are not mere haphazard nonsense. As accusation piles upon accusation, echoes of familiar speech-styles begin to emerge. We become aware that the assault is actually a melting-pot of distorted idioms and clichés, that the questions and accusations share a common ground, evoke a common source despite their diversity.

What we have here is, in fact, a collage of recognizable jargon styles drawn by Pinter from the verbal stereotypes of the gangster movie, the spy novel, the theological sermon, the philosophy lecture, the political rally, the history textbook, the TV advertisement, the children's rhyme. The attack is comprised of jargon intellectualism, genre imitations, and clichés, a heap of common and commonly used verbal debris all the more frightening for its familiarity. From this mass there emerges a fragmented and distorted view of the platitudinous values held by, as Handke would put it, "all right-thinking people." The juxtaposition of these rhetorical styles, and their pointedly clichéd, jargonized nature, make it abundantly clear that Pinter's indictment is not of the "messengers" whom the "organization" has sent, but of the *message*; i.e. an indictment of those all-too-common coins of mechanical speech which have become the replacement for thought and the hallmark of conformity. Stanley is being attacked by the moral and intellectual clichés which he, in his seclusion and rejection of society, has rejected. The aim of the attack is to reimmerse

Stanley in those values by realigning him with the *language* of those values.

Explosions of jargon, which induce threat and tip the power balance, are not uncommon in Pinter's early plays. In *The Caretaker* (1960), for example, Mick, owner of the building in which the destitute tramp Davies has been staying, intimidates the vagrant with a mock offer to sell him the house. Mick's speech (a page and a half long) snowballs into the convoluted jargon of high finance and insurance which includes "down payments, back payments, family allowances, bonus schemes, remission of term for good behaviour [...] disposal of shares, benefit extension, compensation on cessation, comprehensive indemnity against Riot, Civil Commotion, Labour Disturbances, Storm, Tempest, Thunderbolt, Larceny or Cattle all subject to a daily check and double check," and leaves Davies speechless and frightened.[27] In *The Homecoming* (1965), the pimp Lenny suddenly confronts his brother Teddy, a professor of philosophy, with the question: "Do you detect a certain logical incoherence in the central affirmations of Christian theism?"[28] and with this gains power over the stunned and stuttering Teddy. Two things might be noted about the uses of jargon here. Goldberg, McCann, Mick, and Lenny are all low-life gangster types whose control of such specialized language is startling; and all use this language suddenly, out of context, and through it gain mastery over the recipients of their speeches. Such uses of language break the realism of the dialogue and draw attention not so much to *what* is being said, as to the *formulae* of speech themselves. As one critic put it: "The evocative power of jargon creates an image of the impersonal web that society weaves in order to snare the individual."[29] Pinter's control of jargon is immaculate. He echoes with precision formulae of specialized speech which, in their proper context, would seem fully (if annoyingly) appropriate. It is precisely the smoothness of the imitation which is here the point. Its odd familiarity is both soothing and disturbing. We are not asked to believe that thugs like Mick, Lenny, Goldberg, and McCann are capable of such language; we are asked to take note of how the familiar formulae of speech can in fact manipulate and intimidate. In *The Birthday Party* this manipulation is accomplished by two stage-types, Goldberg and McCann, who act not in their own names, but as "agents" of the "organization" which endorses these speech-forms and the values they enact.

Despite their fully drawn and rather colorful personalities, Goldberg and McCann undergo a peculiar change as soon as they enter their "inner" roles, i.e. when they are alone with Stanley in Acts II and III. Their speech accelerates in speed and rhythm, taking on the tone and threatening curtness of public prosecuters. A ritualized pattern of stichomythic dialogue derealizes them as individuals and gives increased emphasis to their language, a language consisting of terms and idioms culled from a stratum of speech beyond their own experience. They seem to be gradually overtaken by the verbal terrorism which is the source of their power, and become instruments of that verbal power rather than speaking individuals: Stanley is not so much being tortured *by* Goldberg and McCann, as *through* them. Pinter's intentional break with realism in this and the following verbal torture scene, and the abrupt change of idiom and stage mood, are significant indicators that interpretation can no longer be rooted mainly in plot. Any reading of this scene must look to the language, to its massive and disjointed idioms and the power which they exercise. Goldberg and McCann function here very much like the Prompters in *Kaspar*: they are *mediums* for socially prescribed speech, vessels for the manipulative power of language – rather than autonomous characters. Stanley is repeatedly accused of betraying the "organization"; it is this "organization" which Goldberg and McCann represent: their jargonized speech and executive style of dress only too clearly expose them as "organization men." It is an "organization" in which Goldberg holds a high "position," attained, as Goldberg later explicitly states, through his total submission and conformity to the rules, through playing the "game," following the "line." "Follow the line, the line, McCann, and you can't go wrong. What do you think, I'm a self-made man? No! I sat where I was told to sit, I kept my eye on the ball" (p. 77). Goldberg and McCann are products of an "organization" for which Stanley, too, is now being molded; and his reshaping is achieved through the process of interrogation.

Interrogation, the art of extracting confession and converting belief through the force of the word, is the root metaphor of Handke's *Kaspar* as well as of his radio-play *Hörspiel* no. 1. Stanley's torture, like Kaspar's, is mental torture; its goal is to control and shape his mind, to gain power over this thoughts. In all of these plays interrogation becomes a projection of the tactics of terror, terror conceived of as the usurpation of an individual's capacity to speak, and thus think, freely. Language is shown to be an instrument of power, the very embodiment of power. Stanley's torture and ultimate conversion recall another, more horrible, but distinctly parallel scene from postwar literature: Winston and O'Brien, tortured and torturer, in George Orwell's *Nineteen Eighty-Four*. In the torture/interrogation scene in that book, O'Brien tries to convert Winston to saying – and believing – words and thoughts approved by the Party. Winston is tortured horribly, but the physical torture is not the point. O'Brien is not interested in merely harming Winston physically, nor is Winston broken through physical pain. O'Brien seeks a conversion – similar to the conversion of Kaspar from speech-lessness into socially accepted speech – a conversion through which O'Brien, like the Prompters, like Mother Jack, and like Goldberg and McCann, would gain total control over the mind of his victim. As in *Kaspar*, the trick, the essence of the conversion, lies in the total identification of "model" sentences, i.e. correct grammatical forms, and molds of thought, i.e. socially or politically endorsed axioms of order. Kaspar reaches successful integration when he finally speaks in the Prompter's voice. Stanley's conversion is imaged in his final appearance in the play, dressed in suit and tie, the very reflection of his torturers. In Orwell's book, O'Brien seeks to force Winston into a similar mold of unswerving conformity; Winston must be made to say "War is Peace," "Freedom is Slavery," "Ig-norance is Strength," and to believe these axioms as true and unquestionable. To do this O'Brien must rid Winston of

"Oldspeak," of the words and grammatical forms which pre-date Big Brother's control and allow for humanistic thought. He must rearrange Winston's mind in the form of a new, in fact *opposed*, language. "Power," O'Brien tells Winston, "is in tearing human minds to pieces and putting them together again in new shapes of your own choosing."[30] It is the "shape" of Stanley's mind which – like Winston's – is under attack; a mind which has rejected the solid clichés, the orderly behavior, the regulated mores of the controlling society. O'Brien's prophecy of Winston's future after the interrogation and torture is very similar to Stanley's fate after his brainwashing:

What happens to you here is forever. Understand that in advance. We shall crush you down to the point from which there is no coming back... You will be hollow. We shall squeeze you empty, and then we shall fill you with ourselves.[31]

In the torture/interrogation scene of Act II Stanley too is squeezed empty. Like Handke's Kaspar, whose one original sentence is "exorcised" by the Prompters through a massive assault of scrambled, vaguely familiar phrases, and who is thus silenced and made ready to be reshaped by socially acceptable language, so Stanley too is emptied of his own language, rendered speechless. In the ensuing torture/reconstruction scene of Act III Stanley is recreated, "filled" by Goldberg and McCann with themselves, just as Winston is filled with O'Brien, and reshaped by the very language which has destroyed him.

On the morning after the birthday party (to which I will return) we learn, through vague hints, that Stanley had spent a horrendous night "... talking" with Goldberg and McCann, an experience which has left even the hardened McCann shaken and weary. McCann: "He's quiet now. He stopped all that... talking a while ago" (p. 73). The fact that Stanley has not spoken since his torture, uttered not a word during the party, and does not speak once he reappears, puts a threatening point on McCann's vague, perhaps euphemistic use of "... talking." When Stanley finally does appear, he looks transformed. His previously derelict, pajama-clad attire is replaced by a well-cut dark suit and white collar; he is neat and clean-shaven. Again he is seated and surrounded by Goldberg and McCann, who, in a long stichomythic exchange, bombard Stanley with words which parallel the previous interrogation but reverse its intention. Stanley does not interrupt their liturgy. In fact, he "shows no reaction," as the stage directions tell us. The entire scene has an incantatory quality; the rhythmic exchange of short one-line sentences is almost hypnotic.

GOLDBERG: You've gone from bad to worse.
McCANN: Worse than worse.
GOLDBERG: You need a long convalescence.
McCANN: A change of air.
GOLDBERG: Somewhere over the rainbow.
McCANN: Where angels fear to tread. [...]
GOLDBERG: But we can save you.
McCANN: From a worse fate. (p. 82)

It is interesting that this is precisely the form of speech used by Handke in the passage right before Kaspar is "cracked open," i.e. before multiple Kaspars appear on the stage and Kaspar finally speaks like the Prompters who have reconstructed him.

KASPAR: I am quieting myself.
PROMPTERS: You were already making a fist.
KASPAR: I was still screaming.
PROMPTERS: You still took a deep breath.
KASPAR: I was already there.
PROMPTERS: The chair still stands in its place.
KASPAR: I was still standing.[32]

After this, Kaspar is told by the Prompters: "When you begin to speak you will begin to think that you speak even when you want to think something different...you must think what you are saying..."[33] Like Kaspar, Stanley too is being molded into someone who is "not allowed to think anything *different*" from what he will say; and what he will in the future say is being fed to him in this section. The use of stichomythia has a similar purpose in both plays: it transposes the dialogue into a derealized chant whose hypnotic effect acts as a prelude to conversion. Moreover, the "spacelessness" of the dialogue, allowing no gap for thought or response, is akin to the methods of advertisement and propaganda attacks. Stanley now no longer stands accused; rather, he is wooed, courted, promised a new life, new health, and a new conformity.

GOLDBERG: You'll be re-orientated.
McCANN: You'll be rich.
GOLDBERG: You'll be adjusted.
McCANN: You'll be our pride and joy.
GOLDBERG: You'll be a mensch.
McCANN: You'll be a success.
GOLDBERG: You'll be integrated.
McCANN: You'll give orders.
GOLDBERG: You'll make decisions.
McCANN: You'll be a magnate.
GOLDBERG: A statesman. (pp. 83–4)

Toward what is Stanley being "re-orientated"? Goldberg and McCann make their plans quite clear not only through the contents of their promises ("rich," "a mensch," "a success"), but, more importantly, through the type of language they use: a language cluttered with the most hackneyed idioms and socially sanctioned aspirations. They promise to save Stanley "from a worse fate" by filling him with clichéd desires, consumer banalities, and the hallmarks of an orderly middle-class existence – all "on the house."

GOLDBERG: From now on, we'll be the hub of your wheel.
McCANN: We'll renew your season ticket.
GOLDBERG: We'll take tuppence off your morning tea.
McCANN: We'll give you a discount on all inflammable goods.
GOLDBERG: We'll watch over you.
McCANN: Advise you.
GOLDBERG: Give you proper care and treatment.
McCANN: Let you use the club bar.
GOLDBERG: Keep a table reserved. [...]
GOLDBERG: Give you a free pass.
McCANN: Take you for constitutionals.
GOLDBERG: Give you hot tips. [...]
McCANN: A day and night service.
GOLDBERG: All on the house. (pp. 82–3)

There is hardly a phrase in this litany which contains spontaneous or original language. The life which Stanley is being promised is composed of trivial materialistic advantages. Stanley will be cared for, watched over, advised. There is no attempt to expand the description of these temptations, to whet his appetite through decorative or inflated rhetoric. On the contrary: these banalities are left in their purely chlichéd form. The cliché is offered as the "model" structure through which Stanley will be reborn a new man. He is "filled" with platitudes, force-fed a diet of pre-formed images which are to replace his wayward individuality, his dropout reclusiveness, and to recreate him – in the mold of his torturers.

The language and content of Stanley's reconstruction can be best understood by comparison with the odd, almost parodic language which Goldberg uses in the "outer" scenes. There is a direct connection between what Goldberg represents, his mode of expression, and Stanley's promised future. In Goldberg we find a perfect union between idea and expression, between moral values and their verbal formulations. Goldberg stands for respectful ties to family, country, tradition; for the values of work, order, and health; and above all for *obedience*, following the "line," playing the "game." In short, he stands for total and unquestioning conformity. The language in which he expresses these values, the language which has in part *composed* these values, is a seamless web of sententiousness, proverbial wisdom, and social clichés, as we see in the following:

GOLDBERG: You know what? I've never lost a tooth. Not since the day I was born. Nothing's changed. (*He gets up.*) That's why I've reached my position, McCann. Because I've always been as fit as a fiddle. All my life I've said the same. Play up, play up, and play the game. Honour thy father and thy mother. All along the line. Follow the line, the line, McCann, and you can't go wrong. What do you think, I'm a self-made man? No! I sat where I was told to sit. I kept my eye on the ball. School? Don't talk to me about school. Top in all subjects. And for why? Because I'm telling you, I'm telling you, follow my line? Follow my mental? Learn by heart. Never write down a thing. And don't go too near the water. (p. 77)

Goldberg – whose motto is "work hard and play hard" – is a model for the new Stanley. Like the Prompters, whose language shapes Kaspar's values, so too Goldberg's language is a blueprint for the new "integrated" Stanley. Stanley's integration, like Winston's and Kaspar's, will entail his total conversion into the mold – verbal, moral, and behavioral – of his tortures. The play ends with a scrubbed and respectably dressed Stanley – in Pinter's 1964 direction of the play, Stanley is dressed in a suit identical to those of Goldberg and McCann – being taken away in Goldberg's black limousine; and a broken, finally comprehending Petey calling after him: "Stan, don't let them tell you what to do!" (p. 86). But it is too late; he has already been told.

The central event of the play, that which gives the play its title, is, of course, Stanley's "birthday" party. It belongs to the "outer" action, the seemingly objective level of the play, and involves all of the characters, except Petey. The status of Stanley's birthday is itself uncertain. Despite his stout denial, Meg insists that today marks the event and, upon Goldberg's suggestion, she plans a family party. The beginning of the party overlaps with the end of Stanley's first torture/interrogation which is, in fact, interrupted by the sound of a drumbeat as Meg enters, all dressed up and carrying Stanley's birthday gift: a toy drum. Stanley remains silent and isolated during the party while the others chat and sing with growing intimacy. The climax of the party involves a game of blind-man's-buff during which Stanley, helpless under his blindfold, tries to strangle Meg and then, during a sudden black-out, to rape Lulu. All of this occurs amid a chorus of banal exclamations, the emphasis being not on the dialogue but on the chaotic action. Stanley's violent behavior is totally incompatible with the harmless, ineffectual character we met before his interrogation. His sudden violence is obviously a sign of derangement, as the stage directions make clear.

Lulu is lying spread-eagled on the table, Stanley bent over her. Stanley, as soon as the torchlight hits him, begins to giggle. Goldberg and McCann move toward him. He backs, giggling, the torch on his face... The torch draws closer. His giggle rises and grows as he flattens himself against the wall. Their figures converge upon him. (pp. 65–6)

Not only has Stanley become a giggling idiot but, as we can discern in the stage tableau which closes Act II, he is also a trapped and dehumanized figure who is "cornered," pinned to the wall, taken over physically by the same two figures who originally broke him mentally.

Thus we have two images of Stanley's destruction: verbal assault, which leads to Stanley's loss of language; and physical assault, of which Stanley is the deranged and giggling perpetrator. If there is a connection between these two images – and I feel that a connection must be assumed – it can perhaps be found in the correlation of the two levels of the plot. In the "inner" or subjective action, Stanley suffers mental violence through verbal attack; this action is introverted, unrealistic, seems to take place out of time, is unknown to the family members, and cannot be interpreted merely on the level of plot. In the "outer" or objective action, Stanley's subjective ordeal receives a psychological, plot-oriented translation: he emerges as deranged and physically out of control. It does not seem to me metaphorically too far-fetched to interpret Stanley's attempts to strangle and rape others as a direct outcome of his own experienced verbal strangulation and rape through verbal assault. This violent action merges the "outer" and "inner" levels of the play both in terms of plot and of metaphor, and marks Stanley's complete rupture from the family into the control of Goldberg and McCann. Thus, the birthday party serves as a controlling image which integrates the two divergent levels of action. Meg may be mistaken in her well-meant assumption that today is Stanley's birthday – Stanley certainly claims that she is – but the image of rebirth and transformation guides the development of the plot and is central to its meaning.

What, however, is Stanley being re-born into? Some critics have suggested that Stanley's abduction is a birth-into-death. The reappearance of Stanley in formal dress, dumb and sightless with his broken glasses, does suggest a corpse "decked out for his own funeral."[34] Goldberg's waiting, black, hearse-like limousine adds to this image. But interpreting these signs as pointing to Stanley's *real* death is perhaps taking them too literally. Such an interpretation ignores too much and renders the entire verbal reconstruction scene senseless. If a funeral awaits Stanley, surely it is the funeral of his individuality; if death awaits him, it is a death-in-life, a death through conventionality, through order and conformity. Moreover, if indeed by the end of the play Stanley looks like a corpse, he acts more like an infant. Following his second verbal attack, Goldberg and McCann ask him what he thinks of his new "prospect." For the first time Stanley tries to speak: but all he can emit are the broken cooing sounds of a new-born not yet educated in language: "Uh-gug...uh-gug...eeehh-gag.... [...] Caahh...caahh..." (p. 84). Stanley is now being taken to Monty who is "the best there is" for "special treatment" (p. 85). The meaning of this is left purposely obscure, but having accomplished Stanley's abduction and the destruction of his individuality, it can be assumed that Goldberg and McCann's mission will culminate in total success. Stanley's new "birth" into shaven and suited respectability augurs the fulfillment of Goldberg and McCann's promises: he will surely emerge "re-oriented...adjusted...integrated."

Part of *The Birthday Party*'s mystification lies in Pinter's characterization of Goldberg and McCann as gangsters, hit-men with the power to destroy and abduct, who, however, carry no weapon other than language. The violence of their attitude toward Stanley, and the success of their brutalization, only deepen the mystification. The mystery, however, disappears once we realize that Pinter's characterization of Goldberg and McCann is parallel to his characterization of language. The brutality and potency of these stereotyped figures, their manipulative and coercive manner, are projections not only of their personalities but equally of the language for which they are a medium, and of which they are themselves composed. Their power to destroy and recreate Stanley is, in a sense, a concrete demonstration of the power which language exercises on us all.

Pinter's indictment of the terrorism of forced verbal conformity – and the subsequent loss of personal autonomy – can be further substantiated by reference to another play: *The Dwarfs*. Originally a novel written before *The Birthday Party* and containing many similar themes, it was later reworked into a radio play and finally into a stage play. *The Dwarfs* contains three characters, Len, Pete, and Mark, young men in their twenties who have been friends since childhood. Len seems to be in the midst of a personal, perhaps a mental crisis; he cannot communicate with his friends who are talkative, back-biting, manipulative, and preoccupied with trivia. He escapes their (to his mind) attempts to control him – to turn him into a "ventriloquist's dummy"[35] – by fleeing into an imaginary world populated by dirty, gluttonous dwarfs.

Just as there are two levels of action in *The Birthday Party*, so there are two levels of speech in *The Dwarfs*: "public" or conversational speech, and "private" or interior speech. Len experiences great difficulty with public speech. The words of others seem to cause him pain; he calls this outside speech "voices" and claims that they pierce him, make "a hole in (his) side." Not only conversation, but also the name-tags of objects seem alien to him. During his first interior monologue – many of the play's sections must be viewed as such – we hear Len rehearsing the names of the objects in his room in short, basic sentences which recall Kaspar's elementary attempts to learn public speech.

LEN: There is my table. That is a table. There is my chair. There is my table. That is a bowl of fruit. There is my chair. There are my curtains. [...] This is my room. This is a room. There is the wall-paper, on the walls. There are six walls. Eight walls. An octagon. [...]
I have my compartment. All is ordered, in its place, no error has been made. I am wedged. Here is my arrangement, and my kingdom. There are no voices. They make no hole in my side. (*Whispering.*) They make a hole, in my side. (pp. 87–8)

To escape from these "voices" Len creates a private fantasy world in which tactile contact is the main form of communication. The dwarfs who occupy this world are purely physical creatures who spend all their time either eating or playing. They never speak, possess no "voices," nor do we ever see them: we only learn of them through Len's descriptions. In his private world Len's language is not only fluent but highly evocative, even poetic. There is a marked discrepancy between

Len's stifled public language and the richness of his described fantasy.

> They nod, they yawn, they gobble, they spew. They don't know the difference. In truth, I sit and stir the stumps, the skins, the bristle. I tell them I've slaved like a martyr, I've skivvied till I was black in the face, what about a tip, what about the promise of a bonus, what about a little something? They yawn, they show the blood stuck between their teeth, they play their scratching game, they tongue their chops, they bring in their nets, their webs, their traps, they make monsters of their innocent catch, they gorge. (p. 96–7)

The Dwarfs centers around a comparison between two types of relationships: that which Len has with Pete and Mark, and that which he imagines with the dwarfs. It is a "rough" play, not totally consistent, and not easy to interpret. There are sections of dialogue in which Len appears quite normal, and then suddenly the conversation of his friends fills him with inexplicable anguish. At one point, while Pete is describing a nightmare he has had, Len "begins to grunt spasmodically, to whimper, hiss, and by the end of the speech, to groan" (p. 92). This extreme physical reaction to the "speech" of his friends recurs a number of times. Len feels threatened by Pete and Mark; he feels they are dishonest, cunning, trying to manipulate him. He fantasizes about them as killers and spiders arranging their web, a web in which he will be caught. He feels their manipulation in even the most trivial situations. In the following conversation, for example, Len tries to discuss Mark's new suit but quickly finds himself repeating Mark's words in almost hypnotic parrotry.

LEN: What's this, a suit? Where's your carnation?
MARK: What do you think of it?
LEN: It's not a schmutta.
MARK: It's got a zip at the hips.
LEN: A zip at the hips? What for?
MARK: Instead of a buckle. It's neat.
LEN: Neat? I should say it's neat. [...]
MARK: I didn't want it double-breasted.
LEN: Double-breasted? Of course you couldn't have it double-breasted.
MARK: What do you think of the cloth?

LEN: The cloth? [...] What a piece of cloth. What a piece of cloth.
    What a piece of cloth. What a piece of cloth. What a piece of
    cloth.
MARK: You like the cloth?
LEN: WHAT A PIECE OF CLOTH!
MARK: What do you think of the cut?
LEN: What do I think of the cut? The cut? The cut? What a cut!
    What a cut! I've never seen such a cut! (*Pause. He groans.*) (p. 88)

The dwarfs, on the other hand, are "a brotherhood. A true
community" (p. 99). Although they are dirty, self-centered
creatures whose only activities are eating and pleasure, Len
feels safe with them. In a beautiful sentence, Len describes the
dwarfs' eating-sounds as "a chuckle of fingers. Backchat of
bone, crosstalk of bristled skin" (p. 95). Note the speech
metaphors – chuckle, backchat, crosstalk – used here to describe not verbal activity but the sensual sounds of oral
pleasure. Len watches with envy as they "yowl [...] pinch,
dribble, chew, whimper, gouge, then soothe each other's
orifices with a local ointment, and then, all gone, all forgotten,
they lark about, each with his buddy" (p. 99). This wordless,
sensuous communion is contrasted with the pragmatic, banal
speech-world which Len finds so threatening. At one point, Len
tries to break away from the overbearing and demanding
friendship of Mark and Pete, and in a telling passage, he turns
on them:

LEN: You're trying to buy and sell me. You think I'm a ventriloquist's
    dummy. You've got me pinned to the wall before I open my
    mouth. You've got a tab on me, you're buying me out of house
    and home, you're a calculating bastard. (*Pause.*) [...] Both of
    you bastards, you've made a hole in my side, I can't plug it!
    (p. 97)

The play ends with Len in hospital suffering, according to
Pete, from "kidney trouble" (analogous to the "hole in my
side"?). He has lost Mark's and Pete's friendship. They too
have fought with each other, and Len, now alone, finds that he
has also lost his dwarfs. Deprived of his inner world, Len
returns to his attempt to grasp outer reality. The last lines of the
play return us to the language of Len's first monologue: "Now

all is bare. All is clean. All is scrubbed. There is a lawn. There is a shrub. There is a flower" (p. 108).

The Dwarfs is generally considered a difficult and unsuccessful play. It is full of mysteries. Little is known of the characters except what is given through Len's unstable mind, and the lack of verifiability is clearly one of its main themes. Len cannot grasp the world around him, never knowing whether what he perceives is "the scum or the essence" (p. 104). Nor can he respond to the world, since socially he is all but linguistically incapacitated. Austin E. Quigley, in an excellent essay, "*The Dwarfs*: A Study in Linguistic Dwarfism," suggests that Len's basic problem is "processing input (perceived complexity) into output (verbal patterns)."[36] This "perceived complexity" always pertains to the objective world, and his stunted "output" is always in terms of "public" language. "What vitally concerns Len," Quigley writes, "is not only his inability to do things with language but also his growing fears about what might be done to him through language."[37] Len feels himself "pinned to the wall" by the manipulative powers of others. This phrase obviously alludes to T. S. Eliot's "The Love Song of J. Alfred Prufrock" in which the eyes of others "fix" the impotent hero into a phrase and leave him "sprawling on a pin," no longer able to get free or to "begin" with words of his own. Like Prufrock, Len feels that he has been formulated "in a formulated phrase," that words outside of himself have robbed him of his identity, have left him "pinned and wriggling on the wall." In his one outright attack on those he accuses of "formulating" him, Len says that he is being treated like a "ventriloquist's dummy," that is, of course, like a lifeless object which mouths the words of others. In another passage, Pinter develops this "mouthing" metaphor:

LEN: You're frightened that any moment I'm liable to put a red hot burning coal in your mouth.
MARK: Am I?
LEN: But when the time comes, you see, what I shall do is place the red hot burning coal in my own mouth. (p. 90)

As a result of this "coal," Len would finally become incapable of "mouthing" the words of others, and thus of being manipulated.

Quigley's conclusion as to the basic theme of *The Dwarfs* can be applied equally well to *The Birthday Party*: "Linguistic control it seems, is the ultimate power in this play. To control what someone is *able to say* is to control to a considerable extent what they are *able to be*."[38] Len and Stanley have much in common. Both are alienated characters, outsiders, escapees from the world of ambition and manipulation. Both choose cop-out lives: Len in his silent fantasy world, Stanley in his passive seclusion. Both feel threatened, almost physically endangered by those who seem to represent the values and language of the "organization," of social norms. And both must finally relearn the language, and thus the norms, which they have rejected: Len from his hospital bed, Stanley through the torture and rehabilitation induced by Goldberg and McCann.

VÁCLAV HAVEL: *THE GARDEN PARTY* AND *THE MEMORANDUM*

Of all the postwar Czechoslovakian playwrights living and writing in their native country, Václav Havel is certainly the best known in the West.[39] His double career under the pre-December 1989 communist regime (before becoming President of his country) was as a political activist for human rights and a man of the theatre. These two activities merge in his plays, which, in a variety of idioms and styles, center on the individual's reaction to stifling outside constraints.[40]

Havel's theatre career began in 1960 when he joined Jan Grossman – director, critic, and theoretician – at the small Prague avant-garde "Theatre on the Balustrade" as dramaturge and resident playwright until 1968. The post-Stalinist political and cultural "thaw" of the mid 1960s made possible the writing and directing of plays which would previously have proved dangerous, and it was during this period that Havel wrote his major early plays: *The Garden Party* (*Zahradní slovnost*, 1963), *The Memorandum* (*Vyrozemení*, 1965), and *The Increased Difficulty of Concentration* (*Ztízená moznost soustredení*, 1968). The fact that Havel was writing in a communist country adds a dimension to his critique of language. The political aspect is more pronounced than in the plays of Ionesco and Pinter, and indeed the socio-political and the personal traits of his characters are almost totally merged. This, however, in no way limits his critique to only local interest. While he is more blunt in his parody of the establishment than either Ionesco or Pinter, language is similarly treated as a form of aggression, a prod to uniformity, and a threat to personal identity and autonomy. Jan Grossman, in his 1965 article "A Preface to Havel," notes that Havel's "key concern is the mechanization of man"[41] – a concern he shares with Ionesco, Pinter, Handke, and others, and which implies the interpenetration of political and personal language.

In both *The Garden Party* and *The Memorandum*, the protagonist is the mechanism which controls the human characters. The mechanism of cliché dominates the former play: man does not use cliché, cliché uses man. Cliché is the hero, it causes, advances, and complicates the plot, determines human action, and, deviating further and further from our given reality, creates its own.

Grossman's remark that in Havel's play "man does not use cliché, cliché uses man" echoes Doubrovsky's comment on Ionesco's use of language: "Instead of men using language to think, we have language thinking for men," and Pinter's line in *The Dwarfs* that language makes of us "a ventriloquist's dummy." Grossman continues:

In *The Memorandum*, the protagonist also comes from human speech: man makes an artificial language which is intended to render communication perfect and objective, but which actually leads to constant deepening alienation and disturbance in human relations... Abstract speech is the subject: it is projected onto the mechanism of cowardice, the mechanism of power, the mechanism of indifference, and each of these in itself – as well as all of them in harmony – creates a stratified, complex picture of human depersonalization.[42]

These themes are as common in the West as in communist east bloc countries, and Havel's accessibility to western audiences is well demonstrated by his success. During the three years following *The Garden Party*'s first performance in Prague in 1963, it was staged in eighteen West German theaters, in

Austria, Switzerland, Sweden, and Finland, as well as in Hungary and Yugoslavia. Both *The Garden Party* and *The Memorandum* were almost immediately translated into all major European languages and, when staged in New York in 1968, *The Memorandum* received the prestigious Obie Award.

The Garden Party and *The Memorandum* are studies of the inhuman absurdities of a centralist bureaucratic system. The system, a tangle of self-perpetuating rules and restrictions, displaces the individual, or rather transforms him into an extension of its mechanism stripped of individuality. Language in both plays floats in a dimension between the system and the character. It exists independently, as a level of reality which continuously threatens, and ultimately succeeds in "taking over" the characters and reducing them into compliance. Both plays center around this encroaching, dehumanizing language. In *The Garden Party* it is the play's only mode of operation; in *The Memorandum* it is, in addition, the subject of the plot. In both, the dramatic functions through the verbal matrix. As Havel himself claims: "In my own work...language...isn't or doesn't care to be merely a means of communication by which the characters express themselves, but a sphere in which drama, as it were, realizes itself directly."[43]

The Garden Party explicitly decodes the connection between language and power. The plot shows the overnight rise to power of Hugo Pludek who, like Handke's Kaspar, begins as a "blank" nobody, barely speaking, and is recreated through his acquisition of language into a powerful, although ultimately faceless, human cliché. The play opens in the Pludeks' home where Hugo spends his time playing chess against himself, thus always winning and losing simultaneously. Hugo's parents are portrayed as absurd specimens of middle-class mentality who, like the parents in Ionesco's *Jack, or the Submission*, tend to speak in extended clichés and confused aphorisms. "He who fusses about a mosquito net can never hope to dance with a goat"[44] quips Pludek-father, typically. His aphorisms, like Ionesco's, have the form of proverbs but their content is nonsensical. Inverted proverbs, false syllogisms, absurd deductions, meaningless verbal noises, all recur repeatedly, automatically, and constitute a speech-style which will later be contrasted by Havel with other, equally automatic speech-styles. Hugo is his parents' one hope since their other son, Peter, "the black sheep of the family" (p. 40), not only looks like an intellectual but insists on being bourgeois as well. Hugo, on the other hand, is compliant; from the first he parrots his parents' words and imitates their warped proverbs. These two images – the chess-player who always both wins and loses, thus inspiring his parents' admiration since "such a player will always stay in the game" (p. 14), and the verbal parrot who stays in the social game by appropriating the words of others – distinguish Hugo and mark him for success. Like Kaspar, Hugo absorbs the speech of others, repeats and expands upon borrowed sentences, finally treating them as his own. The people whom Hugo parrots are also very like Kaspar's Prompters: they are representatives of a society and language which are con-servative, reductive, and intent on maintaining the order of which they are a product. But Hugo, unlike Kaspar, does not rebel against his "speechification" ("Versprachlichung"). On the contrary: he completely appropriates the language of his "Prompters." By the end of the play even his parents can no longer recognize their son Hugo under the speech-object, the personification of jargon and double-talk, which he has become.

Act II shows Hugo's verbal re-education and the beginning of his rise to power. Hugo visits a government bureau, the Liquidation Office, whose function is (purposely) obscure, to meet Kalabis, a former friend of Pludek-father and now a high-ranking official, who has promised to start Hugo on his career. Kalabis never appears but this proves irrelevant, as does the garden party, for which the play is named but which we never see, which is taking place outside. Instead, Hugo meets the Clerk and Secretary of the Liquidation Office, and Falk, a high official at the dialectically opposed and equally mysterious Inauguration Service. All of these characters, like Hugo himself, are no more than stick-figures, vocal tubes who must be viewed only through their use of language: dogmatic, mechanical, and highly absurd. Hugo's education begins in earnest as he is exposed to a variety of rhetorical styles. The Clerk and

Secretary speak in mechanical, doctrinaire terms, as though reading from an official communiqué. Their sentences overlap and sound like one long monologue delivered in two voices. For example, an argument arises when Hugo suggests that Large Dance Floor A in the party area must be larger than Small Dance Floor C, and therefore "Why not move Self-Entertainment with Aids to Amusement to Large Dance Floor A and the dance of Sections to the Small Dance Floor C?"

SECRETARY: At first glance there's logic in it –
CLERK: Unfortunately, this kind of logic is merely formal –
SECRETARY: Moreover, the actual content of the suggestion testifies to an ignorance of several basic principles.
CLERK: You mean you'd approve if the dignified course of our garden party were disrupted by some sort of dadaistic jokerism which would certainly ensue if such an important and, as it were, junctional area as the Large Dance Floor A were to be opened to unbridled intellectualities?
SECRETARY: Moreover, what makes you think that Large Dance Floor A is larger than Small Dance Floor C? Why deceive oneself? (p. 22)

Hugo is overwhelmed and silenced by their formal, textbook style of speech with its long, clausal sentences and convoluted jargon. He retreats into silence and spends most of the second act listening and absorbing.

Falk, who is more powerful than the Clerk or the Secretary, also possesses a more complex set of speech-styles. He is a pompous, self-satisfied man who combines the vulgar phraseology of the common man – whom he claims to represent – with self-righteous slogans and ideological clichés. "I hate phrase-mongering and I resolutely reject all sterile cant," he claims (p. 23), and then expounds his fervent belief that "progress progresses" and "man lives:"

FALK: [...] At a certain stage it's really important that people frankly say to one another that they're sort of people. However, progress progresses and we mustn't get stuck with mere abstract proclamations. You know, I always say man – man lives! [...] You see, chums, life – life is a bloody marvellous thing. Don't you think? [...] And even a liquidation officer has a right to his slice of a really full – I mean, you know – er – full life! [...] I refuse to work with paper abstractions. You may stake your life on that! (p. 28)

This type of pretentious banality reaches a climax when Falk, in a contemplative mood, insists that "a whole damned heap of burning problems in matters of art and technology" need to be discussed. He produces his learned arguments for and against both of these important areas – using virtually identical terms. This absurd discussion proves important to Hugo who begins actively to appropriate key pieties and catch-words.

FALK: Art – that's what I call a fighting word! I myself – sort of personally – fancy art. I think of it as the spice of life. [...] Art ought to become an organic part of the life of each one of us –

SECRETARY: Absolutely! At the very next meeting of the Delimitation Subcommission I propose to recite a few lyrico-epical verses!

HUGO (*to himself*): Lyrico-epical verses –

FALK: Mind you, it's good that you're inflamed by the question of art, but at the same time you mustn't sort of one-sidedly overrate art and so sink into unhealthy aestheticism profoundly hostile to the spirit of our garden parties. As if we didn't have in technology a whole damned heap of burning problems.

CLERK: I was just going to change the subject and mention technology.

FALK: Technology – that's what I call a fighting word! You know, I maintain that we're living in the century of technology [...] Technology ought to become an organic part of the life of each one of us –

CLERK: Absolutely! At the very next meeting of the Liquidation Methodology Section I'll suggest that we reconsider the possibilities of the chemification of liquidation practice.

HUGO (*to himself*): The chemification of liquidation practice –

FALK: Mind you, it's good that you're inflamed by the question of technology, but at the same time you mustn't sort of one-sidedly overrate technology and so sink into perilous technicism which changes man into a mechanical cog in the dehumanized world of a spiritless civilization. As if we didn't have a whole damned heap of burning problems in matters of art!

SECRETARY: I was just going to change the subject and mention art –

FALK: Art – that's what I call a fighting word! (pp. 32–4)

Note the cascading platitudes, the hypnotic, overly-familiar phrases. Each repetition of these stock phrases inspires the Clerk and Secretary, eager to please, to a renewed act of verbal parrotry. The repetitions accelerate, sentences grow shorter and tumble over each other as the whole discussion takes on the mechanical aspect of an irrepressible engine running amok. Falk, the Clerk, and the Secretary fall into a paroxysm of staccato slogan exchanges:

FALK: It's good that you're inflamed by the question of technology. But you shouldn't underrate art.
SECRETARY: Art – that's what I call a fighting word!
FALK: It's good that you're inflamed by the question of art –
CLERK: But you shouldn't underrate technology!
SECRETARY: Technology – that's what I call a fighting word!
CLERK: It's good that you're inflamed by the question of technology!
SECRETARY: But you shouldn't underrate art!
CLERK: Art – that's what I call a fighting word!
SECRETARY: It's good that you're inflamed by the question of art –
   [...] (p. 35)

During this exchange a number of words break away and strike Hugo and he, silent until now, begins repeating them to himself. "Lyrico-epical verses – chemification of liquidation practice – Impressionism – the periodic table of elements – lyrico-epical verses – chemification – [...]" Hugo's first *coup* occurs when he strings all of the jargon, the slogans, and the style he has just learned into a long and overpowering polemic achieving a *synthesis* of both art and technology, thus gaining supremacy over Falk:

HUGO: [...] in the future art and technology will sort of harmoniously supplement each other – the lyrico-epical verses will help in the chemification of liquidation practice – the periodic table of the elements will help in the development of Impressionism – every technological product will be specially wired for the reception of aesthetic brain waves – the chimneys of the atomic power stations will be decorated by our best landscape painters – there will be public reading rooms twenty thousand leagues under the sea – differential equations will be written in verse – on the flat roofs of cyclotrons there will be small experimental theatres where differential equations will be recited in a human sort of way. Right? (p. 36–7)

Every phrase in this monologue is gleaned from the previous conversations. Hugo has conquered the phraseology, absorbed the cant, and with this begins his climb to power.

The third act shows Hugo's conquest of the Director of the Liquidation Office. In it the parody and exposure of ideological bureaucratic rhetoric reaches its peak, accelerating to the point where the speaker completely disappears behind the deadening, self-perpetuating jargon. The Director is a master of jargon and textbook ideology, but Hugo manages to assimilate his words and finally to displace him and assume his position through superior control of the rhetoric. The struggle between the two men is an almost physical power battle carried out over nine pages of text. Its rhythm is that of a boxing match: the two contestants at first carefully dance around each other, then throw out probing jabs, and finally enter into fierce struggle. The Director begins in a superior position of control. Their first "round" concerns the theoretical terminology of inauguration. The Director poses the questions, but is soon overcome by Hugo's talent for synthesizing jargon:

DIRECTOR: Inaugurating, to my mind, is sort of a specific form of education, isn't it?

HUGO: Yes. But it's also its specific method.

DIRECTOR: Well – form or method?

HUGO: Both. It's precisely this peculiar unity which guarantees its specificity.

DIRECTOR: Stimulating!

HUGO: Isn't it?

DIRECTOR: All right, but what is specific for the content of inauguration?

HUGO: Its specific form.

DIRECTOR: Stimulating!

HUGO: Isn't it?

DIRECTOR: All right, but what is specific for the form of inauguration?

HUGO: Its specific method.

DIRECTOR: Stimulating!

HUGO: Isn't it?

DIRECTOR: All right, but what is specific for the method of inauguration?

HUGO: It's specific content.

DIRECTOR: Thrice stimulating!
HUGO: Isn't it, isn't it, isn't it?
DIRECTOR: It is.
HUGO: Yes. And this specific interrelation might be called the basic
    inauguration triangle. (pp. 49–50)

Note the circular application of the terms "form," "method,"
and "content," and its dialectic synthesis into a "basic
inauguration triangle" of terms whose specific character, Hugo
suggests, "is precisely its triangularity." This parody of
dialectic thought and language recurs on many levels in Havel's
play, and I will discuss its significance later. As the verbal
struggle continues, sentences grow in length with certain words
recurring almost ritually. Hugo and the director vie for those
words, often picking up each other's speech in mid-sentence,
until finally both end up reciting the same stock dogmatic
phrases in complete unison.

HUGO: [...] nevertheless there exists a danger of sinking –
DIRECTOR: Into liberal extremism – which would happen to any
    who failed to see these positive short-term characteristics from
    the perspective of the later development of the Inauguration
    Service –
HUGO: And who failed to see behind their possibly positive intent –
    from the subjective point of view –
DIRECTOR: Their clearly negative impact – from the objective point
    of view –
HUGO and DIRECTOR: Caused by the fact that as a result of an
    unhealthy isolation of the whole office certain positive elements
    in the work of the Inauguration Service were uncritically
    overrated [...] (pp. 54–6)

The language seems to churn out on its own with Hugo and the
Director acting as mere vocal instruments for the pre-existing
and self-contained text. The Director is finally reduced to
sputtering monosyllables under Hugo's uninterrupted onslaught and when Hugo shouts "do stop messing about! This is
no time for tongue-twisters!" – the Director "backs out in
terror" (p. 56).

    This climactic duet raises the question: what indeed are
Hugo and the Director struggling over? They consistently
agree on all the issues, so they certainly do not represent varying ideologies. In fact, their struggle is not over the *meaning* of

their words – both say virtually the same things – but over the possession of the words. Power resides in the complete possession and the capacity for total identification with a pre-existing rhetorical structure. Words spew forth automatically, almost by rote, without recourse to intent. Thought is reduced to knowing the right jargon and using it in sufficient mass. Havel's fear and disgust with the strangling power of predigested rhetoric is brought into overt focus through such ironic comments as Falk's "I hate phrase-mongering and I resolutely reject all sterile cant," and Hugo's rejection of "tongue-twisters." At the height of Hugo's victory over the Director, Havel has him spout forth a convoluted condemnation of cliché and cant in the most fluent bureaucratic terms. Hugo rails against "the arsenal of abstract humanist cant [...] reflected in their typical form, for example in/the hackneyed machinery/of the pseudo-familiar inauguration phraseology hiding behind the routine of professional humanism a profound dilution of opinions [...] " (pp. 55–6). These uses of jargon signal the total self-containment of the rhetoric which has even integrated the terms of its own criticism. Karl Popper's critique of pseudo-scientific theories (especially Marxism and Freudianism) is to the point here: scientific theories, Popper claims, must contain, indeed seek, the conditions for their own refutation in order to demarcate the limits of their validity. Dogmatic thinkers, however, are "able to interpret any conceivable event as a verification of their theories."[45] When a theory is "immunized" against criticism, voided of all demarcation and fortified against refutation, it becomes totally closed, self-referential, and ultimately dangerous. Hugo's harangue against cant is a grab-bag of concepts and terms which cannot be refuted since they are their own criteria. Hugo's genius is his ability to assimilate whatever verbal style he meets, to disappear completely behind the self-validating language and to *become* that verbal style. His personality mutates directly into the verbiage, becomes a vessel for the pre-existing rhetoric. With each "conquest" Hugo transforms into the personality of the character he has replaced. He defeats the Director by *becoming* the Director, by stealing his inner being – which consists of nothing more than "Director rhetorics."[46]

The last act, Hugo's "homecoming," shows us the cost of such mutability. The proud Pludek parents have learned that Hugo has been put in charge of liquidating both the Liquidation Office and the Inauguration Service and of establishing on their ruins a Central Commission for Inauguration and Liquidation, which he is to head. The parents excitedly await their son's return, but when he does arrive they don't recognize him, nor does he seem to know them. In what appears as a parody of the sentimental eulogy, Hugo speaks of himself – his old self – in the third person, praising the absent Hugo. He speaks in repetitive platitudes, like a politician covering himself from all sides. When asked what he thinks of Hugo's new appointments, his answer is non-committal and totally self-negating: "Well, I'd say he should have not accepted it, not turned it down, accepted it and turned it down, and at the same time turned it down, not accepted it, not turned it down and accepted it. Or the other way round" (p. 69).

The climax of the act, a long, brilliant tirade by Hugo, testifies to the extent of his mutation and essential mutability. It is also a call by the author, from behind the words, that we beware of our own reduction into mechanical speech formulae. The monologue is pseudo-philosophical in tone and is clearly directed (in intention, although not through stage action) at the audience. Moreover, it is a sharp parody and critique of Marxist dialectic and the thesis of permanent change. In this speech Havel combines his essential faith in the dignity and complexity of man – even at one point alluding to Hamlet's "What a piece of work is man" – with scorn for the reductive, mechanical creature which man can be turned into. Hugo's parents ask him who he *is*, to which he replies:

Me? You mean who am I? [...] You think one can ask in this simplified way? No matter how one answers this sort of question, one can never encompass the whole truth, but only one of its many limited parts. What a rich thing is man, how complicated, changeable, and multiform – there's no word, no sentence, no book, nothing that could describe and contain him in his whole extent. In man there's nothing permanent, eternal, absolute; man is a continuous change [...] the time when A was only A, and B always only B is gone; today we all know very well that A may be often B as well as A; that B may just as well be A; that B may be B, but equally it may be A and C; just as C may be not only C, but also A, B, and D; [...] those who today understand only today are merely another version of those who yesterday understood only yesterday; while, as we all know, it's necessary today somehow to try and understand also that which was yesterday, because – who knows – it may come back again tomorrow! Truth is just as complicated and multiform as everything else in the world [...] he who is too much may soon not be at all, and he who – in a certain situation – is able to a certain extent to not-be, may in another situation be all the better for that. I don't know whether you want more to be or not to be, and when you want to be or not to be; but I know I want to be all the time and that's why all the time I must a little bit not-be. (pp. 73–5)

In this complex monologue Havel implicates two cornerstones of Marxist ideology: the dialectical thesis of permanent change which, as Trensky notes, in communist society became a tool for proving as well as denying everything;[47] and the dialectic method, the basic instrument of Marxist thought. The dialectical struggle of opposites, the Hegelian thesis and antithesis which ideally lead to a synthesis which contains and is qualitatively superior to both, is persistently questioned and parodied. This point is particularly important to the language of the play, for dialectic is not only a method, it is also a thought process which is reflected and incorporated in the formulae of speech. "For all dialectical thinkers to the degree that they are genuinely dialectical," writes the Marxist critic Fredric Jameson, "thinking dialectically means nothing more or less than the writing of dialectical sentences. It is a kind of stylistic obedience analogous to that which governs the work of art itself, where it is the shape of the sentences themselves [...] that determines the choice of the raw material [...] also the quality of the idea is judged by the type of sentence through which it comes to expression."[48] Ideally, such sentences reflect structures of thought which seek the integration of disparate realities much like, suggests Jameson, the surrealist image whose strength "increases proportionately as the realities linked are distant and distinct from each other."[49] Through this, the essential interrelatedness of reality finds expression. But when the link between dialectical thought and its governing ideology is broken, when alienation between method and meaning sets in, as it does in *The Garden Party*, then all that remains are empty forms. The structure is fossilized within the language which, as mere method devoid of meaning, becomes an automatic and deadly verbal game. Everything and its opposite can be said in one breath, and synthesis is no longer qualitatively superior to thesis and antithesis, but only its mechanical agglomeration.

In his excellent essay "On Dialectical Metaphysics" Havel wrote that "a certain type of 'dialectical synthesis' liquidate[s] two one-sided but nonetheless valuable opinions by combining them into one joint opinion which, while not one-sided, is however completely useless."[50] This tendency, he claims, defeats the true meaning of dialectic by becoming "fetish-ridden," a hardened mold of thought, rather than a flexible process. "A way of thinking becomes a formula for thought and the process turns into a scheme; instead of the dialectic confirming itself by serving reality, it is supposed to confirm itself by having reality serve it."[51] This is precisely what happens in the language of Havel's play. Such language can only sound absurd, contrived, empty. The "fossil" principle – i.e. the survival of dialectical structure devoid of its governing ideology and thus alienated from meaning – is found throughout *The Garden Party*. It is evident, for example, in the early chess-playing Hugo who simultaneously wins and loses; in Hugo's sterile synthesis of "art and technology"; in the "basic inauguration triangle"; in Hugo's advice to both reject and accept the new positions; and most explicitly in the closing tirade. The focus of that speech is on "being," on man's mode of existence. Its convoluted, semi-logical forms – "some only are, some are only, and some only are not," etc. – are a mad demonstration of linguistic forms as well as, poignantly, a personal statement on the impossibility of "being" under conditions in which to be is to be pre-determined by dead verbal and ideological structures. Hugo's last sentence reads: "And if at the moment I am – relatively speaking – rather not, I assure you that soon I might be much more than I've ever been – and then we can have another chat about all these things, but on an entirely different platform" (p.75). Hugo is "rather not" in that he has dissolved into a faceless object through his rhetorical subjugation. But the hope is extended, by Havel, that "an entirely different platform" *exists*, a different way of viewing man, a different set of terms, a different vocabulary; and here Havel seems to be speaking for man whom "no word, no sentence, no book" can contain, man who is not reduced to the empty forms of language. This section recalls Kaspar's first "breakdown" in which he recites a long list of variations on the verb "to be" – just when he has lost his "being" as an individual. Like Handke, Havel succeeds in merging a critique of language with a critique of language-engendered thought.

The Memorandum[52] takes place within a large organization, apparently a government bureau, although no name is given. The structure of the play is more schematic than *The Garden Party*: there are twelve scenes divided into four units, each with three alternating locations – the Director's office, the Ptydepe classroom, and the Secretariat of the Translation Center. This artificial structure de-emphasizes plot and stresses process. It is a structure often used in Expressionist plays, station dramas such as, for example, Strindberg's *To Damascus*. *To Damascus* Part I has seventeen scenes: the first eight descend into the Stranger's psyche; the last eight reverse the sequence and trace an ascension. *The Memorandum* follows a similar arc: the first six scenes show the fall from power of Josef Gross; the last six scenes repeat the first sequence precisely, but show his return to power. Here the similarities between Strindberg and Havel end. Strindberg's structure is a poetic, mystical vehicle well suited to the inner psychological landscape he is exploring. Havel's "stations" are no more than mechanical repetitions of sequence, equally well suited to exposing a barren, mechanical bureaucracy.

Gross, the protagonist, is the director of this government institution. As the play opens he is reading an indecipherable memorandum, a note written in some totally foreign language.

He soon discovers that the language is a synthetic creation of his own department, initiated behind his back by his own deputy, Balas, and is now to become the official language of bureaucratic communication. The thin plot of the play shows Gross's failed attempts to get this memorandum translated, an impossible task in view of the contradictory rules and red tape which govern translations. The new language, Ptydepe, is supposed to make misunderstandings impossible. It is to replace the imprecisions and emotional connotations of natural language and thus perfect the bureaucratic machine. Everybody is involved in the perpetuation of this language except Gross who, through his refusal to support Ptydepe, loses his job, is demoted to the lowliest position, and is replaced by Balas. Gross's initial objections to Ptydepe are on humanist grounds: "I'm a humanist," he explains, "[...]the staff is human and must become more and more human. If we take from him his language, created by the centuries-old tradition of national culture, we shall have prevented him from becoming fully human and plunge him straight into the jaws of self-alienation. I'm not against precision in official communications, but I'm for it only in so far as it humanizes Man" (p. 20). Gross is a mixture of sentimental nostalgia, liberal rhetoric, and impotence. In the end his "ideals" turn out to be as hollow as the language he opposes, and as mutable. When Gross finally does get the memorandum translated – illegally, through the aid of Marie, secretary of the Translation Center – it turns out to be a directive from "above" condemning Ptydepe and restoring Gross to power. Gross again becomes director and again installs Balas as his deputy. The ending of the play is disturbing: Marie is fired for her illegal aid in translating the memorandum and Gross refuses to help her; and Balas immediately proceeds secretly to introduce a second synthetic language, Chorukor, to which Gross again succumbs. Like Ionesco's *The Lesson*, this is a circular play in which language is both the central device and the main subject.

Some of the most interesting scenes of the play take place in the Ptydepe classroom where the linguist, Lear, lectures on the nature and function of the new language.

Ptydepe, as you know, is a synthetic language, built on a strictly scientific basis. Its grammar is constructed with maximum rationality, its vocabulary is unusually broad. It is a thoroughly exact language, capable of expressing with far greater precision than any current natural tongue all the minutest nuances in the formulation of important office documents. The result of this precision is of course the exceptional complexity and difficulty of Ptydepe. There are many months of intensive study ahead of you, which can be crowned by success only if it is accompanied by diligence, perseverance, discipline, talent and a good memory. And, of course, by faith. Without a steadfast faith in Ptdyepe, nobody yet has ever been able to learn Ptydepe. (p. 23)

Learning Ptydepe is nearly impossible and has been mastered by only a few linguists, caricatures whose style of speech is close to the bureaucratic jargon found in *The Garden Party*. Ptydepe is devised to attain maximum precision through maximum redundancy. Its basic method is a complex mixture of mathematical models and information theory which parody the scientific pretensions of modern structural linguistics which, after all, originated in Prague. It also has an affinity with Bertrand Russell's "logical atomism" which sought to create a mechanical, mathematical model of language which could be broken down into logical units – meanings and referents. This complex symbolic logic, like Ptydepe, exhibits a distrust of ordinary language as a precise meaning-bearing tool. As Lear explains, bombastically:

You see, a redundancy – in other words, the difference between the maximum and the real entropy, related to the maximum entropy and expressed percentually – concerns precisely that superfluity by which the expression of a particular piece of information in a given language is longer, and thus less probable (i.e. less likely to appear in this particular form), than would be the same expression in a language with maximum entropy; that is to say, in a language in which all letters have the same probability of occurrence. [...] Thus, for example, out of all the possible five-letter combinations of the 26 letters of our alphabet – and these are 11,881,376 – only 432 combinations can be found which differ from each other by three letters, i.e. by sixty per cent of the total. From these 432 combinations only 17 fulfill the other requirements as well and thus have become Ptydepe words. (pp. 24–5)

This intricate tabulation and sophisticated scientific creation leads to a situation in which the word "wombat," for example, has 319 letters, the word "whatever" is rendered "gh," and the exclamation "Hurrah!" becomes "frnygko jefr debux altep dy savarub goz texeres."

Through the discussion of Ptydepe, language theory becomes an overt subject in the play. But Ptydepe also offers a dramatic opportunity: spoken on stage by the linguists it comes across as pure gibberish and thus parodies, and renders comic, the theoretical assertions.

SAVANT: In ptydepe one would say axajores. My colleagues sometimes ylud kaboz pady el too much, and at the same time they keep forgetting that etrokaj zenig ajte ge gyboz.
STROLL: Abdy hez fajut gagob nyp orka?
SAVANT: Kavej hafiz okuby ryzal.
STROLL: Ryzal! Ryzal! Ryzal! Varuk bado di ryzal? Kabyzach? Mahog? Hajbam? (p. 35)

Thus, the audience is confronted with a supposedly rational but in fact totally opaque language. (In the Czech the nonsense is apparently more nuanced as certain letter combinations evoke Czech words. This is lost in the translation.) Ptydepe frustrates and conceals meaning from the audience, forcing them to question its efficacy and to identify with Gross's bafflement.

Ptydepe is an outgrowth of the stifling and counter-productive web of rules which characterize the play's under-lying world: the rule of the Bureaucracy. Like the bureaucracy it represents, Ptydepe is initially meant to be functional, to fulfill a rational need; but it grows, instead, into an ideology, becoming a grotesque and unconquerable mass. As in *The Garden Party*, the device of mechanical proliferation is employed. The rules of Ptydepe, like those bureaucratic rules which make it impossible to obtain translations, allow for endless expansion which finally threatens to destroy even those who created it. Ptydepe begins to usurp control, to *determine* expression. When it is finally outlawed, Lear, swiftly switching sides, delivers a condemnation in which he demonstrates the extent to which Ptydepe had come to master its users, "limiting more and more the possibilities for further continuation of texts, until in some instances either they could continue in only one specific direction, *so that the authors lost all influence over what they were trying to communicate*, or they couldn't be continued at all" (p. 103, my emphasis).

In *The Memorandum*, as in *The Garden Party*, language is the "hero" and the conqueror. For, although Ptydepe is ultimately rejected, a new artificial language replaces it and, with its fall, another will certainly rise. These artificial languages are not merely forms of speech, but forms of ideology. Just as Kaspar learns model sentences and axioms of thought simultaneously, and Hugo mutates into the language and thought patterns of those he replaces, so Ptydepe too conditions, indeed dictates, thought and behavior. Ptydepe has a clear affinity with Orwell's "Newspeak." Like Newspeak, it is meant to replace a natural language which does not embody the forms of a new ideology. "Oldspeak" is outlawed by the Party because of its "vagueness and its useless shades of meaning." The linguist Syme describes Newspeak in terms obviously parallel to Lear's description of Ptydepe: "Every concept that can ever be needed will be expressed by exactly *one* word, with its meaning rigidly defined," he tells Winston; "The Revolution will be complete when the language is perfect."[53] Orwell's appendix, "The Principles of Newspeak," puts the matter even more clearly:

The purpose of Newspeak was not only to provide a medium of expression for the world-view and mental habits proper to the devotees of Ingsoc, but to make all other modes of thought impossible. It was intended that when Newspeak had been adopted once and for all and Oldspeak forgotten, a heretical thought – that is, a thought diverging from the principles of Ingsoc – should be literally unthinkable, at least so far as thought is dependent on words. Its vocabulary was so constructed as to give exact and often very subtle expression to every meaning that a Party member could properly wish to express, while excluding all other meanings and also the possibility of arriving at them by indirect methods.[54]

Ptydepe, ostensibly intended to allow man greater control over his environment, becomes, like Newspeak, the determining structure of his thought. Dictating mental options through its verbal constrictions, it caused men, as Lear admits, to lose "all influence over what they were trying to communicate." As a dehumanizing mechanism, Ptydepe can enter the dictionary beside the word "Robot," invented by Havel's compatriot Čapek in his play *RUR – Rossum's Universal Robots*. Like the Robot, who is an extreme but recognizable version of modern mechanized man, Ptydepe too is an extreme but distinctly parallel version of modern "officialese," the language of rhetorical control which turns Hugo into a facless cog in *The Garden Party*.

The Memorandum, like *The Garden Party*, ends with the protagonist delivering a long speech through which Havel can speak directly to the audience. Gross speaks in the flowery liberal phrases of the humanist he still claims to be; but now this high-minded terminology is used to explain why he must betray Marie, accept the new synthetic language Chorukor, and succumb to the power-structure of which he is a part. The words, therefore, ring as both sincere and ironic, as Havel's and Gross's voices overlap:

> [...] we are irresistibly falling apart, more and more profoundly alienated from the world, from others, from ourselves. Like Sisyphus, we roll the boulder of our life up the hill of its illusory meaning, only for it to roll down again into the valley of its own absurdity. Never before has Man lived projected so near to the very brink of the insoluble conflict between the subjective will of his moral self and the objective possibility of its ethical realization. Manipulated, automatized, made into a fetish, Man loses the experience of his own totality; horrified, he stares as a stranger at himself, unable not to be what he is not, nor to be what he is. (p. 108)

This alienation is as true of Hugo as of Gross, and their total submission to inorganic languages is the signal of their defeat.

There is a strong atmosphere in Havel's plays which derives not from the western tradition of the Absurd, but from a closer source: Prague, the city which produced Kafka and Hašek, Prague, "that ancient, mysterious city with its dark winding streets and haunting legends of the Emperor who was an alchemist or the old Rabbi who made an artificial man, a Golem, from a lump of clay; Prague, the seat of a vast and alien bureaucracy ruling a downtrodden population that did not know the meaning and purpose of the complicated rules and regulations it had to obey," to quote Esslin.[55] Kafka is clearly present in Havel's plays. The bureaucracy of the Liquidation Office and the grotesque intricacies of translating a Ptydepe memo, are mechanical versions of Joseph K's search for the court of justice and, indeed, for the nature of his crime in Kafka's *The Trial.* The airless, oppressive inner sanctuary of Kafka's court house, with its endless mushrooming files and the patiently, hopelessly waiting petitioners, is an image which underlies both of Havel's plays. In addition, Hugo has much in common with Hašek's *Good Soldier Schweik* who carries out his absurd orders *ad absurdum,* precipitating his personal collapse. Like Schweik, Hugo and eventually Gross, too, submerge themselves in the oppressive logic and language of their world, succumbing to a mechanism which they cannot withstand.

Havel's life since the Soviet invasion of Czechoslovakia in 1968 has also shared in the atmosphere and ironies of Kafka and Hašek. He lost his position at the Balustrade Theatre in 1969 and became a "free-lance," i.e. essentially unemployed author, continuing to write plays which were not produced. His unpopularity with the new regime resulted both from his personal views – expressed in various articles and in his plays – and from his political involvement in the Czech dissident movement and in human-rights issues. It resulted in numerous arrests, house arrests, and a combined total of almost five years' imprisonment between the years 1977 and 1989. In 1978 Havel wrote a philosophical–political essay, "The Power of the Powerless" (not published, but circulated among friends and sympathizers), whose theme is directly related to *The Garden Party* and *The Memorandum*. It is a detailed analysis of the nature of post-totalitarian regimes, and of the effects of prolonged exposure to ideological indoctrination on the moral well-being of a people, and on the individual psyche. Eleven years later, and only a month before the regime he so opposed would crumble without a battle and he himself would be elected as the President of Czechoslovakia, Havel wrote an acceptance speech for the Peace Prize of the German Booksellers Association – in which he again warned against the danger of words. "There can be no doubt that distrust of words is less harmful than unwarranted trust in them," he wrote. We should always be suspicious and wary of words, but "this is not just a linguistic task. Responsibility for and toward words is a task which is intrinsically ethical."[56]

THE POLITICS OF LANGUAGE DOMINATION

In a poem written about Joseph Stalin – a poem that would cost the poet his life – Osip Mandelstam creates a stunning image of political tyranny as residing in, and enacted through, verbal domination. Mandelstam depicts "The Kremlin's Mountaineer," as he calls him, as a man who derives and exercises power through his usurpation of language: "He alone talks Russian." The violent images of oppression center around his tyrannical control of speech; he is felt in every whispered half-conversation, his words heavy "as ten-pound weights," his sentences striking out "like horseshoes" never missing their mark. Language has weight and mass, it hits and pounds, torturing, castrating. "He always hits the nail, the balls" – and reduces others, his drained advisors, the half-men with whom he plays, to a subhuman gurgling of "touching and funny animal sounds." This concrete depiction of verbal violence, as George Steiner writes, "images and enacts a notion of language as being itself murderous."[58] Stalin's murderous language contains a political ideology: the ideology of absolute power which controls speech and indeed redefines language in its own terms. This power parallels that of the Professor in *The Lesson* who both creates language and uses it to kill; it also parallels the philosophy of O'Brien in *Nineteen Eighty-Four*: "The object of power is power," he tells Winston; "When finally you surrender to us it must be of your own free will. We do not destroy the heretic…we convert him, we capture his inner mind, we reshape him."[59] No doubt he is reshaped into a half-man who makes "touching and funny animal sounds."

All of the plays studied above, implicitly or explicitly, view language domination as the extension of an ideology. The ideologies vary, but all are encapsulated and propagated through language, and all result in the dehumanization of their victims. It is interesting that the three authors discussed here –

Ionesco, Pinter, and Havel – implicate in these plays the three major ideologies of the twentieth century: Fascism, Capitalism, and Marxism. The implications range from the blatant – the Professor's donning of a swastika-emblazoned armband and Hugo's mastery of dialectical rhetorics – to the subtle – Goldberg's mass of corporate jargon and consumer-oriented promises. In each case, the ideological implications form a backdrop and offer a context for the verbal violence.

The connection between language and politics, between the corruption of language and the loss of autonomy, has been discussed in two outstanding essays: George Orwell's "Politics and the English Language" and Herbert Marcuse's "The Closing of the Universe of Discourse," from his book *One-Dimensional Man*. Both Orwell and Marcuse denounce the corruption of free thought through the mechanical acceptance of pre-formed verbalizations, the "gumming together [of] long strips of words which have already been set in order by someone else," as Orwell put it,[60] and which preclude the development, differentiation, or contradiction of meaning. Marcuse claims that such language is ruled by "operationalism," i.e. the tendency to reduce things and concepts to their function, so that the concept is "absorbed by the word."[61] Concepts thus absorbed induce automatic, single-faceted connotations which are no longer open to criticism or revision. An anti-critical syntax allows for the telescoping and abridgement of ideas into stock slogans; the replacement of tentative propositions by ritual–authoritarian formulae; the reconciliation of opposites (e.g. "clean bomb") which immunize the mind against concepts. "This language speaks in constructions which impose upon the recipient the slanted and abridged meaning, the blocked development of content, the acceptance of that which is offered *in the form in which it is offered*."[62] Ritualized phrases, jargonized terms, debased idioms, are tacked together "like the sections of a prefabricated henhouse"[63] and the result of this automatism is that man is literally "taken over" by language, hypnotized, as it were, and forced to accept frozen formulae which can no longer create, or express, conceptual thought. Such language is often identified with dogma or propaganda but is also found in the slogans of advertising or the reduced lingo of journalism. Thus, Marcuse warns, hallowed and magical formulae of speech, authoritarian, threatening and dangerous, have become the public norm. And Orwell cautions that such language, "if not indispensable, is at any rate favourable to political conformity."[64]

All of these distortions appear, to one degree or another, in the plays discussed. The Professor's method of instruction, for example, is clearly authoritarian. He silences the Student's attempts to ask questions – "Be quiet. Sit where you are. Don't interrupt" (p. 200) – and forces on her a vocabulary, verbal and conceptual, which she has no option to challenge or contradict. Threats of violence – "Silence! Or I'll blow your brains out!" (p. 209) – and their ultimate implementation through verbal rape and murder complete the picture of a dictatorial will forced on its drained victims. The Professor's self-validating, hypnotic language closely approximates Marcuse's description of "magic" authoritarian–ritual speech-formulae which exclude "the process of cognition and cognitive evaluation."[65] Without the mediation of cognition, the "space" between the word and its meaning dissolves, and concepts are reduced to the word which contains them. As the Professor proves, such "magical" language induces pained obedience and powerless subordination. Ionesco's injection of the Nazi armband at the end of *The Lesson*, while dramatically clumsy, underlines the affinity which the play demonstrates between coercive verbal norms and totalitarian practices. The degeneration of the German language under Nazism – a degeneration from which German, according to Sternberger, has yet fully to recover[66] – is only one example of the reciprocal influence of language on ideology and ideology on language.

Although Ionesco has been an outspoken critic of Brecht, Sartre, and other "committed" playwrights, and engaged in 1958 in a public dispute with Kenneth Tynan and others over the role of literature (personal testimony versus social commitment), he is in fact an intensely "committed" writer. His commitment, however, is *against* the spreading of ideologies. Ionesco's basic fear of authoritarianism – personal and political – and of the doctrines and ideologies which foster it, underlies his attack on language.

If anything needs demystifying it is our ideologies, which offer ready-made solutions (which history quickly overtakes and refutes) and a language that congeals as *soon as it is formulated*. It is these ideologies which must be continually re-examined in the light of our anxieties and dreams, and their congealed language must be relentlessly split apart in order to find the living sap beneath.[67]

Hardened ideologies and their fossilized verbal mold impose themselves on the individual and invade the contents of the subjective self. Man thus controlled by verbal codes becomes "a man of slogans, who [...] repeats the truths that others have imposed upon him, ready-made and therefore lifeless. In short the *petit bourgeois*," Ionesco claims, "is a manipulated man."[68] He is manipulated into continuous conformity through the uncritical acceptance of an unfelt mechanical language, a body of pre-determined concepts.

Conceptual dictatorship is even more clearly demonstrated in *The Birthday Party* and *The Garden Party*. In these plays, as in *Kaspar* and *Jack*, language imposes conformity to ideological norms. The means of imposition is through verbal indoctrination; the result is the conversion of the victim and his subsequent perpetuation of the imposed doctrine. Stanley and Hugo differ from each other in a number of important ways. Stanley has rejected conformity to mainstream norms and mores and is forced to return through verbal torture. He fights against his brutal reintegration but loses, to be reborn into the visual mold (clean-shaven, well-dressed), and verbal stereotypes of his torturers. Hugo is a more opportunistic character. Prompted by his parents' ambition, he chooses to "play up, play up, and play the game," as Goldberg would put it, unaware that the process of successful conformity will lead to his personal annihilation. Both emerge, at the end of the play, laced into a straightjacket of clichés: Stanley's well-tailored executive image, and Hugo's faceless cloak of party power. Language has eroded individual consciousness, realizing Orwell's warning that personal subjugation through prefabricated language, "if not indispensable, is at any rate favourable to political conformity."

Pinter and Havel create for their characters language-determined fates which are similar, although rooted in different ideologies. In Stanley's case the materialistic bias of a capital-oriented society becomes apparent through the promises which Goldberg and McCann make, promises with the ring of an advertisement campaign to intensify consumer desires. In Hugo's case the fossilized rhetorics of bureaucratic politics are contained in a "fetish-ridden" dialectical mold which betrays its Marxist bias. In both cases, succumbing to the verbal structures of the ruling norm entails the characters' automatic incorporation into the political power-structures which this language embodies and serves. Stanley and Hugo are *absorbed* by the language and programmed to emerge as perpetuators of the dogma. Stanley's projected future is one of wealth and power; similarly, Hugo attains the heights of power through his verbal parrotry. For both, the possession of the ideologically "correct" rhetoric is *identical* with the possession of power.

Havel's *The Memorandum* attacks not only dogma and cliché, but also the soulless mechanism for their perpetuation: Bureaucracy. Bureaucracy as a system of order and control, a system which Hannah Arendt terms "rule by Nobody," has produced Ptydepe and is to be reinforced through it. If we consider tyranny as government which is not held to give account of itself, then "rule by Nobody," according to Arendt, "is clearly the most tyrannical of all, since there is no one left who could even be asked to answer for what is being done."[69] No one person is responsible for creating Ptydepe, although all are eventually held accountable to its rules. Ideology is directly codified into its synthetic form, and that form becomes the framework for thought. Ptydepe is a more extreme form of dogmatism than Hugo's rhetoric, but both share the same basic nature. Both are authoritarian reductions of meaning which insist, as Marcuse puts it, on "the acceptance of that which is offered in the *form* in which it is offered." That is, the prefabricated formula is offered in lieu of meaning. When the Director and Hugo speak, for example, of "the hackneyed machinery/of the pseudo-familiar inaugural phraseology hiding behind the routine of professional humanism a profound dilution of opinions" (p. 56), this jumble of terms cannot be said "in other words." To rephrase would be to destroy its potency, which resides precisely in the dogmatic compression of incompatible parts into a closed, opaque whole. The *form* in which it is offered – whether it be the jingles of advertisement, the slogans of political demagoguery, or the "scientific" vocabulary of Ptydepe – is the formula which invades our consciousness. "Hammered and re-hammered into the recipient's mind," Marcuse insists, "they produce the effect of enclosing it within the circle of the conditions prescribed by the formula."[70]

In all of these plays language is imposed from without. Its power and efficacy are represented through figures who, themselves, possess both authority and position: a professor, parents, messengers for a powerful "organization," leading bureaucrats. The catch and irony of this is that these figures derive their position and their authority from their *own* conformity to pre-existing verbal norms, and are thus rendered appropriate vessels through which language can subjugate the rebellious or the uninitiated. The abstract quality of this socially and politically imposed "normative" language is paradigmatically captured in *Kaspar*, in which language is embodied in the aural presence of Prompters who through words alone, without the need for physical presence, coerce total conformity to a speech mold. Roland Barthes, in what Susan Sontag called "that instantly notorious hyperbole,"[71] indicts the power of language with the words "language – the performance of a language system... is quite simply fascist; for fascism does not prevent speech, it compels speech."[72] Citing Jakobson, Barthes argues that "a speech-system is defined less by what it *permits* us to say than by what it *compels* us to say":

In French (I shall take obvious examples) I am obliged to posit myself first as subject before stating the action which will henceforth be no more than my attribute: what I do is merely the consequence and consecution of what I am. In the same way, I must always choose between masculine and feminine, for the neuter and the dual are forbidden me. Further, I must indicate my relation to the other person by resorting to either *tu* or *vous*; social or affective suspension is denied me. Thus, by its very structure my language implies an inevitable relation of alienation. To speak, and, with even greater reason, to utter a discourse is not, as is too often repeated, to communicate; it is to subjugate [...][73]

Barthes concludes that: "Once uttered, even in the subject's deepest privacy, speech enters the service of power."

The French philosopher Bernard-Henri Lévy, in agreement with Barthes, develops these arguments eloquently, and more overtly politically, in his book *Barbarism with a Human Face*. The barbarism to which the title refers is political: its sources are both in the Left and in the Right, and its weapon is an absolutist ideology. "There is an obvious relationship between the forms of power and the shape of language, between the orders of a Prince and the images of a sentence," he writes, quoting Oswald Spengler.[74] Speech "*is* simply power, *the very form of power, entirely shaped by power* even in its most modest rhetorical expression[...] To speak is inevitably to pronounce and articulate the law. There is no full speech which is not full of prohibition, no free discourse not stamped with the seal of tyranny[...] Grammar is a police force, syntax a court of law, writing a pair of handcuffs [...] to speak is to become, in every sense of the term, a *subject*."[75] Lévy develops this idea of language as power and control in connection with the totalitarian state:

What does a State do when it hatches the mad project to become identical with the society it administers? It imposes a language on it, its own language, its own discourse, claiming to have found it in society and simply to have transcribed it; for Stalinists this is known as "democratic centralism." What is to be understood by a total State and its negation of division and social polyphony? This must mean not the State but the total discourse, the one it offers about itself and indirectly about the society it denies [...][76]

It is this active function of language as a shaping, manipulative force, outside of individual control and in constant conflict with man's will to individuality, which is heightened and revealed in these plays. Ionesco, Pinter, and Havel posit language stage center and allow it to take over and undermine their characters. The absurd quality of these plays derives largely from the seeming ridiculousness of the "direct leap" from word to power. A middle link – the link of *action* which is normally assumed to implement language – is almost totally missing. There are few actions in these plays. Goldberg and McCann carry no weapons, the Professor need not brandish a real knife, Hugo uses no physical force. The only threat and the only weapon is language. And this is the point of the plays: verbal control is shown to be an action which is as powerful, and dangerous, as control through force of arms.

CHAPTER 4

Language as a prison: verbal debris and deprivation

In Peter Handke's play *They Are Dying Out* (*Die Unvernünftigen sterben aus*, 1973), the loquacious tycoon Quitt – who throughout has been seeking words with which to recreate himself – accuses his servant/confidant Hans of making fun of his language:

I would much prefer to express myself inarticulately like the simple people in that play recently, do you remember? Then you would finally pity me. This way I suffer from my articulateness being part of my suffering. The only ones that you and your kind pity are those who can't speak about their suffering.[1]

Quitt explains, sarcastically, that the characters of that play moved him, for, despite their speechlessness, their poverty and seemingly dehumanized demeanor, they too seek contact:

They too want tenderness, a life together, et cetera – they just can't express it, and that is why they rape and murder each other...The animalistic attracts me, the defenceless, the abused and insulted.[2]

Handke's semi-mocking remarks are obviously directed against a fellow playwright who, like Handke, is obsessed with the relationship between language and power, language and debasement: namely, the German Franz Xaver Kroetz. But unlike Handke's Quitt, Kroetz's socially depressed characters cannot protest their deprivation through meaningful speech – which is what they most basically lack.

Inarticulateness is not a new phenomenon in drama, but it has never in the past been used as the subject and entire substance of a play. Even Büchner's Woyzeck, the first and most famous of the modern inarticulates, is surrounded by more explicit characters who can control their language – and therefore also control him. Another famous inarticulate, O'Neill's Yank of *The Hairy Ape* represents, like Woyzeck, the natural goodness of the oppressed, warped by a fluent and uncaring world. Whatever Yank cannot say is made clear by the other characters; the burden of verbal expressiveness is not on him alone. Moreover, both Woyzeck and Yank transcend their verbal inadequacy through their heightened and expressive literary significance. The inarticulates discussed here don't have this advantage. They in no way transcend their deficient verbal lives, nor do they evidence any "natural goodness"; they are shaped and shackled, culturally and morally, by their deficiency.

Three playwrights – the German Kroetz, the English Edward Bond, and the American David Mamet – have written a group of plays which enclose us in the stunted and violent world of the verbally debased. Kroetz's early plays – I will concentrate on three – are dedicated to the problem of restricted language and diminished lives. Bond, in his plays *Saved* and *The Pope's Wedding*, and Mamet, in his powerful *American Buffalo* and *Glengarry Glen Ross*, deal with similar themes. In each of these plays a certain environment is reproduced, and a cohesive, if usually fringe group, speaking an undifferentiated and highly restricted language, is portrayed. The playwrights demonstrate the inter-relationships between character and social milieu, between the milieu and the restricted language available, and between the language and the overt and covert violence which erupts with sudden and mindless brutality in their plays. They center our attention on the diminished verbal world of their characters, showing it as not merely the result, but the *source* of their maimed existence. All of the plays are characterized by realistic depiction, and by a language consisting largely of fragmented sentences, uncommunicative banalities, and repetitive clichés. They are plays in which a very limited verbal world imprisons the characters, drastically stunts their relationships with the outer world and their inner selves, and leads to disproportionate aggression.

FRANZ XAVER KROETZ: "NO HARM IN TALKING"

When two one-act plays by Kroetz opened in Munich in 1971, they created a minor scandal. Shouting crowds, throwing stinkbombs and rotten eggs, protested the showing of *Homeworker* (*Heimarbeit*, 1969) and *Stiff-Necked* (*Hartnäckig*, 1970) in which an attempted abortion, masturbation, copulation, and the drowning of an infant were to be shown on stage. Marieluise Fleisser, who came out of retirement to attend the premier of her "favorite son," later wrote that "The little people who protested on the streets didn't understand that these plays were about their plight."[3]

Kroetz belongs to a group of German and Austrian playwrights who emerged in the mid-60s with a drama which has been termed the "New Realism" or, as some prefer to view it, "the new Folk-play" ("das neue Volksstück"). Writers such as Martin Sperr, Rainer W. Fassbinder, Jochen Ziem, Harold Sommer, Peter Turrini, all wrote plays about the socially underprivileged, demonstrating their helplessness and oppression through their verbal inarticulateness. Like Kroetz, they preferred some form of dialect to *Hochdeutsch* (high or standard German) and emphasized their characters' limited, banal language. In addition, these writers – especially Fassbinder, Sperr, and Ziem – shared with Kroetz a debt to the "rediscovered" playwrights Ödön von Horváth (1901–38) and Marieluise Fleisser (1901–73) who had been virtually unread and unproduced since the early 1930s. Horváth, an Austro-Hungarian, and Fleisser, a Bavarian, wrote so-called "Critical Folk-plays" in the 1920s and '30s, and both documented the corrupt, clichéd language of the *Kleinbürgertum*. Similarly, the "new realists" wrote about the "common man" – usually of a lower-class milieu – and employed a vernacular rather than a literary style of speech. Kroetz, who has repeatedly declared his indebtedness to both Horváth and Fleisser, went further than his contemporaries in demonstrating and indicting a class-connected language which had become an alienating and distortive tool. Like Horváth, he viewed the "little man" as disinherited, fiercely restricted and unable to fashion his own fate. Like Fleisser, he gave his characters a language "which is of no use to them, because it's not theirs."[4]

Kroetz's plays fall roughly into three periods: the early plays (1968–71); those written after he became an active member of the German Communist Party in 1972; and the more recent plays written after he had distanced himself from the Communist Party. The plays written after 1972 differ from the earlier work in a number of ways: the milieu shifts from the rural lower class to an urban lower middle class; the shocking brutality, which had previously earned Kroetz both fame and notoriety, is here reduced; and most importantly, the characters are given a greater, and sometimes didactic, verbal capacity. These changes are conscious, ideological, and interesting in themselves; I will, however, limit myself to Kroetz's early plays.

All of those plays deal with a marginal social group living outside of industrial German society and excluded from the mainstream economic prosperity. These are essentially "family" dramas set almost exclusively within the home or its immediate environment. The plots tend to center on an aberrant occurrence which threatens the "order" of family life – usually an unwanted pregnancy or an accident – and almost always leads to violence. In Kroetz's first play *Wild Crossing* (*Wildwechsel*, 1968), the pregnant thirteen-year-old Hanni refuses to give up her lover and ends up both shooting her father to death and losing the child. In *Homeworker*, Martha tries to abort her illegitimate child with a knitting needle, thus deforming the infant. Her husband Willy will later drown the mutilated child in a tub, calling the murder "a death like any other." In *Michi's Blood* (*Michis Blut*, 1970), a strange two-character play consisting almost entirely of the painful attempt of a man and a woman to make some meaningful verbal contact, the one action of the play is the crude abortion of Marie's child by Karl, the father: and her resulting death. *Farmyard* (*Stallerhof*, 1971) and its sequel *Ghost Train* (*Geisterbahn*, 1971), Kroetz's most important plays of this period, include graphic scenes of rape, defecation, masturbation, nudity, and finally an infanticide carried out on stage by its mentally and verbally retarded fourteen-year-old mother.

All of this is presented with spare economy and almost claustrophobic tightness in short, close-up scenes, focusing on a few characters all of whom speak the same language and are on the same level of verbal and existential consciousness. Even more disturbing, the plays contain virtually no authorial intrusion: no character who speaks for the author, no *raissonaire* who represents an alternative voice, no character whose level of consciousness is above that of the others. This is perhaps the major reason for the hopelessness in the plays, the sense of total, unreprieved imprisonment. Also absent is the authorial device of slanting blame, or passing judgment on his characters: all the characters are presented in an equal light, all are victims who exist on the stage without comment, without blame. An author can intrude through stage directions or prefigurations (in language or actions) which prepare an audience for vital events. A famous example of this is Hedda Gabler's gun; the numerous references to it and its symbolic significance prefigure her suicide. Ibsen organizes the elements of his stage reality so that they reinforce and explain each other. Kroetz rarely does so. Violence and graphically distasteful scenes all occur suddenly, without preparation or aftermath, with a stubborn refusal of comment. The audience, like the characters, is denied any privileged information. All this, as will be shown, is most prominently contained and demonstrated through the characters' empty, transparent language which harbors no "unexpressed" depths – unlike, for example, that of Chekhov's characters, whose banality masks profound longings and helps bridge over great personal unhappiness. With Kroetz the banal is all there is. That which Kroetz's figures cannot express is, tragically, that which they also cannot think or feel. Their language is the limit of their consciousness, and as such it is painfully insufficient, incapable of intimacy, of understanding, of compassion.

Kroetz has claimed that the speech of his characters does not function properly, that their problems lie so far back and are so advanced, they can no longer express them in words. He blames the social power-structure for his characters' hollowness, accusing society of "verbal expropriation."[5] But the impression of a language expropriated, "stolen" by society, is not available in the plays themselves. The social situation is given by the author without comment and accepted by the characters with hardly a thought. Poverty and social deprivation are the realities, but they are rarely the issue. They underlie all of Kroetz's plays, are implied by the settings and circumstances; but Kroetz, in these plays, does not analyze a social situation, does not point out sources, structures. Nor does he condemn. He merely reproduces the reality, turning the audience into witnesses. Paradoxically, from within their strangled language the characters' poverty and moral vacuity become most explicit.

The plot of *Farmyard* and *Ghost Train* centers on Beppi, the fourteen-year-old, marginally retarded daughter of the Farmer and his Wife. At a country fair, after soiling her pants in fear during a ride on the "ghost train," Beppi is casually, almost unwittingly "deflowered," raped, and made pregnant by her friend, the elderly farmhand Sepp. A love relationship develops between them, much to the parents' horror. When, after she gives birth to a son, her parents insist she give it up to a Home, Beppi runs away with the child to live in the city with Sepp. There they live in dire poverty, though with mutual love. Sepp soon falls ill and dies; the parents refuse to come to the funeral; Beppi remains alone with the child. When she is informed that the child will be taken from her by a state agency, she kills the baby and leaves his body in a box on the ghost train. The play ends with Beppi in juvenile prison. This potentially sensational plot is given by Kroetz in numerous short, understated scenes. An example of his style can be seen in the following, in which the Farmer confronts Sepp with the evidence of Beppi's pregnancy.

(*Farmer and Sepp in Sepp's room. Pause.*)
FARMER: This is gonna cost you ten years and me my honor.
SEPP: But not 'cause it was on purpose.
FARMER: As if that helps. (*Long pause.*)

It leaves you speechless. (*Pause.*)...
FARMER: Wanna hear a secret? She's pregnant.
SEPP: Why?
FARMER: That's right.
SEPP: Not true. That's a lie.
FARMER: We got proof.
SEPP: Can't be.
FARMER: Exactly.
SEPP: Not right.
FARMER: They do a test. Costs ten marks.
SEPP: Why?
FARMER: It's made from piss.
SEPP: Whose?
FARMER: Hers....
SEPP: (*Pause.*) But it wasn't on purpose.
FARMER: 'Cause you're a pig. No way around that.
SEPP: Exactly... (*Farmyard*, II, 7)[6]

Kroetz's language, as we see here, manages to sound natural, almost Naturalistic: but it is actually highly stylized (this is particularly evident in the German original). The plays are written in a German colored by Bavarian diction and using some of its typical idioms, but by no means in dialect. Certain characteristic linguistic elements, already apparent above, recur in all of Kroetz's early plays. These elements define the speech of his characters; they also mark the limits of their verbal capacity. The language is composed almost entirely of pre-formed, standard, and repetitive units of speech strung together. These units fall into three groups: clichés and cliché-idioms; proverbs and other quotations; and semantic blanks, such as the use of "why" and "exactly," above. The cliché is the most extensively used form. It is the staple of communication among the characters, spiced and reinforced by proverbs and axiomatic wisdoms. The two main characteristics of the cliché are its total absence of originality and a sense of automatism, of unthinking, pre-conditioned response. Whole sections of dialogue often consist of such clichés and cliché-idioms which, as opposed to the clichés studied in the previous chapter, are neither absurd nor comic:

WIFE: We should'a gone to the burial.
FARMER: A pauper's grave...

WIFE:... (*Pause.*)Whatever you do is wrong. [*Wie mans macht, is es falsch.*]

FARMER: Exactly. [*Genau.*]...

WIFE: Where there's a will there's a way. (*Pause.*) Better late than never. [*Wer die Wahl hat, hat die Qual. (Pause.) Besser spät wie nie.*]

FARMER: Why? [*Warum?*]

WIFE: Better late than never. [*Besser spät wie nie.*]

FARMER: Yea. It's never too late! [*Ja. Es is nie zu spät.*] (*Pause.*)

WIFE: This is no time to lose heart. [*Das is jetzt keine Zeit zum Kopfhängenlassn!*]...

WIFE:... (*Pause.*)Time cures all ills. [*Wenn die Zeit vergeht, kann man alles richtn, wie man sieht.*]

FARMER: That's a fact. [*Das is bewiesn.*] (*Ghost Train*, III, 4)

These typical German clichés (freely translated) comprise almost the entire content of the above "discussion." But clichés rarely appear alone; they are usually reinforced through a quote. Quotes in Kroetz's dialogue are used in counterpoint to the clichés. Quotes are always in *Hochdeutsch*, a "foreign" language to these characters, one of authority and wisdom.[7] To quote is to participate in this wisdom, to gain a momentary sense of borrowed power. Quotes are of two sorts: the quotation proper, i.e. biblical verse or well-known proverbs – such as the above adage on time – and axiomatic wisdoms, "Volksweisheiten" (street wisdoms), which usually include the explanation "es heisst" or "man sagt" ("they say" or "it is said").

SEPP: I just had no luck in life, that's it. When someone has no luck, he can't do nothing. (*Pause.*)

FARMER: Every man forges his own fate, they say. [*Jeder is seines Glückes Schmied, heisst es.*]

SEPP: Not every. (*Farmyard*, I, 4)

Whenever profundity is attempted by Kroetz's characters we invariably find them quoting. These two types of language – the cliché which the characters treat as their own creation, and the quote which they use to support their cliché – create the powerful impression of a "found" language, a language superimposed upon them, uncreated and unowned.

What is meant by "unowned" language? Let us set up for the moment an opposition: owned/unowned language. Owned language is language which is constantly being created out of a personality to fit a situation. It is language which both reflects and engenders thought; which draws on a public net of words and grammar but reshapes them in order to express a private thought or intuition in words and grammar which can, in turn, be understood by at least a segment of the public world. "By the same act through which man spins language out of himself, he also spins himself into it..." wrote Wilhelm von Humboldt, [8] reflecting on the interrelations between public and private language. Each nation (according to Humboldt) is to an extent determined by the language which is peculiar to it alone; yet that language is also a creation *of* that nation: they are interdependent and form an organic whole. "Owned" language partakes of the public word, but recreates it in the private personality. This is a symbiotic process which always contains the germ, the potential, for originality. Without this concept there could be no meaning to the word cliché – i.e. a word or phrase so overused as to become automatic, insincere, devoid of private recreation.

It is precisely this private recreation of which Kroetz's characters are most incapable; and since they do not "own" their language, they also reject responsibility for what they say. "Redn wird man durfn" – "No harm in talking" – becomes a common defense for even the most indefensible utterances. In Act III, scene 1 of *Farmyard*, for example, the Farmer and his Wife are on their way to church with the pregnant Beppi. The Farmer is worried that her pregnancy may already be visible and declares "There must never be anything there to see." The following "discussion" between the Farmer and his Wife is an attempt to find a solution to the crisis which Beppi's pregnancy has created.

WIFE: It is said that backward people don't feel death the way we do.
FARMER: Course not, a fly doesn't notice anything either. (*Pause.*)
WIFE: Fifth Commandment: thou shalt not kill.
FARMER: Sixth Commandment: thou shalt not be unchaste. (*Pause.*)
    I'll square that with the Lord God myself. (*Pause.*)
WIFE: It is said that the child goes on living in the mother's belly for
    hours after.
FARMER: No way. (*Pause.*) ...

wife: Blessed are the meek, for theirs is the kingdom of heaven.
farmer: I don't believe that.
wife: The thoughts that come into your head. Unthinkable.
farmer: We're only talking. [*Man redt ja bloss.*]

The Farmer and his Wife, quoting biblical verse and the Ten Commandments, discuss in disconnected sentences, between long pauses, the possibility of killing their own daughter as a way out of the shame which her pregnancy will bring upon them. Twice the Wife claims "it is said" and repeats the most fantastic superstitions as though they were fact. The use of "it is said" frees her to speak of her daughter's death and even to consider the fate of the unborn child – who, it is said, will live on for hours in the dead mother's womb. "It is said" removes from her the responsibility for such thoughts: the quoted form gives them the air of objectivity. This is followed by quotations from the Ten Commandments. Without explanation or pre-amble, the Wife quotes the fifth Commandment; the Farmer counters with the sixth. The two Commandments clash; yet they do not develop into a discussion. The quote is not an introduction to discussion, it *is* the discussion. In them the characters express their contrasting moral views without ever owning their positions. The meaning of their remarks is not elaborated, the intention behind them is never made explicit. Nor do they gather cumulative strength, since sentences do not build on each other. Each unit stands on its own, depleted, inconclusive. When the Wife finally protests against the thoughts they are having the Farmer counters: "Man redt ja bloss." This defense – we're only talking, no harm in talking – is a recurring denial of any inherent power in words, since the words which they possess cannot mediate between their desires and the occurrences in their lives. Axiomatic language and quotations, a borrowed code, thus give the characters the impression of having thought and discussed, while in fact brutally putting an end to any individual reflection.

Not only do Kroetz's characters speak and think in clichés and borrowed idioms, they also *feel* in second-hand, pre-formed emotions. In Act III, scene 4 the Farmer and his Wife are in

bed talking, refusing to blame themselves for the tragedy which
has occurred. After a pause, the Farmer says:

FARMER: If we at least had another child, a boy, that would be a ray
of light.
WIFE: Why?
FARMER: It's obvious.

Why is it obvious that a son, if only they had one, would be a
ray of light in their lives now? The answer here too, we can
assume, is "it is said." This cliché sentiment, like the language
used, is borrowed. The conventional wisdom both creates the
emotional longing for a son as consolation, and justifies that
desire. When the Wife attacks the Farmer for having that wish
– he knows that she has been barren since Beppi's birth–the
Farmer answers defensively, "Redn wird man durfn..." – "No
harm in talking."

The extent to which pre-formed speech comprises personal
identity is pointedly demonstrated in *Ghost Train*. This play
begins after the birth of Georg, Beppi and Sepp's son. Beppi,
who had been virtually dumb in *Farmyard*, now speaks far
more, especially to her child for fear that he will turn out to be
like her. "Now she talks more, since the birth. Can't help
noticing," says her father. "Cause the kid can't talk, she talks"
(I, 2). Beppi's parents have decided to send Georg to a Home,
in order to put an end to Sepp's visits to his son, a right which
the law gives him, "it's official." When Beppi learns of this she
forms her first true sentence, her first expression of will: "If
Georg goes to the Home, I'll kill myself" (I, 6). She repeats this
sentence to herself, privately rehearses it until it becomes her
own, and with this threat finds the strength to leave home and
go with the child to the city to live with Sepp. Act II, scene I
has Beppi proudly telling Sepp her sentence. They celebrate
with a game of clichés which is in fact far more than a game:

BEPPI: Who dares, wins!...
SEPP: That's just a saying, nothing more.
BEPPI: Who dares, wins!
SEPP: (*Laughing.*) Every man forges his own fate! (*Pause.*)

BEPPI: The bold will inherit the world.
SEPP: Where there's a will there's a way! (*Pause.*)
SEPP: And?
BEPPI: Who dares, wins!
SEPP: We did that one already.
BEPPI: More?
SEPP: Man is the measure of all things!
BEPPI: Exactly. (*Both laugh.*)

With poignant irony these two outcasts find momentary courage in those same cliché forms which have, all their lives, imprisoned them. The cliché is lifted into a series of liberating mottos, formulae for courage. But the contents of these aphorisms – which claim that through courage, will, and selfhood, man can forge his own fate – are in pathetic contrast to the meek lack of power and will which characterize both Sepp and Beppi. Ironically, while Beppi seems to find momentary liberation from her fate by forming a sentence which is her "own," it is precisely the nature of this sentence, and of those used in their "game" of quotes, which undermines true self-expression in Kroetz's plays.

Aside from the cliché and the quote, Kroetz employs various linguistic devices which render his language almost useless for communication. Semantic blanks, the third type of speech mentioned above, consist of certain words or phrases which recur incessantly in the dialogue as replacements for response, or as ways to stem discussion. The most common words are "exactly" ("genau"), "right" ("ebn"), and "why" ("warum"), all of which lose their lexical meanings.[9] When the Farmer confronts Sepp with the information that Beppi is pregnant and that this will cost Sepp ten years "and me my honor," we get a mere collection of non sequiturs:

FARMER: She's pregnant.
SEPP: Why?
FARMER: Right.
SEPP: Not true. All lies.
FARMER: We have proof.
SEPP: Can't be.
FARMER: Exactly.

SEPP: Not right.
FARMER: A test is made. Costs ten marks.
SEPP: Why?

The words are reduced to sounds, as though the emotionality of this subject can only evoke grunts. Sepp's "why," "can't be," "not right," are used to fend off blows. The Farmer's "right" and "exactly" are not, as they would imply, words of agreement, but emphatic gestures, exclamation points. These lexically voided words also function as safety valves. They neutralize contradictions, stem the breakdown of communication which at all times threatens Kroetz's dialogue. At one point Beppi tries to hit her parents. The Wife taunts the Farmer with his lack of reaction:

WIFE: Are you scared of your own child?
FARMER: Why?
WIFE: Right. (*Pause.*) (*Ghost Train*, I, 7)

"Right" is not an answer to "why," nor is "why" a plausible response to the Wife's accusation that her husband fears his own child. "Why" here is not used to mean: "Why do you say that?" or "How do you mean?" "Why," as in Sepp's use of the word above, is a defensive act. "Right," which is normally a term of agreement, an affirmation, is then used by the Wife to contain the potential quarrel, to neutralize tension.

Another empty verbal form common in Kroetz's plays is the tautological sentence: "If it can't be helped, then it can't be helped" (*Farmyard*, III, 4); "What is, is" (*Ghost Train*, II, 2); "Better is better" (*Ghost Train*, II, 11). This type of sentence carries a sense of finality, of fatality and resignation. It serves to justify things as they are. Like the cliché-idiom, tautological sentences are circular, self-validating, and function to close off venues for response:[10] "I'm leaving you Willy, 'cause I'm going away" (*Homeworker*, 12). "It's not your fault when you're sick, 'cause you don't feel well" (*Ghost Train*, II, 10).

The repeated usage of the above verbal forms, and the extreme unoriginality of Kroetz's characters' language, suggest an inherently restricted language code. This term, Restricted Code, belongs to a socio-linguistic theory developed by Basil Bernstein in the sixties, and which, though still controversial, has gained wide approval.[11] Bernstein's theory of Elaborated and Restricted Codes probes the relationship between language, social milieu, and the potential for communication. Bernstein postulates two speech systems, or linguistic codes, which are generated by different social structures and which condition the way a speaker conceptualizes and expresses himself. Speakers of an Elaborated Code select from a wide range of syntactic alternatives, making it hard to predict which option they will choose. These speakers expect their listeners to be different from themselves, shared assumptions are not taken for granted, and they therefore tend toward a verbal elaboration of meaning. An Elaborated Code user comes to regard language "as a set of theoretical possibilities available for the transmission of unique experience." His/her concept of self will be verbally differentiated and therefore complex, and will become the object of perceptual activity.

Speakers of a Restricted Code, on the other hand, own a reduced range of syntactic alternatives. They tend to presuppose shared assumptions between speaker and listener and thus do not elaborate intent verbally or make it explicit. The Restricted Code is predicated upon, and serves to reinforce, the form of the *social* relationship between the speakers: parent/child, husband/wife, boss/employee, etc. The Elaborated Code is rooted in the recognition and expectation of psychological difference; in the case of a Restricted Code it is the status relationship between speakers which is dominant. The fixed relationship, not the specific circumstance, determines the form of speech. Elaborated Codes are person-oriented and therefore flexible, while in Restricted Codes the concept of self will tend to be refracted through the rigid implications of the status arrangement. In addition, the range of the latter code is defined by what speaker and listener have in common; thus the code is not available, and indeed tends to depress, "the transmission of unique experience."

These codes, according to Bernstein, are learned, not

inherent, and are entirely dependent on sociological constraints. Bernstein concludes that the codes are largely
connected with learning procedures within different social
classes and are culturally induced. Middle-class children tend
to possess both an Elaborated and a Restricted Code, while
children socialized within some sections of the working class,
and especially the lower working class, tend to be limited to a
Restricted Code. Moreover, the functions of the codes tend to
determine the options and self-image of its users. One serves to
emphasize individuality, uniqueness, conceptual abstraction,
and therefore freedom; while the other focuses on and
presupposes the social role and relation, depresses a sense of self,
and is oriented toward concrete, limited, narrative statements.
This second function is typical of Kroetz's language.[12]

The fateful tie between social status and verbal ability,
between social and verbal determination, is at the heart of
Kroetz's early plays. The language of his characters is never
explicit and always assumes common understanding and
mutual intent. The extensive use of cliché-idioms, quotes and
axiomatic speech supports this: they comprise a verbal
shorthand which reinforces an assumed (never explicitly stated
or discussed) consensus of opinion ("it is said"). The resultant
language is highly unoriginal and fragmented. Another of
Bernstein's points which is particularly valid for Kroetz is the
lack of selfhood which a Restricted Code seems to generate: the
self is subordinated to a social role. This does much to explain
the rigid formulae which pass for communication between
child and parent, man and woman, employer and employee.
As Sepp says of himself, "It's only 'cause I was always the
weaker one…You can't defend yourself when you're the
weaker one" (*Ghost Train*, ii, 1). Women particularly suffer:

KARL: All you know how to do is cry.
MARIE: I'm not sayin' nothing.
KARL: Yea, it's better if you're quiet.
MARIE: I believe you; you're the man and I'm the woman.
KARL: Exactly. Just remember that. (*Michi's Blood*, 4)

It is Karl who forces Marie to abort her child. It is Willy who

leads Martha to try to abort hers (*Homeworker*). The best
example is backward Beppi who is never consulted by her
parents on any of the crucial decisions they make about her life.
When told that her son would be put into a Home she threatens
to hit her parents. This act of self-assertion draws a reaction –
but not to her as an individual. The Farmer explains her
aberration quite simply: "It's because she's a Mother now. We
underestimate that" (*Ghost Train*, 1, 7).

The restrictedness and essential dumbness of Kroetz's
characters are best evidenced in the rhythm of his dialogues.
Those dialogues are composed not only of speech but also of
silences, of pauses which are an inherent part of the language
itself. Kroetz himself continuously stresses their importance; as
he wrote: "The most distinctive behavior of my characters is
their silence; because their language doesn't function."[13] In
the stage directions of *Farmyard*, Kroetz allots the various types
of pause-signs (dash, pause within dialogue, pause between
sentences, long pause) exact time values varying from five to
thirty seconds each. He insists these be strictly adhered to if the
play is to become "clear and understandable." In *Homeworker*
he goes so far as to indicate the minimum time a scene should
last on stage, often demanding three to four minutes for a scene
of only twenty lines. In *Farmyard* and *Ghost Train* the most
prevalent conversational pattern is a unit of three to eight lines
ending with a pause. Often, especially if the subject under
discussion is emotional, pauses will follow every line or two.

Kroetz's pauses are blank spaces, transitions from one
fragment of speech to another, from one cliché to the next.
Unlike Pinter's pauses, for example, they are not uneasy or
menacing. Pinter's pauses are a direct continuation of the
dialogue. They are emotionally charged; within them meanings
multiply, centers of power shift, tension builds. Kroetz's pauses
are the opposite; they mark the end of a unit of tension, a
sudden dissipation of whatever slight interaction the dialogue
may have created. Like timid boxers, Kroetz's characters say
their few lines and then scuttle to their corners. The subject
may be continued in the next round, but no cumulative power
is carried from one unit to the next. This serves to increase the

terrible isolation in which Kroetz's dialogue exists. Since each unit exists in isolation, continuity and consistency of opinion are neither expected nor found. Speech and thought are disjointed, almost arbitrary, making it nearly impossible to reach rational decisions. When discussions are attempted (as in the attempt to decide what to do about the pregnant Beppi, quoted above) they usually end in a stalemate, in confusion, in the claim that "We're only talking."

Kroetz's splintered dialogue is paralleled by sudden out-bursts of violence; more precisely, it *underlies* the violence. Acts of brutality occur in isolation, unreflected, unelaborated. When language does precede violence, it is usually in the form of a banal cliché. The abortions in both *Homeworker* and *Michi's Blood* are preceded by the comment "Action speaks louder than words" ("Probieren geht über studieren"). But on the whole violence occurs in bestial silence, without warning, without direct aftermath, as isolated and hopeless as the units of dialogue. Kroetz masks his intentions, allows no foreshadowing. Beppi suffocates her baby suddenly, without a sound. Willy's drowning of Martha's infant in *Homeworker* is done completely in pantomime. In a long, silent scene Willy carefully prepares the bath-water, heats it and tests the temperature. He then washes the baby "thoroughly and not without skill. Then he drowns the baby in the tub. He leaves the baby lying in the tub and dries his hands on a towel...Then he cleans up" (scene 16). The murder gains in horror by the banal description he later gives to Martha: "A death like any other" (scene 19). Beppi's rape by Sepp is even more sudden and unexpected, and Beppi never utters a word during the entire scene. Sepp helps Beppi clean herself after the ride on the "ghost train;"

SEPP: You dirtied your pants? Yea, you did. Were you scared? (*Beppi is all confused.*)

SEPP: Or was it the drink. Come, we'll take care of that... Pantshitter. Let me. (*He cleans her.*) Take off your underpants, you can't go around like that. (*Beppi does it.*)

SEPP: Here, clean yourself with this. Let me. (*He cleans her up with a handkerchief.*) That's better. Come here. (*He takes her and deflowers her.*) (*Farmyard*, II, 1)

The switch from paternal care to brutal rape is sudden and presented without comment or aftermath. Sepp takes Beppi like an animal. Her silence and helplessness seem to elicit it. Later, in *Ghost Train*, when Sepp and Beppi are living together, Sepp says to her: "Beppi is like a dog that can't talk" (II, 10). The inability to communicate is not innocent, it is not natural to man. Bestiality becomes evident in the violence which replaces language, and in the lack of a dimension of mind for which man, unlike dogs, must suffer.

Kroetz has written that "People who have learned how to talk can make contact, or, even more important, they can *defend* themselves."[14] The connection between language and self-defence, or language and power, is implicit in all of the above plays. In scene 5 of *Michi's Blood*, titled, significantly, "The Restoration of Order," this is overtly discussed. Marie lies with her legs spread, passively accepting the soap-water solution which Karl pours into her womb in order to abort the child who threatens their "orderly" life. While this horrifying and eventually fatal procedure takes place – three times, since "All good things are three" – Marie, grunting but hopeful, expresses her faith in the superiority of man over beast, of which this act of abortion is supposedly an example:

MARIE: Ah. This is the difference, an animal can't defend himself when something goes wrong.
KARL: We defend ourselves.
MARIE: Exactly.

The irony is wrenching. The speechless, like beasts, are in fact defenceless; and the equation of the two is itself a recurring theme. *Michi's Blood*, a short one-act play, places this theme overtly within the text. The play consists of fifteen short scenes of almost pure dialogue. It contains only two characters, Marie and Karl, and takes place entirely within their one room. The central events are an unexpected pregnancy, a crude abortion, and the resultant painful death of Marie. So far the play is consistent with most of Kroetz's early plays. It differs, however, in a few important aspects. *Michi's Blood* contains a rawer, more vulgar language, full of obscenities and invective – sad, depleted abuse, totally lacking in originality. And the play contains no stage directions or comments: no setting is given, no stage action is described and, most surprising, no pauses are indicated. Directions for actions – such as the abortion scene (5) which occurs graphically on stage – must be inferred from the dialogue itself. Silences too emerge only from what is said; MARIE: Why have ya stopped talking? (5). Yet, while Kroetz appears to have removed the last traces of any authorial intrusion, he introduces a (for him) new device: each of the fifteen scenes is preceded by a title which, often ironically, comments on the following dialogue and thus returns the author to the text. This device also offers a telling reflection, and a point of comparison, with the language of his characters: for the scene titles have a literary ring. They pin-point in a few well-chosen words the theme or content of a scene, and those words are drawn from a vocabulary to which his characters have no access: "Thoughts about Love," "Formulating a Plan," "Restoration of Order," "Accounts and Balances," "Salvation Attempts." The titles are conceptualizations, and as such they demonstrate a language unavailable to the characters, whose lack is the source of their suffering.

In each of the fifteen dialogues, Karl and Marie seek ways to make contact. Marie still believes in speech and has the urgent need to say something which might break through the meanness and the misery of their lives. Karl has no faith in speech "that anyway never did us no good" (15). Speech only leads to abuse, and he seeks relief – or perhaps denial – through silence.

The first scene, ironically entitled "Table Conversation," opens in mid-dialogue and consists entirely of seemingly unmotivated invective:

MARIE: 'Cause we only have one room you can go to the John.
KARL: It's cold there.
MARIE: I won't put up with just everything.
KARL: Exactly.
MARIE: 'Cause you're a pig.
KARL: That's what you are, what's it make me?
MARIE: You're stupid.
KARL: That's what you are, what's it make me?

MARIE: You're horny, but you can't get it up.
KARL: That's what you are, what's it make me? Who cares.

The ugly, childish taunting is obviously a stock response in their fights and bickerings. However, it masks a deeper struggle, one that finds strangled expression in almost every scene: the struggle for contact. As the scene continues Marie tries to elicit some word of affection from Karl but fails, because "their language doesn't function":

MARIE: When you need someone and he sees that, then he doesn't know how to appreciate it. You want'a get rid of me.
KARL: I just want some peace.
MARIE: No one's said nothing.
KARL: I can't take it...Stop crying, if ya can't understand what I say.
MARIE: I understand plenty...
KARL: Why do ya keep talking and mixing in?
MARIE: I have my rights.
KARL: You have nothing.

Karl is sick of the inevitable aggression which speech evokes. He is drawn to an animal dumbness which is in any case inherent in their incapacity for meaningful speech. Marie's defensive "No one's said nothing" and "I have my rights" are revealing. After two dozen lines of cruelties nothing has been said, but as a human being she senses that she has the right to be able to speak and create meaning.

MARIE: 'Cause I'm a person too.
KARL: Big deal. (13)

Karl and Marie speak exclusively in stock phrases and semantic blanks. When Marie tells Karl that she's pregnant, they break into confused clichés which recall Sepp and Beppi's game. Marie claims, illogically, that "You gotta look at the sunnyside and everything looks different. But accept things as they are." To which Karl replies "We gotta make do...At night all cats are gray. And that's the truth" (4). The lack of coherence in these dialogues verges on the absurd, except that clearly no parody is intended. The dialogue is meaningless because speech is no longer available to these characters. The following scene, "Restoration of Order," in which irrelevant sayings accompany a brutal abortion, best demonstrates the horrifying disjunction between language and action. The lack of stage directions makes this scene particularly incongruous and horrifying:

MARIE: Ya feel it?
KARL: Yea.
MARIE: What?
KARL: A kid...Here are the feet, here's the stomach, here the head. Ya feel?...
MARIE: It hurts, but it's nice.
KARL: Pain is pain.
MARIE: Yea.
KARL: Then get rid of it.
MARIE: You crazy? I won't, 'cause it's my happiness, see?
KARL: Ya gotta let people have their happiness.
MARIE: Right.
KARL: Now open up. It's gonna hurt, but it don't matter.
MARIE: I can take it...Oww...
KARL: Hold it open, now we'll do it again. If this don't work, I don't know what.
MARIE: Action talks louder than words.
KARL: Right. Feel anything?
MARIE: Doesn't hurt at all anymore.
KARL: 'Cause now you're used to it.
MARIE: You can get used to anything, they say.
KARL: Now you can let it out. All good things are three. A horse couldn't take this...Let it out and everything's over and forgotten.

Kroetz does not explain the sudden switch from parental joy to painful abortion. Motives, feelings, thoughts, are never made explicit. All we are offered are the bare bones: strings of clichés and sudden, seemingly unmotivated actions. Richard Gilman wrote of the play's frustrating language that:

...the painfulness of these exchanges rises both from their substance, naturally, but even more from their relation to the play's events or, more accurately, the expected significance of those events, their "values"...The clichés, the repetitions of banalities, the bromides all testify to the stricken nature of their speech...the queer and terrifying sense it gives of not having been created by them but of having instead passed through them, as it were. It is as though their language has been come upon, picked up, scavenged ...[15]

After the abortion Marie lies bleeding and dying for days. No action is taken; they sit and wait for it to pass, while Marie tries, unsuccessfully, to find a way to talk about what is happening to her. Scene 14, "Salvation Attempts," shows a dying Marie attempting to make sense of the death of her aborted child, to find some "salvation" through an understanding of her fate. Typically, this is done by quoting a cliché notion of human suffering:

MARIE: Every minute a child dies of hunger, they say.
KARL: Ya want something?
MARIE: No. But I still got a right to talk.
KARL: Talk is silver, silence is gold, they say. Don't ya know that?
MARIE: Sure I know that.
KARL: Then be quiet if you know.
MARIE: It's easy to shut up a person like me, who's dying.

These lines contain both of their positions. Marie's need for speech; Karl's for silence. Karl has given up seeking "meaning" but Marie, realizing that she is dying, seeks some final comfort in the knowledge of the universality of death: "Every minute a child dies of hunger." This bit of "folk-wisdom" places her child's death, and her own, within a universal – if banal – context. It also denies responsibility for her own act, over which she seems to have had as little control as over those anonymous deaths by hunger.

Lack of originality is insidious; its verbal manifestation covers, and produces, a deeper lack of morality and compassion. Compassion for the suffering of others, a trait so lacking in Kroetz's early plays in which rape and child murder are almost routine, depends on the ability to imagine another's pain. But a stunted, pre-formed, unowned language alienates the characters from their feelings and stifles imagination. The last line of *Michi's Blood*, spoken by Karl to the now dead Marie, is: "Can't ya hear me? Those who won't listen have to feel, understand?" The irony of this sentence is, of course, that those who cannot listen and understand each other, can not in fact feel. Verbal and emotional imagination are inseparable. To call the murder of an infant "A death like any other," to compare the death of one's child with that of a fly, requires a peculiar lack of imagination – and compassion. In this, Kroetz's characters are almost interchangeable.

There is a sense in which these characters seem to have all been formed by the same mold, an almost mechanical mold of language which recurs, undifferentiated, unelaborated, in play after play. Despite the surface realism of Kroetz's language, he does not try to create nuanced, spontaneous speech. In fact, his dialogues studiously avoid those devices which might give the illusion of verbal spontaneity. Spontaneous speech is typified by false starts, hesitations, interjections, retractions: i.e., the struggle to verbalize is part of the speech itself. Such langauge is common in dramas which attempt realistically to create the speech of a given milieu. Kroetz's language lacks such false verbal planning completely. His syntax is unvarying, the language is foreshortened, emphatic, extremely lean. Characters do not interrupt each other, sentences do not overlap, and there is no attempt to create atmosphere or mood through language. All those elements which transfer dialogue into lived and felt speech are missing. The reason is perhaps that, unlike Naturalist language – which tends to *characterize* its speaker – Kroetz's characters are not differentiated through a verbal style. Style connotes individuality, the interplay of personality and emotionality within language; Kroetz's figures all seem to speak the same language: their inner life, their personal idiosyncrasies, do not break through the verbal mold. Language is imposed upon them, not created out of them.

This imposed, restricted language not only usurps their individuality but finally becomes their fate. As Harald Burger and Peter von Matt suggest in an article titled, with Bernstein in mind, "Dramatic Dialogue and Restricted Speech," the element of fate within a play can be understood as those factors which objectively limit the characters' freedom, and determine their options. The language-structure of Kroetz's characters is so dominant in its influence on their lives that, they write, "we must recognize in it the dramatic function of a *fate* – similar to heredity in Naturalism, blind vitality in Sternheim, or socioeconomic factors in Brecht."[16] To say that Kroetz's characters are determined by their language is not to deny the role of social oppression and poverty; but the connection between language and oppression can only be made by the audience. The characters themselves accept their limitations almost without question – since to question would be to begin a process of change, and change is inconceivable without language through which thought is not only expressed but, more importantly, formed. "When you learn to talk you'll be a different person," Sepp promises Beppi (*Ghost Train*, II, 3). Although this never comes true for Beppi, it does happen in Kroetz's later plays in which greater verbal capacity leads to a questioning of the molds of thought and behavior. In *The Nest* (*Das Nest*, 1974), for example, Kurt's wife accuses him of being no better than a "trained monkey" who blindly repeats what he is told to think and do. This critique leads to discussion, awareness, and to the responsible (if didactic) final action which differentiates Kroetz's post-1972 plays from his early ones.

In the early plays no such awareness is evidenced, no hope of change is offered. This is poignantly demonstrated by Sepp who, after the birth of Georg, tries to express a dream he has for his son's future. As Sepp puts it: "The kid'll show 'em who we are! He won't ask 'em if he's being asked, he'll just tell 'em, without being called on" (*Ghost Train*, II, 3). Sepp's innermost hope is rooted in his son's verbal freedom, in his ability to "tell 'em" without being called upon, to exercise free verbal options; and thus to control his fate. Ironically, in his stilted, undeveloped sentence Sepp demonstrates only too clearly the limited, hopeless language which the son will inevitably learn from his father – and which will certainly determine *his* future, as it has Sepp's.

EDWARD BOND: *SAVED* AND *THE POPE'S WEDDING*

Language deprivation has also been dramatically explored outside of Germany. In England, Arnold Wesker centred his play *Roots* (1959) around the power and potential of language.

Roots shows the "re-education" of Beatie Bryant, originally of rural Norfolk, who comes to London and is politicized through her relationship with a Socialist intellectual, Ronnie Kahn. Beatie eventually returns for a visit with her poor, uneducated family, bringing her new social and verbal consciousness home with her. Thus, unlike Kroetz, Wesker offers us, somewhat didactically perhaps, a spokesman for a different verbal world:

> BEATIE: Do you know what language is?... It's bridges, so that you can get safely from one place to another. And the more bridges you know about the more places you can see... Use your bridges... It took thousands of years to build them, use them! (Act I)

Beatie tries to awaken her family to their own oppressed lives and debased language, and although she fails – "Whatever she will do they will continue to live as before" – the outcome of the play is not totally pessimistic. She herself does escape their fate, and by the end of the play is deemed to be "articulate at last." Beatie Bryant is perhaps not unlike Shaw's Liza Doolittle who is also "recreated" through speech, a change which Shaw, in his Preface to *Pygmalion*, claims "is neither impossible nor uncommon." Wesker and Shaw present verbal deficiency as an essential deprivation, but not a hopeless one. They are far more optimistic than their fellow Englishman, Edward Bond.

The scandal which accompanied Kroetz's introduction to the German audience in 1971 was played out in England six years earlier around the opening of a similar play: Edward Bond's *Saved*, in which an infant is sadistically tortured and murdered on stage. *Saved* was actually banned by the Lord Chamberlain from being shown on a public stage; the suit which followed eventually led to the demise of the Chamberlain's control over the theater. The similarities between Bond and Kroetz go beyond their overt and shocking depiction of brutality on stage, and beyond the hostile receptions both initially received. In both, socially and culturally deprived characters are shown as the prisoners of a severely circumscribed language and the victims of their own violence.[17] In both, a stylized "slice-of-life" is recorded, blow by blow, cliché by platitude, and left unexplained for the audience to analyze.

Saved, and to an extent Bond's previous play *The Pope's Wedding*, present groups of characters who are just as inarticulate as Kroetz's – but with a difference. Kroetz's language is sparse and lean; it is an empty language, fragmented, weak, isolated, and accompanied by violence which is equally sporadic and dumb. Bond's language in these early plays (and, as with Kroetz, his style and language change in his later plays) is much more insistent and fluent. It is a mean-spirited speech, goading, full of taunts, curses, barbs, and threats. Herbert Kretzmer of the (London) *Daily Express* wrote after the opening of *Saved* that the characters "almost without exception, are foul-mouthed, dirty-minded, illiterate and barely to be judged on any recognizable human level at all."[18] The coarse barrage of language grates, annoying the audience, provoking the characters; and the violence of the play is a direct continuation of verbal malice. Bond's language seems naturalistic to a fault. The characters in *Saved* speak the dialect of South London, and the realism of the language sets up the socio-linguistic reality within which they exist. It is a reality as limiting and stultifying as Kroetz's, but with the added agility of an urban animal manoeuvring within the pressures of impoverished city life. The language is vulgar and strikes out in repetitive, almost automatic, attack. As in Kroetz's plays, this language reflects, and imbues, an inability for thought or compassion. The characters in *Saved* and *The Pope's Wedding* are all of the lowest social class, products and progenitors of a socially induced violence. "I write about violence as naturally as Jane Austen wrote about manners," claims Bond; "Violence shapes and obsesses our society... It would be immoral not to write about violence."[19] This violence is the fabric of his characters' lives, bred and reflected in the language which maintains and perpetuates it.

Saved consists of thirteen scenes. Its large cast of characters fall into two groups comprising two plot-strands, and two types of verbal relationships. The first group is the family members: Mary and Harry, a middle-aged working-class couple who have not spoken a word to each other in over twenty years; Pam, their daughter, twenty-three, vulgar; and Len, a young man she picks up and seduces in scene 1 who consequently moves in as a paying tenant and substitute son. The second group is a street-gang of young, uneducated manual laborers, bullies who almost always appear together. Their leader Fred, with whom Pam is desperately in love, is also Len's "mate." Although the story evolves over a number of years, the characters remain consistent in attitude and language throughout, implying a pessimistic view of their ability to change. The first three scenes show the courtship of Pam and Len. Scene 4 has the family together at home. Pam now has a baby, but it is not Len's; she has long since tired of him and has taken up with Fred who, in turn, is sick of her. The center of the play is the notorious scene 6 in which Pam, to spite Fred, abandons her infant in the park, whereupon the gang torture and stone him to death. For this Fred is arrested and sent to prison, Pam waits for him and continues to pursue him after his release. The rest of the play shows the degenerating and increasingly brutal relationships within the family, especially between Pam's estranged parents. The last scene, scene 13, is almost totally silent as the family sits together in the living room while Len mends a chair. It is, in its silence, the most eloquent scene in the play.

There are two basic modes of speech: the aggressive and compulsively abusive "group-lingo"; and the occasionally more restrained, almost laconic form of dialogue which often occurs between two speakers, usually when some form of intimacy threatens. Both of these modes are highly restricted. Speech in *Saved* is basically a form of attack whose general function is to repel contact. Paradoxically, the group-language, impersonal and vicious as it is, also serves as a common bond among its members.

PETE: 'Ow's it then?
MIKE: Buggered up.
COLIN: Like your arse.
MIKE: Like your flippin' ear in a minute.
PETE: I – I!...
MIKE: Laugh. (scene 6)[20]

COLIN: 'Ere we are again.
BARRY: Wipe yer boots.

MIKE: On you!
BARRY: Where we sitting'?
MIKE: On yer 'ead!
BARRY: On me arse!
LIZ: Don't know 'ow 'e tells the difference. (10)!

Aggression is easily sustained within the gang where personal identity merges into the larger social unit and, so it seems, the individual draws comfort from the expected style of flippant abuse. No member is ever affected by the insults they hurl at each other, nor does any member feel responsibility for what is said or done. Undifferentiated in language or action, the gang speaks, like the poisonous Hydra, with one multi-tongued voice. Bond stresses the integrative nature and vile potential of the gang by having them invent odious sketches, playing off each others' lines:

COLIN: It was in the park, yer 'onour!
MIKE: This girl come up t' me.
COLIN: An' drags me in the bushes.
BARRY: Yer 'onour. (*He laughs.*)
COLIN: I knew she was thirteen.
MIKE: But she twisted me arm.
COLIN: An' 'er ol' dad'd bin bashing' it off for years.
BARRY: Yer 'onour. (*He laughs.*)
COLIN: Twisted yer what? (3)

It is ironically Fred who, in prison, says: "I don't know what'll 'appen. There's bloody gangs like that roamin' everywhere. The bloody police don't do their job" (7).

This easy aggression is not true of the family unit where attacks are personal and emotionally straining. The family members suffer from their incapacity to communicate. Pam speaks of growing "ill" from all the fighting (4): "It's got a stop! It ain't worth it! Juss round an' round," she screams (8); "Yer can't call it livin'" (11). Len is "sick a rows"; "I don't give a damn if they don't talk, but they don't even listen t' yer...No one tells yer anythin' really" (12). For the family, the pattern of verbal violence is an insidious breeder of lovelessness. To talk is to destroy, nothing else is possible, nothing else is known. The only way out of the aggression of speech is through

silence, the alternative which Mary and Harry have chosen.
"Don't speak to 'em at all," Harry advises Len, "It saves a lot
a misunderstandin'" (12).

At the other extreme Bond sets the interpersonal dialogue
which, at its more benign, is merely used to ward off contact.
Scene 2, the only idyllic scene in the play, shows Len and Pam
in a rowboat in the park – the same park in which the infant
will later be killed. Len, the central character of the play,
whom Bond describes as "naturally good, in spite of his
upbringing and environment," is trying to learn a bit about
Pam and her family. Len, in contrast to the other characters of
the play, is truly curious, basically loyal, and willing to make an
attempt at intimacy. He asks questions – which are usually
repelled – and even has hopes for the future. Bond suggests in
his "Author's Note" to the play that Len "remains good in
spite of the pressures of the play... He lives with people at their
worst and most hopeless... and does not turn away from
them."[21] But Pam is incapable of responding to Len's probings.
When asked whether her mother likes Len, Pam's response, in
form as well as content, is typical:

PAM: Never arst.
LEN: Thought she might'a said.
PAM: Never listen.
LEN: O.

Later Len asks about the silence between the parents:

LEN: 'Ow'd it start?
PAM: Never arst.
LEN: No one said?
PAM: Never listen. It's their life.

Len's curiosity is aroused. How do they communicate? Do they
write notes to each other?

PAM: No need.
LEN: They must.
PAM: No
LEN: Why?
PAM: Nothin' t'say... Talk about something else.

Never asked, never listen, nothing to say. This monosyllabic, unelaborated response replicates the emotional numbness characteristic of the family members. "No one listens," Pam will later cry (11), and the connection between not listening and not responding – verbally and emotionally – becomes one of the themes of the play. This is painfully demonstrated in scene 4, in which we see the family together for the first time, setting the pattern for their interrelationship throughout. Pam watches TV and puts on make-up; Mary sets the table for Len's dinner; Harry sits in silence. The dialogue is all fragments of trivial, circular bickering, but it is lifted into something quite horrible by the fact that throughout, "without a break until the end of the scene," we hear the baby crying. Its cries get louder and more frantic, but nobody moves to help it.

> (*The baby screams with rage. After a while Mary lifts her head in the direction of the screams.*)
> MARY: Pam-laa! (*Slight pause. Pam stands and puts her cosmetics in a little bag. She goes to the TV set. She turns up the volume. She goes back to the couch and sits.*) There's plenty of left-overs.
> LEN: Full up.
> MARY: An' there's rhubarb and custard.
> LEN: O. (*Pause. The baby chokes.*)
> PAM: Too lazy t' get up an' fetch it.
> MARY: Don't start. Let's 'ave a bit of peace for one night... (*Pause, to Len.*) Busy?
> LEN: Murder.
> MARY: (*Watching TV*) Weather don't 'elp.
> LEN: (*Still watching TV*) Eh? (*The baby whimpers pitifully.*)

It's a fairly long scene and the only humane – though useless – reaction to the child's suffering is Len's hopeful "It'll cry itself t' sleep." The baby's cries are treated as noise to be drowned out by the noise of the TV set or the trivial chatter ("Weather don't 'elp"); of no more concern than the yowls of an animal (PAM: I thought the cat was stuck up the chimney). The family's baffling incapacity to respond to the infant, to treat him as human, sets up the violence which will be directed against him in scene 6.

The infant murder in scene 6 is complex and carefully structured. Unlike the violence in Kroetz's early plays, it does not suddenly "erupt:" it develops, evolves through dialogue, is twice foreshadowed earlier in the play. Indeed, the first time we meet the gang, in scene 3, Pete, Barry, Mike, and Colin are all assembled in the park. Pete is dressed up for a funeral, the funeral of a boy "only ten or twelve" whom he has run down with his car:

PETE: 'E come runnin' round be'ind the bus. Only a nipper. Like a flash I thought right, yer nasty bastard. Only ten or twelve. I jumps right down on me revver an' bang I got 'im on me offside an' 'e shoots right out under this lorry comin' straight on.

MIKE: Crunch.

COLIN: Blood all over the shop.

MIKE: The Fall a the Roman Empire...

COLIN: What a giggle, though.

MIKE: Accidents is legal.

COLIN: Can't touch yer...

PETE: Rraammmmmmmmmmmm!

COLIN: Bad for the body work... Ruined 'is paint work.

Barry, jealous of the attention Pete is getting, claims that he's "done blokes in" too. "More'n you 'ad 'ot dinners. In the jungle. Shootin' up the yeller-niggers. An' cut 'em up after with the ol' pig-sticker. Yeh." The repulsiveness of this dialogue warns us of violence to come.

The murder is also foreshadowed figuratively. Scene 6 begins with Len and Fred fishing in the park. Len tries to talk about Pam who is suffering from Fred's neglect, but Fred, like Pam, repulses any attempt at intimacy: "I come out for the fishin'. I don't wanna 'ear all your ol' crap." Fred cuts Len off by turning the discussion to the bait which has wriggled off his hook. He then proceeds in graphic detail to teach Len how to hook a worm.

FRED: Right, yer take yer worm. Yer roll it in yer 'and t' knock it out. Thass first. Then yer break a bit off... Now yer thread yer 'ook through this bit. Ta. Yer thread yer other bit on the 'ook, but yer leave a fair bit 'angin' off like that, why, t'wriggle in the water... Main thing, keep it neat.

There are a few connotations to this "lesson." One is sexual: Fred is teaching Len his superior technique. The other connotation of the indifferent torturing of a worm is of course to point us toward the torture of the child, which will follow. In the next section Pam enters the park pushing the baby carriage. She has come to beg Fred to spend the night with her "juss this last time." Their "discussion" is carried out in short fragmented sentences, in the pared-down line which characterizes the blunt rhythm of Bond's stifled speech. The child is used by Pam as "bait" with which to capture Fred; she appeals to him as a father and at the same time promises that the child won't disturb them, "Won't wake up till t'morra:" it's been drugged with aspirins. When Fred finally rejects her she explodes, and as revenge leaves the child behind with him: "An' yer can take yer bloody bastard round yer tart's!"

At this point the gang enters the park in mid-conversation, taunting each other as usual. They see the carriage and direct their aggression toward it, but it is at first playful aggression; the type which characterizes their mutual relationships. It is important to note that their smirking, vulgar humor will take on its exact parallel in physical action:

BARRY: 'Oo's 'e look like? (*They laugh.*)
MIKE: Don't stick your ugly mug in its face!
PETE: It'll crap itself t' death…
FRED: You wake it up an' yer can put it t' sleep. (*Colin and Pete laugh.*)
BARRY: Put it t' sleep?
COLIN: 'E'll put it t' sleep for good.
PETE: With a brick.

The threats are not seriously meant, but once they have been made they become possibilities: in fact the baby is eventually smeared in its own excrement and the "brick" becomes stones which do "put it t' sleep for good." The references to death and murder multiply, with a growing sense of real aggression. Barry, pushing the pram, sings the child a mock lullaby:

BARRY: Rock a bye baby on a tree top,
    When the wind blows the cradle will rock,
    When the bough breaks the cradle will fall,
    And down will come baby and cradle and tree an'
    bash its little brains out an' dad'll scoop 'em up and use 'em for bait. (*They laugh.*)

FRED: Save money.

Again the child is equated with Fred's worms, a helpless victim of indifferent violence; and like the worm, the gang notices that the child is quivering and shaking, apparently awake but unable to utter a sound. They pull its hair to draw a response.

BARRY: It don't say nothin'.
COLIN: Little bleeder's 'alf dead a fright.
MIKE: Still awake.
PETE: Ain't co-operatin'.

The drugged infant is not responding as they expect, and its silence, its lack of human response, seems to enrage them. To stop it from quivering Barry suggests they "Gob its crutch." The violence grows as the gang members egg each other on.

PETE: Give it a punch.
MIKE: Yeh less!
COLIN: There's no one about! (*Pete punches it.*) Ugh! Mind yer don't 'urt it.
MIKE: Yer can't.
BARRY: Not at that age.
MIKE: Course yer can't, no feelin's.
PETE: Like animals...
MIKE: What a giggle!
PETE: Cloutin's good for 'em. I read it.

The child, unresponding, is compared to an animal without feelings – reminiscent of the Wife's remark in *Farmyard* that the retarded do not feel pain at their death. Like her, Pete believes what is "said," common knowledge, cliché notions such as that "Cloutin's good for 'em." Like Kroetz's characters, these brutal men cannot begin to imagine the suffering of another, and their lack of moral imagination is directly bound to their limited verbal imagination. These limits become particularly clear with the stoning of the child. "Play" gives way to deadly seriousness: they intend to kill it. The group taunts Fred – unparticipating until now – to throw the first stone. Note the platitudes with which they goad each other on and justify their intentions:

MIKE: (*Quietly*) Reckon it's all right?

COLIN: (*Quietly*) No one around.
PETE: (*Quietly*) They don't know it's us...
BARRY: Might as well enjoy ourselves.
PETE: (*Quietly*) Yer don't get a chance like this everyday.
   (*Fred throws the stone.*)

The excitement mounts; the same smutty, low-minded drivel accompanies all the acts of violence, the pinching, beating, burning and stoning which lead to the child's death. The child's silence is a provocation, a seeming invitation, not unlike the silence which draws Sepp to rape Beppi. The inability to respond dehumanizes it. Martin Esslin wrote of this scene:

Bond has succeeded in making the inarticulate, in their very inability to express themselves, become transparent before our eyes. ... the baby does not respond to the first casual and quite well-meant attentions of the gang. Because it does not respond, they try to arouse it by other means, and that is how they gradually work up to greater and greater brutality, simply to make the mysteriously reactionless, drugged child show a sign of life... The baby in the pram is neglected because his mother cannot picture him as a human being like herself; the boys of the gang kill him because having been made into an object without conscience they *treat* him like a mere object.[22]

This shocking murder is not the culmination of the play, as is Alen's murder in *The Pope's Wedding.* The infanticide occurs only halfway through and resolves nothing, neither Pam's desire for Fred, nor Len's for Pam, nor the violence and despair. The remaining seven scenes center on the unhappy family and set up an emotional equation between the warring young "couple," Pam and Len, and Pam's silent, loveless parents.

Both here and in *The Pope's Wedding,* Bond seems to posit two interrelational options for his characters: violence or silence. The young crowd, the gang, and Pam herself communicate through constant aggression; Pam's parents, more experienced, have chosen silence as the only way to coexist. These two options are painfully juxtaposed in scene 8 in which Pam and Len tear into each other while Harry, ignoring them, calmly irons a shirt. As long as this silence is maintained, Mary and Harry live in cold, loveless peace. But when it is finally broken

– following an incident between Mary and Len which has some sexual overtones – the couple fall right into the expected pattern of verbal and physical violence.

MARY: Don't you dar talk to me!…Dirty filth! Worse! Ha!…Don't
      you dare talk to me!…Mind out of a drain…
HARRY: I don't want to listen.
MARY: Filth…Don't talk t' me! You!…
HARRY: I 'ad enough a you in the past!…
MARY: Yer jealous ol' swine!
HARRY: Of a bag like you? (11)

Mary hits Harry with her teapot, wounding him, and he stands there shocked and bleeding. "'Ope yer die…Use words t' me!" she says. "Whass 'e done?" Pam asks, horrified; "Swore at me!"

The brutal action results almost inevitably from the act of speech. This same pattern of aggression occurs repeatedly between Pam and Len, and Pam and Fred. In fact, most of the speech between two characters follows the same violent pattern. "I've heard it all before," Len says wearily of their fights (12). Mary hits Harry not merely because he swore at her, but because speech for these characters is a circular trap; it goes "round an' round" with no exit available except violence or silence. Not even Len – who alone among them makes some attempt to break out of the verbal viciousness – escapes. As in Kroetz's plays, a sense of fated entrapment prevails. There can be little doubt that Len and Pam will one day be like Mary and Harry; they too will either live together in cruel silence – which scene 13 seems to suggest – or do each other physical harm. "I won't turn out like that," Len had promised Pam in scene 2, referring to her parents. But the fact that he is kinder and more honest than the others seems to make little difference; he is caught in the same snare and cannot break through. "Yer don't wan'a go," Harry advises Len when he speaks of leaving, "no point…no different any other place" (12). Harry had once left and returned; his claim is that Len too would have no other option. When Len speaks of escape the only thing that occurs to him is to emigrate. ("Yer're too young t' emigrate," Harry tells him, "do that when yer past fifty.") To emigrate is not necessarily to leave England, but to leave his world; and this, precisely, is shown as quite futile. Bond offers no "real" solution for Len, other than hanging on.

"*Saved* is almost irresponsibly optimistic," Bond writes in the "Author's Note"; "The play ends in a silent social stalemate, but if the spectator thinks this is pessimistic that is because he has not learned to clutch at straws." The final scene shows the family in their usual positions, Pam staring at the *Radio Times*, Mary clearing the table, Harry filling out a football coupon. The tableau is similar to the opening of scene 4, but, in contrast, here barely a word is spoken. The only action is Len mending a chair. The interaction between Len and the chair, a long and varied series of physical positions, is the most intimate action of the play. It is tender and forceful, almost an act of love, sexual but without any aggression.[23] The silence between the family members is not a communicative silence; each character is isolated, none looks at Len or at each other, and it is, no doubt, only a temporary silence. But the play ends in that silence, and with Len embracing, slipping his arm around, resting his chest against – a chair. This pathetic communion is the "straw" of optimism which Bond offers us. No more than a silent gesture, located outside of deforming speech, this final tableau suggests an incipient humaneness and possible hope extended.

The Pope's Wedding, Bond's first performed work (1962), contains many of the same components as *Saved*. Here also, two sets of social and verbal relationships are set up, and communication, the need for response, is a central motif. Scopey, the main character, is in many ways Len's precursor, just as Pat, his wife who later leaves him for her former boyfriend, is an early sketch of Pam. Instead of parents, Bond creates a mystifying outsider figure, the hermit Alen, who becomes the metaphoric and dramatic center of the play. The play's sixteen scenes alternate among three locations: village life with its bored street-corner gangs, pub banter, or cricket games; the home life of Scopey and Pat; and the isolated hut where old Alen lives. The shifting short scenes trace Scopey's dislocation from each of these environments, as each fails to supply some "answer" which he, inarticulately, perhaps not quite consciously, seeks. In the end, having distanced himself from gang, wife, and community, Scopey severs all ties by killing the old man and taking his place.

For the first two scenes of the play Scopey is indistinguishable from the other members of the crude, brawling gang of bored, young day laborers. As in *Saved*, the gang relates through barely articulate verbal and physical aggression and, here too, this aggression serves as a bond and integration point among them. Ironically, as long as Scopey remains within the gang he is "safe," protected by the anonymity and limited desires of the group-will. Scopey moves to center stage in scene 4 when he emerges, unexpectedly, as the local hero of the annual cricket match. His sudden success earns him the sexual attention of Pat, Bill's girlfriend, who is taken by the image of the heroic Scopey, "beautiful all in white." "Yoo looked beautiful this afternoon," she tells him; "I keep seein' yoo standin' there with that bat" (5).[24] From the moment Scopey begins his relationship with Pat, in a grove outside the pub where the group is noisily celebrating its victory, he will no longer be seen with the gang. "They'll 'ave t' doo without me," he tells Pat, who keeps insisting they join their friends (5). Domesticity replaces group anonymity. Pat, a simple, unambitious girl, is both an extension of and counterpoint to Scopey. They share the same background, social ties, and limited vocabulary; and are seemingly fated to share the same drab future.

JUNE: Take the weight off your feet.
SCOPEY: (*Sitting*) An' on t' me arse.
PAT: If it ent corns it's piles. (7)

Pat's desires are limited to the "fags" she never has enough of; her imagination ends with the "nice" sandwiches she prepares for lunch; her dreams extend no further than the pre-packaged image of a clean-swept American town pictured on a postcard from her friend Betty Legs. The discussion between Pat, her girlfriend June, and Scopey, as to the desirability of that postcard image, shows, for the first time, Scopey's distrust of surface illusions and his need to know, to verify reality. Pat shows Scopey the card with the words "Nice, ent it?"

SCOPEY: Yoo can't tell.
JUNE: I like it.
SCOPEY: Yoo need more than that. Yoo'd 'ave t' see more.
JUNE: It's nice.
SCOPEY: Yoo need more.
JUNE: I know what I like – they keep the streets swep'...
SCOPEY: Nothin's like that. No more yoo ent seen sky like that.
JUNE: Never said I 'ad. I just said I like it.
SCOPEY: Yoo can't tell. (7)

If Scopey had hoped for a different type of communication with Pat, that hope is soon thwarted as the only intimacy they achieve, short-lived and banal, is sexual. The next time we see Pat and Scopey together, in scene 9, newly married, Scopey is eating Pat's "nice" ice cream in the dark, since the fuse has blown. The atmosphere is tense as they exchange accusations and bicker over petty domestic problems in, Bond tells us, "the clichés of argument, but they sound friendly." By scene 11, a few months later, their arguments no longer "sound friendly." Scopey has been working late to make the money they need to put down a payment on a house. They no longer go out together at all and Scopey is too tired, or uninterested, to have sex with Pat. Their conversation is mean, trite, unloving.

Parallel, and in counterpoint to this empty marriage, Bond traces the growing relationship between Scopey and the recluse, Alen. Alen's corrugated-iron hut is the setting for every second scene, beginning with scene 6; and the contrast between Alen's world and that of Pat or the group is sharply caught in the verbal register which Bond allows the old hermit. The opposition between violence and silence, which also figures in *Saved,* emerges early in this play. Alen's first appearance, in scene 3, is totally non-verbal. His silent, measured movements, which consist of shifting newspapers from one pile to another, contrast with the volatile gang racket of scenes 1 and 2. Moreover, whereas their rowdy, vulgar behavior had been transparent, all on the surface, Alen's is mystifying, secret. Alen inspires in Scopey the belief that he knows something through his rejection of community, his seeming lack of desires, his refusal to interact. Alen's communication is minimal and seems, to Scopey, to harbor depth. Scopey's fascination with Alen must be seen in contrast to the hopeless banality of his relationship with Pat. He meets Alen through Pat who, for reasons unclear, takes care of Alen's basic needs. Pat shops and cleans for Alen without warmth, but also without making any demands; probably because she had promised her dying mother to do so. The first time Scopey comes to Alen's place (scene 6) he waits outside. After Pat leaves he calls to Alen through the door: "What yoo doo all day?" (*Longer pause.*) ... "What yoor 'obbies?" The interrogative mode characterizes Scopey's dealings with Alen and is opposed to his communication with Pat, where Scopey shows neither curiosity nor interest.

The next time Scopey comes to Alen's hut (scene 8), he forces his way in under the pretext of looking for Pat's bag. His curiosity is kindled by the piles of papers which Alen claims are for "My bloody work!" and by the old man's refusal to communicate. He convinces Pat to let him "poke the owd broom round the corners" at Alen's instead of her ("I reckon I pass 'is owd sty every time I come 'ome a work.") Thus, when he appears there in scene 10, he comes as Pat's replacement, much to the old man's displeasure. Scopey's behavior with Alen is, again, in stark contrast to his behavior with Pat. While he expects Pat to cook, shop, and prepare his cocoa (which he likes "milky"), he caters to Alen as though he were a child, going so far as to spoon-feed him. Wearing an apron, Scopey cooks, sweeps, and cleans, all the while speaking to the grunting Alen and asking questions which the old man ignores.

SCOPEY: What yoo been dooin' since last Thursday? Eh? Chew it. Yoo been washin' yoorself? ... What yoo get up to all day? Yoo must 'ave plenty a time, yoo ent put a finger t' this place for months ... Where you sleep? That's it? ... I thought you might fancy a smoke or a chat. (*Slight pause.*) Yoo don't smoke.
ALEN: Eh?
SCOPEY: You don't smoke.
ALEN: Smoke?

SCOPEY: 'Ow long yoo been 'ere?
ALEN: Dont want no trouble...
SCOPEY: ...What's yoor first name?
ALEN: Eh?
SCOPEY: I'm Sco.
ALEN: What?
SCOPEY: That's just a name.

As a result of Scopey's growing fascination he stops working late and spends the evenings with Alen, ignoring Pat. He even spends nights outside the hut, watching over Alen. The degeneration of his marriage and social ties thus spills over into his work: he withdraws from all in search of something he believes Alen can supply. Scopey's downfall is that he misreads all the signs, ascribes significance where there is none, and by insisting on solving a mystery, finally creates one. In the climactic and longest scene of the play (scene 12), the false significances are first elaborated and then exposed. Alen's hut is a perfect location for such misreading since it is strewn with false clues. It's clutter and filth, the puzzling stacks of newspaper, the lack of any comforts, and the absolute isolation all hint at an alternate understanding of life, in powerful contrast to the town and home which Scopey knows. "I'm fussy for bein' clean myself," Scopey tells Alen, "yoo got 'ords a little vermin runnin' round 'ere." Scopey is struck by the clothes Alen wears – "No wonder Pat did yoor washin' 'ere. I can't see 'er 'angin' that out our place" (10); and by his lack of personal hygiene and manners. The objects in Alen's room all seem to Scopey to be imbued with meaning: "What's the paper for?...What's this for (*Touches a box with his boot.*) What's this? (*He taps the couch with his boot.*)" But mainly, he is intrigued by Alen's self-containment, his seeming lack of desires and aversion to contact. "You ought a keep a dog. Good company," Scopey suggests (8); and later volunteers to buy him a radio; "Yoo can pick 'em up cheap, good second 'and." Alen ignores Scopey's offer of "a smoke or a chat," of tea or "a 'ot water bottle" (10), as he ignores all of Scopey's offers and questions. In scene 12 Scopey tries to unravel some of the clues. He questions Alen about an old photograph he has found there, "shaped like an

egg, in brown an white, an' there's fly-blows round the edge."
All Alen can remember is where he bought it, but the lady in
the picture means nothing to him. Later, Alen gives him an old
army greatcoat. "That goo back long afore the great war,"
whose pockets are still sewed shut "T' keep the shape." Scopey
immediately wonders what might be hidden in the pockets:

SCOPEY: Ent yoo 'ad a look?
ALEN: Why?
SCOPEY: There might be somethin' inside.
ALEN: I don't want nothin'.
SCOPEY: Where's the scissors?...Chriss yoo might 'ave anythin' in
    'ere.

Just as Scopey seems on the verge of discovering something,
he is interrupted by Pat, who has come to see how Alen is faring
without her. During the few minutes in which Alen speaks with
Pat, while Scopey hides, all of his images of Alen are reversed.
Alen receives Pat joyfully, not like one indifferent to contact;
Pat casually reveals that Alen talks to himself, something
Scopey had not known; and when she leaves, Alen "goes to the
stack of papers by the wall. He climbs on to them. He peers
through a chink in the wall."

SCOPEY: (*Stands and looks at Alen.*) I never 'eard yoo talk a yoorself.
    Why's she say that? (*Pause.*) That what yoo use them papers for?

Scopey erupts in violent disillusionment, as the mystery sinks
into wretched banality.

SCOPEY: I got the sack t'day.
ALEN: O.
SCOPEY: That's count a spendin' too much time 'ere when I should
    a been a work.
ALEN: That ent my fault...Yoo ont get no money out a me.
SCOPEY: I never arst for money!...Yoo owd nut! I thought yoo 'ad
    them papers for keepin'. All yoo want 'em for 's t' stare outside.
    Yoo owd fake!...You're at that crack all day! Starin' out! It all
    goos on outside an' yoo just watch...Yoo're a fake! There's
    nothin' in this bloody shop!

Alen tells Scopey that he had once owned a "wireless" on
which he listened to church services until it was taken away

from him. "I never stopped gooin' after people," Alen explains in an effort to calm Scopey down, "They stopped gooin' after me." Having learned that Alen's needs are just like everybody else's, that his life has no hidden significance, Scopey says, after a pause: "Pockets're empty."

In scene 14 we are given a double view of Scopey: as he was, and as he has become. In the previous scene the gang, bored and looking for some action, discuss going to Alen's place to "sort the owd sod out...Just for a laugh." Unknown to the others, Scopey has replaced Alen as the hermit in the hut and we see him, standing on the pile of papers looking out, dressed in Alen's greatcoat. Scopey goes through a set of silent movements which recall Alen's first appearance in scene 3. Only this time the gang, unseen, is heard outside, snickering and vicious, shouting insults and throwing stones. In those voices we recognize Scopey as he was in the first two scenes, but see what he has become: silent and isolated, in a separate world. Scopey's change is also contrasted with the lack of change in the gang. A year has passed. One harvest season has given way to another, another cricket match has been played and, this time, lost. But in the gang we see cycle without growth: nothing has changed for the youths who move in the expected groove, unquestioning, locked into their limitations. Pat, too, has returned to her former boyfriend Bill, a typical hard-drinking member of the group. Only Scopey has escaped the fated cycle, defecting into tragedy.

Scopey is in many ways similar to Len: basically decent, sensitive, inquisitive. Like Len, he wants to know more than his environment or nature can offer. Len tries to understand how it *feels* to kill a child: "Wass it feel like?... When yer was killin' it... Wass it feel like when yer killed it?... Whass it like, Fred?" (10); just as Scopey wants to understand what it means to live outside of the groove which awaits him. But Scopey, more strongly than Len, embodies the spiritual need to break out, whatever the cost, of the emptiness of his environment and, especially, of the limited communication if offers. According to Bond, Len is "good" because he has seen people at their worst and stays with them. But Len is also realistic and unambitious:

with him Bond seems to be saying that the contact offered in scene 13, the benign communion in silence, is as much as can be hoped for, as much as Len will ever get. Len stays, but he changes nothing. *The Pope's Wedding* is a more poetic and mystifying play, and in it Bond went further, almost romantically further, by allowing his "hero" to reject the mean banality of his life and to seek, go on a quest, for the unfathomable, the unknown, that impossible "Pope's Wedding with another kind of life," as John Worthen put it.[25] Scopey's relationship with Alen recalls, in a way, Len's relationship with the mysterious dwarfs in Pinter's play by that name. Like the dwarfs, Alen seems to offer an escape from the expected and limiting type of contact demanded by the outside world, and to pose the option of a different form and format of being.

In the final scene of the play, Pat finds Scopey in Alen's hut, dressed in Alen's greatcoat, surrounded by five hundred (!) tins of food. This enigmatic, powerful image is contrasted to Pat, who appears dressed in "an old white mack. The cuffs, collar and hem are dirty grey. She wears on her head a dingy white and red scarf." Bond's detailed description of Pat's clothing is meant to situate her firmly within her "dingy" work-day reality. Her speech too is unchanged, colorless, flat. Scopey, on the other hand, both looks and speaks like someone out of a different world. While Pat tries to find out, through simple, direct questions, where Scopey has been and why he killed Alen, Scopey obsessively describes, in cryptic metaphors, as though speaking to himself, the *way* he killed Alen, with his own hands.

PAT: Hello. (*She comes down towards Scopey.*) Where's the owd boy? (*She looks at the tins.*) Scopey? (*She sees the bundle on the floor and starts to go to it.*)
SCOPEY: I 'oisted the flap a month back. 'Is 'ead's like a fish.
PAT: 'E's dead.
SCOPEY: All silver scales.
PAT: Why 'ent yoo come?
SCOPEY: I took one 'and on 'is throat an one 'eld 'im up be the 'air.
PAT: Why?
SCOPEY: One 'and...
PAT: They'll 'ang you.
SCOPEY: One be the 'air.

PAT: Stay there.

With images of fish and silver scales, of a strangulation carried out in mid-air, it is Scopey who now becomes a figure of mystery and unexplained depth. Visually and verbally differentiated from Pat and her world, Scopey becomes an alternative to the groove. But what does his choice represent? We never learn why Scopey killed Alen. Nor is it clear whether he is, in the end, mad or transposed to some higher understanding. What is clear is that by killing Alen, Scopey has become Alen, and by becoming him he has entered the mystery he had wanted to solve, and passed the need for solution on to the audience.

DAVID MAMET: *AMERICAN BUFFALO* AND *GLENGARRY GLEN ROSS*

One further example of a playwright who imprisons his characters within crippling verbal debris is the American, David Mamet. In two obsessively, almost unbearably verbal plays, *American Buffalo* (1975) and *Glengarry Glen Ross* (1983), Mamet studies the relationships between groups of people who interact through a radically restricted, highly jargonized, and painfully "unowned" language. As with Kroetz and Bond, Mamet's surface realism, his reproduction of a seemingly ultra-naturalistic cast of class-connected speech is implicitly critical of a society, a social ethos, and a political system which can produce such a debased verbal – and moral – existence. Also as with Kroetz and Bond, Mamet's characters are soldered into their language. The identity between persona and speech is gapless, i.e., no self-critical distance exists, and no alternate speech idiom or option is offered. Mamet's landscape, like Bond's, is urban. It is, however, a landscape which is reflected solely through the rhythms of its language. Unlike *Saved*, with its park and street scenes, *American Buffalo* and *Glengarry Glen Ross* are both restricted to indoor locations: a junk-shop, a restaurant, a real estate office. The city is reproduced through the manic tempo, the crude brutality of the speech, and through the implicit equation of a bankrupt business morality with verbal manipulation.

American Buffalo is a two-act play which takes place, fittingly, in a junk-shop: "Don's Resale Shop." The stage, cluttered with debris and decayed household objects, as well as cast-off cultural souvenirs from the "Century of Progress" exhibition of the 1933 Chicago World's Fair, visually reflects the broken, displaced speech which is the play's core. Walter Kerr, in his review of the Broadway production (1977), complained that there is altogether too much talk and not enough action in the play:

...when words become an end in themselves, when they tend to constitute a playwright's entire stock in trade...then, I think, we've got trouble...it's surely a mistake to urge him to make whole evenings out of logorrhea, out of the compulsive, circular, run-on and irrelevant flow of words that tend to spill from folk when they're otherwise impotent...they fatuously, foolishly, furiously speculate... decorating their outbursts liberally with obscenities...staking everything on the verbiage that is the only thing left to them or to us.[26]

The speakers of this "circular, run-on and irrelevant flow of words" are Don, a man in his forties, owner of the shop; Bob, his gopher, a young punk and ex-junkie; and Teach, a "friend and associate" of Don's. All three are petty hoodlums, and the central "action" of the play is the incoherent planning of a finally unaccomplished robbery. Almost nothing happens, the action is all within the language – a compulsively obscene, almost unintelligible junk-pile of sordid expletives, clichés, and verbal distortions. Clive Barnes called it "one of the foulest-mouthed plays ever staged, at a time when very few writers produce dialogue that actually smells of roses."[27] *American Buffalo* is a study of non-talking. The characters circle around the words like wary animals, sniffing out meanings which are never explicitly given. The inexplicitness of the language, its restricted, fragmented, and elliptic quality, breeds endless misunderstandings. Overburdened by incoherence, the language repeatedly breaks down into verbal – and eventually physical – assault.

The play's central image is the buffalo-head nickel for which it is named. This remnant from America's past (an ironic reminder of the mythic frontier, of open spaces and heroic challenges) is found in the shop by a customer who, much to Don's surprise, offers him a huge sum for it. The coin's value eludes Don, but its price – "Ninety dollars for a nickel...I bet it's worth five *times* that" (p. 31)[28] – and the automatic assumption of having been suckered, become the occasion for the planned robbery. The characters discuss this robbery as a business venture whose motive is rightful profit – as Teach puts it, America is *founded* on the Individual's right "to secure his honest chance to make a profit" by "Embark(ing) on Any Fucking Course that he see fit" (p. 73). The terminology of classical liberalism employed in the service of burglary functions for the characters as a justification, but alerts us to a warped value system which is Mamet's main concern. Neither *American Buffalo* nor *Glengarry Glen Ross* contains any female characters. In both, the "male" world of business manipulation intermingles with the values of male friendship; and in the distortion of both – business ethics and personal loyalty – Mamet offers a sharp criticism of the moral disintegration of a capitalist society.

Like Bond's *Saved*, this is a play about violence; and like both Bond and Kroetz, Mamet writes about the impossibility of human contact or compassion among the verbally and morally debased. The relationship between the older Don and young Bob is shown as part paternal, part utilitarian. Bob is passive and speaks little. He is good-natured although slow-witted, rather like a child with good intentions, and like the children in Kroetz's and Bond's plays, he too will suffer the fate of the silent and the weak. Don views himself as a man of experience, a businessman, and is given to sententious philosophizing spiced with street-wise proverbs like: "Action talks and bullshit walks" (p. 4). We know little about Walter Cole, called Teach, except that he is apparently a small-time crook, paranoid, and given to violent fits of aggression. His first words on entering Don's shop are:

TEACH: Fuckin' Ruthie, fuckin' Ruthie, fuckin' Ruthie, fuckin' Ruthie, fuckin' Ruthie.
DON: What?
TEACH: Fuckin' *Ruthie*...

DON: ...yeah? (p. 9)

Ruthie has, it seems, made a remark in a tone which Teach interprets as insulting. In an attempt at a "fair" assessment of the situation, Teach explains:

TEACH: Only (and I tell you this, Don). Only, and I'm not, I don't think, casting anything on anyone: from the mouth of a Southern bulldyke asshole of a vicious nowhere cunt can this trash come... This hurts me, Don. This hurts me in a way I don't know what the fuck to do. (*Pause.*)
DON: You're probably just upset.
TEACH: You're fuckin' A I'm upset. I am *very* upset, Don... The only way to teach these people is to kill them. (pp. 10–11)

A few pages later Teach gets cornered into admitting that part of his anger stems from the fact that he lost a lot of money to Ruthie at cards the previous night. He back-tracks on his words, stumbles, and finally, in tangles, gives up on words completely:

TEACH: And I like 'em too. (I know, I know.) I'm not averse to this. I'm not averse to sitting down. (I know we *will* sit down.) These things happen, I'm not saying that they don't... and yeah, yeah, yeah, I know I lost a bundle at the game and blah blah blah...(*Long pause.*) So what's new?
DON: Nothing.
TEACH: Same old shit, huh? (p. 16)

In the absence of explicit verbal intent, the *sound* of the speech becomes very important, since tone acts as the main indicator of meaning. Mamet indicates the tone of the speech by italicizing words to be emphasized – e.g. Don's recurrent "*Oh* yeah" – and by placing sections of dialogue in parentheses which, according to Mamet, "serve to mark a slight change of outlook on the part of the speaker – perhaps a momentary change to a more introspective regard" (p. 5). This reliance on tone is noted by Bernstein in his description of Restricted Codes. Bernstein argues that an undeveloped code may be so redundant and predictable that the speaker's intention can only be fathomed through "extra-verbal channels" of gesture or intonation. Furthermore, he claims, those who are limited to a Restricted Code often become very sensitive to such cues and highly dependent on them.[29] Mamet's carefully detailed intonation and his strict attention to verbal rhythm, verge on stylization. Speech is orchestrated to reproduce the crude pace and violent energy of caged urban animals. Mamet himself has claimed that "the language we use, its rhythm, actually determines the way we behave rather than the other way around."[30] Since the dialogue is elliptic in the extreme, expressing emotional nuance rather than logical connections, interpretation depends on the characters' ability to "read" these extra-verbal cues – at which they usually fail. The result of this style is to create tension and immerse us in sub-textual aggression. Teach's manic speech pattern, his over-emphatic obscenities and sudden changes of tone are an early indication of the violence which he will later exercise: "The only way to teach these people is to kill them."

Don and Bob plan to rob the coin-buyer's apartment that night. Bob claims to have "spotted" the man and discovered that he has left his house for the weekend, thus clearing the coast. When Teach enters the shop he senses some "action" in the air and wants a part – only without Bob: "We both know we're talking about some job needs more than a kid's gonna skin-pop go in there with a *crowbar*..." (p. 34). Teach convinces Don to betray Bob, despite the friendship between them, and take him instead as a partner: "Loyalty... You know how I am on this. This is great. This is admirable... This is swell. It turns my heart the things that you do for the kid... All I mean, a guy can be too loyal, Don... What are we saying here? Business... don't confuse business with pleasure" (pp. 33–4). Don gets rid of Bob – with twenty-five dollars as compensation. C. W. E. Bigsby, in his monograph study of Mamet, suggests that capitalism "offers a model and a vocabulary for human relations, substituting exchange value for personal relations":[31] at twenty-five dollars, Bob's exchange value is certainly low. Don's betrayal of Bob is an extension of the focal opposition between "business" and "friendship" assumed by the characters. As both Don and Teach assure us, human behavior depends on being able to keep the two concepts separate:

DON: 'Cause there's business and there's friendship Bobby... there are many things, and when you walk around you *hear* a lot of things, and what you got to do is keep clear who your friends are, and who treated you like what. Or else the rest is garbage, Bob, because I want to tell you something.

BOB: Okay.

DON: Things are not always what they seem to be. (pp. 7–8)

TEACH: We're talking about money for chrissake, huh? We're talking about cards. Friendship is friendship, and a wonderful thing... But let's just keep it *separate* huh, let's just keep the two apart, and maybe we can deal with each other like some human beings. (p. 15)

Mamet creates two types of language which correspond to this opposition of personal relations and business relations, and, like the opposition itself, the two interpenetrate and undermine each other. The basic interpersonal mode of speech consists of petty attack and retreat, a profusion of words with little surface meaning which mainly serve to indicate a rising and subsiding aggression. Since speech is a web of subjective connotations, every remark is open to interpretation. Thus, questions such as "What the fuck does that mean?" and defenses such as "I didn't *mean* anything" (p. 60) are common. No thought is ever fixed; the characters change their positions and attitudes from line to line. The language has no center and the result is inherent uncertainty and mutual wariness.

A second level of speech corresponds to what the characters consider "objective," i.e. talk which has to do with business. Here they draw on cliché concepts presented as truth and thus unassailable. The jumble of conceptual confusion is just as great as in the more personal level of speech but, as with Kroetz's use of quotation and proverbs, "business" clichés carry a certain authority. As Teach says, "I am a businessman, I am here to do business. I am here to face facts" (p. 83). Such self-confident platitudes are more than slightly ludicrous since the "facts" change at whim, and neither he nor Don is capable of the logical analysis which such statements imply. "You have your job, I have my job, Don. I am not here to smother you in theory," Teach advises when Don asks how he plans to break into the house. From this a "professional" discussion of "business strategy" evolves:

DON: We can use somebody watch our rear.
TEACH: You keep your numbers down, you don't *have* a rear. You know what has rears? Armies... Hey Biiig fucking deal. The shot is yours, no one's disputing that. We're talking business, let's *talk* business: you think it's good business call Fletch in? To help us.
DON: Yes.
TEACH: Well then okay... Somebody watch for the *cops*... work out a *signal*...
DON: Yeah.
TEACH: Safety in numbers.
DON: Yeah...
TEACH: You, me, Fletcher.
DON: Yeah.
TEACH: A division of labor. (*Pause.*) (Security, Muscle, Intelligence.) Huh?
DON: Yeah.
TEACH: This means, what, a traditional split. Am I right?...
    (pp. 52–3)

For Teach, this board-room jargon – "a division of labor," "a traditional split" – supplies an "objective" justification for Don's apparent lack of faith in Teach's capacity to carry out the "shot" on his own.

Mamet said in an interview that *American Buffalo* "is about the American ethic of business: about how we excuse all sorts of great and small betrayals and ethical compromises called business."[32] Unlike *Glengarry Glen Ross*, in which the business ethic is explicitly portrayed through characters who are salesmen, *American Buffalo* attacks the distorted morality of American capitalism metaphorically: petty crooks mouthing the vocabulary of free enterprise within a moral void. Words are no longer anchored in a conceptual structure; no value system imbues words with connotations. Language does not reverberate: it merely proliferates. Robert Storey noted that:

The making of Mamet's America is founded upon a verbal busyness, glib, deft, quick; the parenthetical asides that lace his dialogue (destined, undoubtedly, to become as celebrated as Pinter's pauses) suggest minds that abhor verbal vacuums, that operate, at all levels, on the energy of language itself.[33]

Like the corpse in Ionesco's *Amédée*, language expands to fill any empty space. Mamet's characters seem almost incapable of *choosing* their words; words tumble out of them, barely digested, barely connected. The following dialogue is a pivotal example of the disruption between personal morality and public rhetorical pieties, or what Bigsby calls "an American past plundered for its rhetoric but denied as the source of values."[34]

TEACH: You know what is free enterprise?
DON: No. What?
TEACH: The freedom...
DON: ...yeah?
TEACH: Of the *Individual*...
DON: ...yeah?
TEACH: To Embark on Any Fucking Course that he sees fit.
DON: Uh-huh...
TEACH: In order to secure his honest chance to make a profit. Am I
    so out of line on this?
DON: No.
TEACH: Does this make me a Commie?
DON: No.
TEACH: The country's *founded* on this, Don. You know this... without
    this we're just savage shitheads in the wilderness.
DON: Yeah.
TEACH: Sitting around some vicious campfire. (pp. 72–3)

The extreme alienation of these characters from their language, the disintegration of all moral coherence in the arguments they present, is alarming. Market values and jargon have infiltrated their language and eroded the ethical basis for action. Teach and Don are unaware of the vacuity of their communication. Worse, the ability to manipulate the shell of once meaningful concepts gives them the impression of participating in, even upholding, the basic tenets of American liberalism. They cannot think beyond their fragmented speech-world, but through these dislocated fragments they repeatedly seek to give meaning to their personal and moral isolation. Speech is, after all, an activity which simulates contact, and although almost every attempt at communication leads to confusion and aggression, Mamet's characters do not give up. They would like to believe, as Don puts it, that "we're human beings. We can *talk*, we can negotiate, we can *this*..." But with "*this*" their capacity to negotiate, and the extent of their humanity, are at an end.

The climax of the play dramatically melds physical and verbal violence, demonstrating their obvious equation. The eruption of brute force occurs simultaneously with the disruption of realistic speech. Don and Teach are waiting for a third partner, Fletch, in order to "go in" and "take the shot." It is very late and he has not shown up, "Cocksucker should be horsewhipped with a horsewhip" (p. 72). Instead, Bob returns with the news that Fletch has been mugged and is in hospital. Don and Teach immediately read multiple meanings into this statement – betrayal, conspiracy – and attack Bob, blaming him. Bob's only defence is the incessantly repeated words: "I *came* here." Don and Teach interrogate him, but his confusion and retractions stoke their suspicions. At a loss for words forceful enough to express his pent-up frustration, Teach suddenly grabs a nearby object and hits Bob viciously on the side of the head. Bob falls to the floor with blood running out of his ear. Finally, semi-conscious, he admits – "I eat shit" – that he lied about spotting the coin-collector that morning, only said it in order to please Don. This admission renders their entire "enterprise" as absurd as the language Teach and Don had used to defend it. With the stage now in shambles, and even the illusion of rationality destroyed, Teach, and his language, go completely out of control. Teach wildly destroys the shop while shouting a list of disjointed mottos – almost credos – which no longer resemble naturalistic speech, but are more like speech gone mad:

> My Whole Cocksucking Life...
> The Whole Entire World.
> There Is No Law.
> There Is No Right and Wrong.
> The World Is Lies.
> There Is No Friendship.
> Every Fucking Thing. (*Pause.*)

Every God-forsaken Thing...
We all live like the cavemen... (*Pause.*)
I go out there. I'm out there every day. (*Pause.*)
There is nothing out there. (*Pause.*)
I fuck myself. (pp. 103–4)

Teach's verbal break-down, his frenzied and elliptic litany of deeply felt accusations, push the language beyond realism. Mamet's use of capitalization here alerts us to the fact that this is no longer conversational speech: Teach's language has entered the oracular mode. Pushed to the limit of his capacity to feel and to verbalize, Teach erupts in a row of fragmented and negative postulates which testify to his spiritual emptiness and the conceptual void they all inhabit. The wild accusations are not directed against anyone in particular. They are almost metaphysical, decrying the grotesque and violent disparity between human needs – contact, communication, comprehension – and the moral and verbal poverty which prohibit their attainment.

The play ends with Don and Bob alone on a destroyed stage, softly muttering confused and pointless words of apology and forgiveness, drawn together in a fragile bond, broken and useless as the cast-off objects which surround them.

Glengarry Glen Ross is more sophisticated, and even more devastating, than *American Buffalo*. It won Mamet the 1984 Pulitzer Prize and established his reputation as a master of the slippery vernacular facade which both harbors and exposes American ethical vacuity. Like *American Buffalo*, it is concerned with the infiltration of individual morality and interpersonal contact by the values and jargon of business. Also like *American Buffalo*, it is an oppressively verbal play in which deformity and violence are performed through a highly limited and opaque language.

We have, however, moved up a rung in the not-quite-social ladder of Mamet's dehumanized landscape. No longer a play about petty crooks incapable of carrying out an incoherent robbery, we now have experienced real estate salesmen in their forties and fifties who *do* manage to "knock off" the office for which they work. As in *American Buffalo*, criminal action is conceived and discussed in the same commercial jargon through which both personal and business interaction is conducted. *American Buffalo*'s obscenities are here supplemented by a dense technical jargon, almost a "code" language of salesmanship, which both frustrates and entices the audience into a closed world. The play opens with the following baffling references:

LEVENE: John...John...John. Okay. John. John. Look:...All I'm saying, you look at the *board*, he's throwing...wait, wait, wait, he's throwing them *away*, he's throwing the leads away. All that I'm saying, that you're wasting leads...all I'm saying, put a *closer* on the job. There's more than one man for the...Put a...wait a second, put a *proven man out*...and you watch, now *wait a second* – and you watch your *dollar* volumes...

WILLIAMSON: Shelly, you blew the last...

LEVENE: No. John. No. Let's wait...One kicked *out*, one I *closed*... (p. 3)[35]

LEVENE: ...When was the last time *he* went out on a sit. Sales contest. It's *laughable*. It's cold out there now, John. It's tight. Money is *tight*...

WILLIAMSON: ...The hot leads are assigned according to the board. During the contest. *Period*. Anyone who beats fifty per...

LEVENE: That's fucked. That's fucked. You don't look at the fucking *percentage*. You look at the *gross*... (pp. 6–7)

This terminology is sustained throughout the play; it is repeated, "hammered and rehammered" as Marcuse put it,[36] until the audience is totally enmeshed within a windowless world of "leads," "sheets," "sits," "boards," "shots," "dollar volumes," and "closings"; a world which is totally self-contained, and at the same time transparently reflects the audience's own. "Always be closing" is the motto with which Mamet prefaces his play. It is that "sales maxim" which pressures the characters into a robbery to attain the "leads" (addresses of potential serious customers) through which they might sell ("close") a property and thus gain a higher position in the hierarchy ("board") of the company's competition. This competition tests the salesmen's capacity to survive: the winner gets a Cadillac, the runner-up a set of steak knives, the losers will be fired. Mamet claims that criminality is an inherent element of business as such. Drawing on his own experience as a former real estate agent, Mamet disingenuously explains that the potential customer is "called a *lead* – in the same way that a clue in a criminal case is called a *lead* – i.e. it may lead to the suspect, the suspect in this case being a *prospect*."[37] The image of the salesman as a detective hunting the "culprit" is developed in the play's dialogue as well as in its thematic moral inversions. Levene, an experienced and fierce salesman, talks of his job in terms we usually associate with police jargon:

> LEVENE: You can't learn that in an office... You have to learn it on the streets. You can't *buy* that. You have to *live* it... Cause your partner *depends* on it... Your partner *depends* on you... You have to go *with* him and *for* him... or you're shit, you're *shit*, you can't exist along... (pp. 57–8)

The prey being stalked out there "on the streets" is the potential buyer, and the salesman, the last of "a dying breed" of real *men* – as Roma (a totally ruthless man, therefore first on the board) puts it – must catch his prey through talk alone.

The act of talking, which already in *American Buffalo* is ambiguously treated by the characters themselves, is here developed into a schizophrenic term: to "talk" is to *act*, talk is power, *men* know how to "talk." When Williamson, the office manager, ruins an important sale for Roma by saying the wrong things, by not "talking the game," Roma attacks his masculinity:

> ROMA: You stupid fucking cunt. *You*, Williamson... I'm talking to *you*, shithead... You just cost me *six thousand dollars*. (*Pause.*) Six thousand dollars. And one Cadillac... Where did you learn your *trade*. You stupid fucking *cunt*. You *idiot*. Whoever told you you could work with *men*?... Anyone in this office lives on their *wits*... What you're hired for is to *help* us... to help *men* who are going *out* there to try to earn a *living*. You *fairy*. You company man... You fucking *child*... (pp. 56–7)

Cunts, fairies, and children are incapable of "talk" and have no place working with "men." "Talk" in this usage opposes the individualistic frontiersman, the tongue-slinging man of action who "lives on his wits," with the sit-at-home, effeminate "company man." As with the buffalo-head nickel which evokes images of America's mythic past, these descriptions, too, ironically contrast pioneer images of masculinity ("last of a dying breed,") with the visionless, self-centered reality of these salesmen. In an earlier scene, Levene also attacks Williamson's lack of male street experience, and at the same time demonstrates the second meaning of "talk":

WILLIAMSON: ...my job is to marshall those leads...
LEVENE: Marshall the leads...marshall the leads. What the fuck, what bus did *you* get off of, we're here to fucking *sell. Fuck* marshalling the leads. What the fuck talk is that? What the fuck talk is that? Where did you learn that? In school...? *(Pause.)* That's "talk," my friend, that's "talk." Our job is to *sell*. I'm the *man* to sell. I'm getting garbage. (p. 5)

Levene opposes action (i.e. talk which *sells*) with the other meaning of "talk" developed in the play: talk as "the blah blah blah" (p. 13), talk divorced from action, talk as theory, as idea. Levene is offended by Williamson's phrase "marshall the leads" because it is not an action term – and because Williamson is using this "educated" phrase to hold Levene off. The opposition between "talk" and talk is pointedly developed in a strategic conversation between Moss and Aaronow, two failing salesmen no longer "on the board." Moss broaches the idea of breaking into their own office and stealing the leads, which they will then sell to a competing Agency:

AARONOW: ...are you actually *talking* about this, or are we just...
MOSS: No, we're just...
AARONOW: We're just "*talking*" about it.
MOSS: We're just *speaking* about it. *(Pause.)* As an *idea*...
AARONOW: We're not actually *talking* about it.
MOSS: No.
AARONOW: Talking about it as a...
MOSS: *No.*
AARONOW: As a *robbery*...
MOSS: ...I said 'Not actually'. The fuck you care, George? We're just *talking*...
AARONOW: We are?
MOSS: Yes. *(Pause.)*
AARONOW: Because, because, you know, it's a *crime*.

MOSS: That's right. It's a crime. It is a crime. It's also very safe.
AARONOW: You're actually *talking* about this?
MOSS: That's right. (pp. 18–19)

Aaronow, a weak man, is willing to "talk" about the robbery
– "No harm in talking," as Kroetz's characters would put it –
but not to actually *talk* about it. To "actually talk" is
equivalent to acting, as Aaronow soon finds out. When Moss
tells him, in typical jargon, that "to the law, you're an
accessory. Before the fact," Aaronow answers: "...we sat down
to eat *dinner*, and here I'm a *criminal*..." (p. 23). Talk is not
innocent. For these characters, who have no use for words
which do not activate or manipulate, participating in talk
means taking a risk.

MOSS: ...In or out. You tell me, you're out you take the consequences.
AARONOW: I do.
MOSS: Yes. (*Pause.*)
AARONOW: And why is that?
MOSS: Because you listened. (p. 23)

Mamet's salesmen "go *out* there to try to earn a *living*"
through talk. To succeed is to succeed in selling, to (as Levene
says) "generate the dollar revenue sufficient to *buy*" – leads,
which must then be *sold* (p. 6). There is no goal beyond the
selling, no need beyond success. Levene builds a mythology
around his early success as a salesman. Much like Arthur
Miller's Willy Loman, he recreates a past in which the Agency
owners "*lived* on the business I brought in" (p. 7). Toward
the end of the play Levene seems finally to manage to close a
deal and is euphoric at having broken a "losing streak." He
has "sold" "Harriett and blah blah Nyborg," selling them
"something they don't even *want*" (p. 44). Levene repeats his
spiel to Roma, describing how he overpowered them with his
rhetorical force until finally "They signed, Ricky. It was *great*.
It was fucking great. It was like they wilted all at once... They,
I swear to God, they both kind of *imperceptibly slumped*. And he
reaches and takes the pen and signs..." (pp. 42–3). Levene's
victory, retold in mock-heroic terms, is in the defeat of the
suspect, i.e. the prospect. When Moss tells him "I don't want

to hear your fucking war stories" (p. 38) the implication is clear: each sale is a battle, and the victor's weapon – like that of Pinter's Goldberg and McCann – is his language.

In the plays of Pinter (with whom Mamet is often compared, and to whom this play is dedicated), jargon is usually a tool of intimidation; here it is the scum and the essence of language. No other idiom exists in this world: business terminology has invaded and colonized the minds of Mamet's characters. Even intimacy is expressed in business terms. When Roma tries to convince a client of his capacity to decide on a purchase alone, despite his wife's disapproval, he describes their marital ties as "a contract ... You have certain things you do *jointly*, you have a *bond* ..." (p. 55). Despite an awareness of some vague unsatisfied need within them, Mamet's characters are incapable of real intimacy or emotion. "The problem is," Bigsby writes, "that they have so thoroughly plundered the language of private need and self-fulfilment and deployed it for the purpose of deceit and betrayal that they no longer have access to words that will articulate their feelings." Language has only one function: to generate an advantage. Morality is a by-product of gain. To steal the company files is theft; to deceive a client, to sell useless land to weak victims – is simply good business.[38] In such a world the very act of speech is a betrayal. To talk is to become an accomplice; to listen is to be implicated ("Because you listened"). Words can only buy and sell, and they sell trust and friendship just as easily as land.

Glengarry Glen Ross is a study of betrayal. Each dialogue charts a verbal manipulation; nothing can be believed, no fraternity exists – not even the proverbial fraternity among thieves. When Moss tries to convince Aaronow to steal the files with him, he promises to split the profit "half and half." Later, caught in an inconsistency, he admits, "I lied ... Alright? My end is *my* business" (p. 23). Roma, supposedly an admirer of Levene, proposes that they go out on "sits" together and "split everything right down the middle" (p. 63). He then tells Williamson, behind Levene's back: "My stuff is *mine*, whatever *he* gets, I'm talking half ... Do you understand? My stuff is mine, his stuff is ours" (p. 64).

Neither *American Buffalo* nor *Glengarry Glen Ross* has a central character or "hero." Both plays are group portraits of interdependent characters who share an unarticulated but clearly felt "thought-world." Their language, gestures, desires, and values are social products: not expressions of individual will. There is a sense in *Glengarry Glen Ross* that the words available to the characters are pre-determined, pre-packaged, infected and contagious, spreading a perversity which is beyond the characters' grasp or control. All partake of the same inarticulate obscenities, the same limited vocabulary and repetitive jargon. These almost seem to *precede* them, and to mold them. We meet six salesmen in *Glengarry Glen Ross*, and hear of half a dozen others. Yet all seem reduced to the words at their disposal or to what Benjamin Lee Whorf calls the "patternment," the unconscious structures of their specific language and thought-world. These patterns, according to Whorf, are pre-conscious and culturally determined: "...significant behavior is ruled by patterns from outside the focus of personal consciousness." Whorf opposes "patternment" (structuring) to "lexation" (word choice), arguing that the former "always overrides and controls" the latter.[39] It is perhaps to this rule of pattern over reference that Mamet refers when he claims that the rhythm of our language "actually determines the way we behave." Mamet's emphasis on rhythm, on the aural patterning of speech which enables the characters to ignore lexical contradictions, even nonsense, seems to intuitively translate Whorf's ideas into concrete prose – and is cardinal to the production of a sense of determinism in his plays. This device, common to all the characters, is parallel to Kroetz's repeated use of "semantic blanks" and pauses. Both abstract language from mere personal idiosyncrasy and embed it in a social milieu. Thus Mamet's implications, like Kroetz's and Bond's, go beyond the individual instance. Mamet draws a portrait of a culture in which the language of exploitation and deception is the inevitable bedfellow of a concept of success which is wholly materialistic and geared only toward personal gain.

It is hard to "like" these characters. Bond, in *Saved* and *The*

Pope's Wedding, gives us Len and Scopey with whom we can identify, whom we can pity. Kroetz too has characters who move us: Beppi and Sepp are certainly figures we might care about. Mamet, however, is pitiless. Despite the obvious misery of his characters, they are so thoroughly infected, so basely motivated as to awaken more revulsion than pity. This is especially true of *Glengarry Glen Ross*, in which ethical perversity and verbal restrictedness are totally interwoven and breed a bestiality which, Mamet seems to be saying, endangers an entire society.

CHAPTER 5

Wrestling with language: "head to head"

Edward Albee's *Who's Afraid of Virginia Woolf?* and Sam Shepard's *The Tooth of Crime* are examples of plays in which language is wielded between two combatants as a tool and weapon: language with the power to destroy but also to create, to reinvent. These two very different plays focus on language as interaction, on style as identity. Language is both reduced to a face-to-face battle "to the death" and expanded into an act of creativity and self assertion. In both plays relationships are developed not through, but *within* language, and verbal mastery is equated – through metaphor and theatrical image – with physical prowess. Characters and authors are very conscious of the words they use, and they wield to win.

Albee's George and Martha are unusually language-conscious – unusually, that is, for a realistic dramatic couple. They obsessively discuss their words, bicker over their verbal styles, win or lose at language-games as though these were concrete realities. Their communication system is to a great degree dependent on verbal imagination and a lust for verbal control. This verbal activity climaxes with the revelation that their son, the object of so much of their verbal aggression, is himself only an invention who is given life, fleshed out and brought up, within language. Albee's insistently vituperative play displays verbal vindictiveness which is first and foremost of the surface. John Gassner and John Mason Brown nominated the play for the Pulitzer Prize in 1962, and when the advisory board rejected their recommendation for this "filthy play,"[1] both Gassner and Brown resigned their positions as members of the Pulitzer Jury.[2] Despite the outrage, *Who's Afraid of Virginia*

Woolf? received both the New York Drama Critics' and the Tony awards for the best play of the 1962–3 season, and was a popular success, running on Broadway for two years.

Shepard's career was made outside of the usual Broadway venue. He is part of a generation of American playwrights who revitalized "fringe" theater and opened the stage to a new dramatic language. Shepard has written more than forty plays, eleven of which (including *The Tooth of Crime,* 1972) received Obie Awards, and in 1979 he won the Pulitzer Prize for his play *Buried Child.* Shepard's futuristic singer/warriors in *The Tooth of Crime* are competitors for "stardom" who do battle "head to head till one's dead"[3] solely through language. Hoss and Crow represent two generations and two styles of expression and experience. Like *Who's Afraid of Virginia Woolf?, The Tooth of Crime* develops various language codes, discourses which define reality and vie with each other for dominion. Unlike Albee, Shepard makes no pretence to dramatic realism. He invents a world and a language through the imaginative exploitation of the jargons of popular culture, and peoples it with characters who evoke the fragmented contexts of popular American myths.

EDWARD ALBEE: *WHO'S AFRAID OF VIRGINIA WOOLF?*

In *Who's Afraid of Virginia Woolf?* Albee returns verbal assault to the realistic and seemingly well-made bourgeois living-room where August Strindberg had first placed it in *The Father,* in *The Creditors,* or in *The Dance of Death.* George and Martha are descendants of Strindberg's warring couples. They continue Strindberg's "dialogues of cruelty" – in Ruby Cohn's coinage[4] – using a similar strategy of verbal thrust and parry, wounding through revelation and insinuation, teasing, taunting, and "hacking away at each other, all red in the face and winded" (as George puts it)[5] through words alone. Like the Captain and Laura of *The Father,* George and Martha carry their battle to dangerous extremes, "trickling poison [...] – like herbane" into each other's ears,[6] doing battle "to the death." Strindberg's "brain-battles" determine one level of Albee's play.

But its flavor and modernity, its manic excessiveness and verbal self-consciousness indicate another influence: Alfred Jarry's bawdy *King Ubu*. With Jarry, words become game objects: self-reflective, inventive, joyously perverse, they both shocked the sensibility (at least, when originally staged)[7] and called attention to themselves as acts which can crack the shell of convention. Ubu – that dirty-mouthed literary spoof whose vitality and toilet-brush humor, whose appetite, ambitions, and verbal obscenities challenged both the conventionality of the theater and the hypocrisy of bourgeois morality – underlies much of the savagery and excess of George and Martha. As with Ubu, their language is often explosive and exhilarating, with vulgarity as a measure for imagination. George and Martha revel in their excesses: they continue beyond reason – indeed, beyond realism – in the throes of a murderous verbal orgy.

Albee harnesses the childlike and self-reflective destructiveness of Jarry's explosive language to the deadly intensity and realistic malignancy of Strindberg's interpersonal power struggles. In *Who's Afraid of Virginia Woolf?* "merdre" no longer merely shocks, it shakes our faith in verbal communication. When Martha strikes out verbally the effect is deeply wounding, leaving "blood in [her] mouth" (p. 208). "Aimless...butchery" (p. 193) Nick calls it, aghast at the brutalities which exceed their ostensible cause and redirect our attention toward the language itself.

The plot of *Who's Afraid of Virginia Woolf?* unfolds along two parallel lines. On the surface, we have a conventional three-act play set in the naturalistic living room "of a house on the campus of a small New England college" named New Carthage. The action extends from 2 a.m. to dawn of a Sunday morning and includes four realistically delineated characters. On this level we have the story of the unhappy marriage of a middle-aged couple, George, Associate Professor of History at New Carthage College, unambitious, contemplative, "hair going gray"; and Martha, daughter of the college President and founder, frustrated, vulgar, alcoholic. Over three acts, this sado-masochistic couple "exercise...what's left of [their] wits" (as George puts it, pp. 33–4) and flaunt the ugly disintegration of their marriage before a young, new faculty couple: Nick, a blond, attractive, and cold-blooded biologist; and his simpy, "rather plain" wife, Honey.

Parallel to these naturalistic details we find a mythic landscape: New Carthage, with its overtones of an ancient city whose success had contained the seeds of its own destruction, a destruction so complete that it became a synonym for doom. In his book *The Decline of the West*, Oswald Spengler, the nineteenth-century historian so admired and quoted by George, drew a parallel between Carthage and modern America, emphasizing a shared sterility and implying a possibly shared fate. George sets New Carthage within the broader mythic context of "Illyria...Penguin Island...Gemorrah..." (p. 40), places of illusion, dashed hopes and destruction.[8] George and Martha reign over the mythic evocations with names that invoke the image of America's first White House couple, father and mother of the "land of the free." By extension, their behavior hints at the intellectual and moral disintegration of the "American Dream" which Albee had already taken to task in his earlier play by that name. The titles of the three acts of the play—"Fun and Games," "Walpurgisnacht," and "The Exorcism" – prepare us for the ghosts and ghouls which metaphorically inhabit George and Martha and which will finally be expulsed. Albee had originally intended to name the entire play "The Exorcism,"[9] thus stressing the ritual rhythm which undermines the play's surface realism in both action and language.

Realism and ritualism are tied together in this play through the strategy of game-playing. George and Martha name four of their games – "Humiliate the Host," "Get the Guests," "Hump the Hostess," "Bringing up Baby" – and their use of alliteration is an early indication of the verbal wit which is a requirement for winning. These are strange, ugly games which demand little action, only an abundance of verbal energy. Even "Hump the Hostess," the only game with a physical correlative, consists mainly of verbal foreplay and, after the failed infidelity, a barrage of verbal backlash. Games and

language are inseparable in *Who's Afraid of Virginia Woolf?*
After George has lost the first round of "Humiliate the Host"
– a game which (perhaps) exposes his past as a patricide and
matricide (truth or illusion?) and leads him to try to strangle
Martha – he says: "Well! That's one game. What shall we do
now, hunh? [...] I mean, come on! We must know other
games, college-type types like us...that can't be the...*limit of
our vocabulary*, can it?" (pp. 138–9, my emphasis). The identification of "vocabulary" with "games" is central to Albee's
dramatic strategy throughout.

From the start, Albee characterizes George and Martha
through their differing verbal styles. Martha initially appears
crass and domineering, while George seems more passive and
restrained. Within the first few pages of the play she imitates a
Bette Davis line taken from some "goddamn Warner Brothers
epic," patronizes George with the sing-song nursery rhyme
"Poor Georgie-Porgie, put-upon pie," and repeats, with relish,
her version of the Disney song "Who's afraid of the big bad
wolf," which she had performed earlier that evening at the
faculty party. Their discussion of that performance is an early
example of Martha's coarse and adolescent vocabulary, and
George's use of restraint and irony.

MARTHA: What's the matter...didn't you think that was funny?
Hunh? (*Defiantly*) I thought it was a scream...a real scream. You
didn't like it, hunh?
GEORGE: It was all right, Martha...
MARTHA: You laughed your head off when you heard it at the party.
GEORGE: I smiled. I didn't laugh my head off...I smiled, you
know?...it was all right.
MARTHA: (*Gazing into her drink*) You laughed your goddamn head
off.
GEORGE: It was all right...
MARTHA: (*Ugly*) It was a scream!
GEORGE: (*Patiently*) It was very funny; yes.
MARTHA: (*After a moment's consideration*) You make me puke!
GEORGE: What?
MARTHA: Uh...you make me puke!
GEORGE: (*Thinks about it...then...*) That wasn't a very nice thing to
say, Martha.
MARTHA: That wasn't *what?*

GEORGE: ...a very nice thing to say. (pp. 12–13)

We note that what Martha considers "a scream!" was for George "very funny." Indeed, not only the reader, but George and Martha themselves have noted their stylistic differences, and later, in front of Nick and Honey, will (again in their own styles) discuss the implications of this disparity:

MARTHA: I thought I'd bust a gut; I really did... I really thought I'd bust a gut laughing. George didn't like it... George didn't think it was funny at all.

GEORGE: Lord, Martha, do we have to go through this again?

MARTHA: I'm trying to shame you into a sense of humor, angel, that's all.

GEORGE: (*Over-patiently, to Honey and Nick*) Martha didn't think I laughed loud enough. Martha thinks that unless... as she demurely puts it... that unless you "bust a gut" you aren't amused. You know? (p. 25)

Thus George turns the table on Martha by replacing the subject under discussion with the *way* it is being discussed. By implication, he equates Martha's coarse vocabulary with her vulgar mode of experience.

From the outset a pattern is established whose focus – as indicated by George and Martha themselves – is on the very words they use. Language seems to be less of a communicative tool for relaying information than a relational gauge through which the definition of their reality is constantly, and violently, negotiated. To control that definition, to determine whether a song was "a scream" or "very funny," whether to "bust a gut" is a sign of vitality or vulgarity, is to control their reality. The equation of verbal control with reality control occurs within a number of syntactic models. Struggles erupt over the fitting style of a phrase, the correct usage of a word or appropriate grammatical structures. Dialogues proceed haltingly as each usage is self-consciously scrutinized, and each scrutiny occasions a power struggle. Just before Nick and Honey arrive, the central metaphor of the play, the son, is mentioned by George. The subject is, however, immediately displaced by an argument about the way it is presented:

GEORGE: Just don't start on the bit, that's all.

MARTHA: The bit? The bit? What kind of language is that? What
   are you talking about?
GEORGE: The bit. Just don't start in on the bit.
MARTHA: You imitating one of your students, for God's sake? What
   are you trying to do? WHAT BIT?
GEORGE: Just don't start in on the bit about the kid, that's all.
MARTHA: What do you take me for?
GEORGE: Much too much. (p. 18)

A "bit" is theatrical parlance for a short scene either rehearsed
or improvised on some known subject. Albee's use of "bit"
here, the first mention of the son in the play, alerts us to the
son's fictive nature, to his status as illusion. Martha, however,
reacts not to the subject (the son) but to George's style, to the
"kind of language" he is using.

   In both of the above examples, the subjects ostensibly under
discussion – George's sense of humor and Martha's lack of
discretion – are viewed through the style of their presentation.
The way the subject is discussed replaces the subject itself and
becomes the source of dispute. The difficulty Nick and Honey
– and indeed the reader – have in validating George and
Martha's reality results from this endless displacement of facts
or information by their mode of presentation. "Truth or
illusion?" becomes increasingly hard to determine. Did George
really kill his father and mother? Is his novel autobiographical
or fictive? Is George really the only man Martha ever loved?
"True or false? Hunh?" (p. 141). George and Martha seem to
believe that the nature of reality is determined by its
formulation. When Martha mistakes handsome Nick for a
mathematician, she is quickly corrected by George:

MARTHA: So? He's a biologist. Good for him. Biology's even better.
   It's less... abstruse.
GEORGE: Abstract.
MARTHA: ABSTRUSE! In the sense of recondite. (*Sticks her tongue out at
   George*) Don't you tell me words... (p. 63)

To know "words" is a mark of both competence and control.
To misuse language is, in this play, a sign of weakness, and
carries an immediate loss of power. This is brilliantly shown in
Act II, where George and Nick vie for position and superiority

through a game of "confessions" which includes the following section:

GEORGE: You know what they do in South America...in Rio? The puntas? Do you know? They hiss...like geese...They stand around in the street and they hiss at you...like a bunch of geese.
NICK: Gangle.
GEORGE: Hm?
NICK: Gangle...gangle of geese...not bunch...gangle.
GEORGE: Well, if you're going to get all cute about it, all ornithological, it's gaggle...not gangle, *gaggle.*
NICK: Gaggle? Not gangle?
GEORGE: Yes, gaggle.
NICK: (*Crestfallen*) Oh. (p. 113)

Nick's attempt to "tell" George words is a way of attaining position, in which he fails. The knowledge, and thus the power, remains with George. Lexical definition gives way to the definition of relational power.

George and Martha's use of language has received an unusual reading by the sociologists Paul Watzlawick, J. H. Beavin, and D. D. Jackson in their book *Pragmatics of Human Communication: A Study of Interactional Patterns, Pathologies, and Paradoxes.* The authors devote an entire chapter of their theoretical study to an analysis of the verbal moves in *Who's Afraid of Virginia Woolf?*[10] viewing the relationship between George and Martha as a model of a derailed communication system. Intriguingly, they read the play as an interactional system which, despite its being a product of Albee's imagination, is considered "possibly even more real than reality."[11] The authors chose to analyze *Who's Afraid of Virginia Woolf?* because of its manageable size, independent data (i.e. not influenced by the researchers), and public accessibility – qualities hard to come by in a real-life test situation. Their choice acknowledges Albee's verbal realism and his focus on language in an interpersonal context. It should be remembered, however, that the authors treat *Who's Afraid of Virginia Woolf?* as a "test-case" through which to study the pathology of communication, not as a literary construct. As literature, George and Martha's entrapment within mutually binding verbal violence has no (necessary) antecedent in outside reality. Albee's eccentric concentration on their verbal interaction is a freely chosen literary device aimed at a *thematic* concern – not at pathological description. Watzlawick *et al.* do not ask why Albee focuses so obsessively on shared verbal cruelty, and what meaning can be ascribed to its final banishment; they are more interested in describing the *how* of George and Martha's relationship, in abstracting structures which can then be generalized for their purposes.

An interactional system is defined by the authors as "two or more communicants in the process of, or at the level of, defining the nature of their relationship."[12] Interrelational communication emphasizes the response which a communication incites and the respective counter-response. This process is akin to Eric Berne's "transactional analysis"[13]; both endeavor to define all communication as depending on the interaction *between* speakers, rather than on the intention or verbal style of any single communicant.

The authors demonstrate the double aspect of every communicative activity. On the one hand, the informational aspect relays semantic information; on the other hand, the relational aspect defines the interpersonal relationship between the speakers. The interplay between information (semantic) and how it is understood (relational) creates a continual tension within the dialogue of *Who's Afraid of Virginia Woolf?* which is sometimes neutralized through wit, and at other times through brawling. When, for example, Martha compliments George's original toast ("for the mind's blind eye, the heart's ease, and the liver's craw") by saying "You have a poetic nature George...A Dylan Thomas-y quality that gets me right where I live," George turns the semantic meaning against her with the words "Vulgar girl! With guests here!" (p. 24) and thus re-opens their relationship conflict. At another point, Martha accuses George of causing Honey to throw up:

GEORGE: I did not make her throw up.
MARTHA: You most certainly did!
GEORGE: I did not!...
MARTHA: (*To George*) Well, who do you think did...Sexy over there? You think he made his *own* little wife sick?

GEORGE: (*Helpfully*) Well, you make *me* sick.
MARTHA: THAT'S DIFFERENT! (p. 118)

Watzlawick *et al.* claim that George and Martha's relationship is "a system of mutual provocation" which proceeds through "symmetrical escalation" – the constant need to compete and outdo each other – and forms a circular "game without end" from which neither can escape.[14] This sociological perspective does much to explain the formal mechanism of the aggression between George and Martha, but it leaves two important questions unanswered: Why is so much of the "symmetrical escalation" centered around language? And why, as the authors themselves point out, is "the constraint on their symmetry [...] that they must be not only effective but witty and daring,"[15] i.e. the requirement of imagination? A closer look at the second question may also help to answer the first.

Language aggression moves in two directions in this play. On the one hand, language is treated as a power tool, to be controlled and possessed. Within language George and Martha develop and fight their relationship struggle: within language their self-enclosed reality is defined and given substance. In this sense, "reality" is always at a remove from the words which give it a shifting form, and the balance of power tips in favor of whoever maintains verbal control at any given moment. But there is another sense in which George and Martha wield language *together* against the numbing platitudes of the outside world – as represented by Nick and Honey. In this sense verbal power is not given through linguistic control or by "knowing words," but through wit and creativity. "Martha's a devil with language, she really is" (pp. 20–1) George warns his newly-arrived guests. Surprisingly, George and Martha's "devilish" verbal ingenuity express certain shared values which go beyond Watzlawick *et al.*'s analysis, and which distinguish the elder couple from their verbally banal and conventional guests.

These values are already hinted at early in the play when George admonishes Martha that it "wasn't very nice" of her to say that "you make me puke!" The passage continues as follows:

MARTHA: I like your anger. I think that's what I like about you

     most … your anger. You're such a … such a simp! You don't even
     have the … the what? …
GEORGE: … guts? …
MARTHA: PHRASEMAKER! (*Pause … then they both laugh*) (pp. 13–14)

Why this moment of communion here? Besides enjoying their
successful teamwork in creating the cliché, George and Martha
recognize in each other a shared attitude *toward* that cliché.
George and Martha recognize the difference between the
clichéd and the creative, the imitative and the imaginative.
And unlike any of the other characters I have discussed, they
are on the side of the creative use of language.

    George and Martha rarely let a platitude slip by unremarked
and are quick to jeer at any "phrasemaker." This is especially
obvious in their contempt for simpy Honey who giggles and
whines and is totally devoid of self-irony. Honey's speech is a
mixture of inane maxims – "Never mix – never worry" (p.
23); and vacuous hyperbole – " … it was a *wonderful* party …
And your father! Oh! He is so marvelous! … He's a wonderful
man" (pp. 25–6). When at one point Honey coyly expresses
the need to "put some powder on my nose," George
sarcastically asks Martha to "show her where we keep
the … euphemism" (p. 29).

    Honey almost seems to have slipped into *Who's Afraid of
Virginia Woolf?* straight out of Albee's absurdist comedy *The
American Dream* (1960), a farce on Middle America that is
composed almost entirely of platitudes and euphemisms. It's
"story" is curiously similar to *Who's Afraid of Virginia Woolf?*,
although in a completely different idiom. We have a
domineering Mommy and a weak Daddy, an unbelievable son
whose existence and death are no more than literal realizations
of speech-coins, and two outsiders: the conventional Mrs.
Barker and the tough Grandma, the most interesting character
in the play. The relationships and dialogue of these stick-
characters is reminiscent in many ways of Ionesco's *The Bald
Soprano*. They go to the "johnny" to do their "johnny-do's";
they "feel misgivings, … definite qualms, … right around where
the stitches were"; they "move around a lot, from one
apartment to another, up and down the social ladder like mice,
if you like similes" – which Mrs. Barker claims she does not."[16]

Except in the case of the straight-talking Grandma, who comes from "pioneer stock" and whose death, suggests Ruby Cohn, is the result of the "clichés of middle-class America,"[17] the dialogue does not emanate from within the characters. They are but mouthpieces for Albee who manipulates his characters through every verbal trick, all the while winking at his audience and inviting them to recognize themselves, their language, their attitudes. "We live in the age of deformity," Grandma quips, and while the other characters may not grasp her wit or the tediousness of their own fatuous babble, the audience, presumably, always does.

This constant authorial presence is exactly the opposite of, for example, Kroetz's use of cliché in his ultra-realistic plays. In *Farmyard* and *Ghost Train*, cliché relationships and language emanate solely from within the characters' limited consciousness. Platitudes are not ridiculed, they are simply given: no other speech form is offered and the author is nowhere to be found. *Who's Afraid of Virginia Woolf?* stands somewhere between these two styles. Its characters, like Kroetz's, are realistic, and their language too emanates from their personalities, not from the author's. But unlike Kroetz's limited characters – indeed, unlike the stick-figures of *The American Dream* – George and Martha are conscious of the language they use. In a sense, authorial consciousness has been internalized within the characters of George and Martha who seem to be both the *dramatis personae* and the directors of their play.[18]

Paradoxically, wit and imagination, which George and Martha seem to use almost as a conscious rebellion against the banal, have also displaced and replaced the authentic. George and Martha "know" words. They move easily from academic glosses – such as George's elaboration on the Spenglerian thesis of the fall of the West (p. 117) – to teeny-bopper slang; from the vulgar to the poetic. But they do not know – or at least will not acknowledge – reality. Existence is constantly verbalized, *versprachlicht*, restructured in a phrase. Even the central event of their lives – their joint son – is no more than a verbal elaboration, a fiction akin to Mommy's "bumble of joy" in *The American Dream*. George at one point sums up his life and existential situation through a surprising grammatical innovation: "Dashed hopes, and good intentions. Good, better, best, bested. How do you like that for a declension?" (p. 32). It is fitting that a declension should be used to define an existence which, for all its originality and self-consciousness, is trapped within the verbal matrix.

The centrality of verbal communication for George and Martha is brought into sharp focus through their meta-communication. Acts II and III contain four separate discussions about the rules and boundaries of their communication. These discussions have two functions: they alert us to the logocentric reality which Albee is setting up (and which he will destroy by the end of the play); and the terms in which the communication is discussed, the metaphors used, confirm the violent and even deadly potential of language. In each of these metacommunications the verbal communication in question is described in metaphors of physical violence. The communicants then enact that brutal verbal style, as their metacommunication itself escalates into aggression; and the aggression sets off another round of verbal violence. It is a cyclical communication pattern which Watzlawick *et al.* rightly call a "game without end" and within which violence is not merely expressed but actually created.

Act II begins with a short discussion between George and Nick on the interaction witnessed in Act I. George admits that he and Martha have been "disgusting" and angers Nick by implying that he is not a worthy audience for their fights. Nick counters by suggesting that if George and Martha "...want to go at each other, like a couple of...animals" they needn't subject others to the spectacle:

GEORGE: (*Considers it*)...Well, you're quite right, of course. It isn't the prettiest spectacle...seeing a couple of middle-age types hacking away at each other, all red in the face and winded, missing half the time.
NICK: Oh, you two don't miss...you two are pretty good. Impressive. [...]...sometimes I can admire things that I don't admire. Now, flagellation isn't my idea of good times, but...
GEORGE: ...but you can admire a good flagellator...a real pro. (pp. 92–3)

This initial description of George and Martha's style of

communication sets up metaphors which will be developed and strengthened over the next two acts. George's "hacking" metaphor evokes the image of a ring-fight, boxers or wrestlers "all red in the face and winded," footing for position, striking out relentlessly, "hacking away" in frenzy. Nick counters with his "flagellation" metaphor, connecting it with "good times" and thus evoking the sado-masochistic context of George and Martha's behavior. Both of these metaphors are drawn from the field of physical violence: for although George and Martha's battles are almost totally devoid of action, they function as violent acts. Later, after George has revealed to Honey that Nick betrayed the secret of her hysterical pregnancy, Nick threatens George with the words: "You're going to regret this... I'm going to make you regret this... I'll play the charades like you've got 'em set up... I'll play *in your language*..." (pp. 149–50, my emphasis).

Martha too attacks George's indiscretion against the young couple, calling it "pigmy hunting" (p. 151). George, who had expected Martha to celebrate his victory, is upset by her derision and opens a discussion of the rules which guide their mutual mutilation:

GEORGE: It's perfectly all right for you... I mean, you can make your own rules... you can go around like a hopped-up Arab, slashing away at everything in sight, scarring up half the world if you want to. But somebody else try it... no sir! [...] Why baby, I did it all for you. I thought you'd like it, sweetheart... it's sort of to your taste... blood, carnage and all. (pp. 151–2)

George rebukes Martha for not playing fair. After all, she slashes and scars up "half the world"; and since brutality is part of their game, he argues that he was playing by the rules. Now the discussion of the rules and reasons for their games escalates into a battle in which each threatens to finish the other off, culminating in a pact of "total war."

MARTHA: (*Fake-spits at him*) You're going to get it, baby.
GEORGE: Be careful, Martha... I'll rip you to pieces.
MARTHA: You aren't man enough... you haven't got the guts.
GEORGE: Total war?
MARTHA: Total. (*Silence. They both seem relieved... elated*). (pp. 158–9)

"Total war" implies that the limits which until now had regulated their game-moves are no longer valid. It is an invitation to renewed imaginative daring in strategy and tactics, an upping of the stakes.

The result of this challenge is Martha's game of Hump the Hostess and George's feigned indifference, which provokes Martha into really seducing Nick. The seduction, however, proves unsatisfactory as Nick, saturated with alcohol, turns out to be one more "flop." Martha's taunts at Nick's failure to "perform" lead to some of the strongest equations of words and mutilation.

MARTHA: Ohhhh! The stallion's mad, hunh. The gelding's all upset. Ha, ha, ha, HA!
NICK: (*Softly*; *wounded*) You... you swing wild, don't you.
MARTHA: (*Triumphant*) HAH!
NICK: Just... anywhere.
MARTHA: HAH! I'm a Gatling gun. Hahahahahahahahaha!
NICK: (*In wonder*) Aimless... butchery. Pointless. (pp. 192–3)

For Nick, Martha's verbal butchery is so excessive as to become itself an object of wonder. Pragmatic, unimaginative Nick remains a spectator at the ring of battle. All he can finally think to say, fittingly choosing a cliché, is "There's no limit to you, is there?" (p. 194).

The final battle of the play, the one called "Bringing Up Baby," will be fought between George and Martha, fought like two gladiators out for a kill. George initiates the final game; he also sets the rules, which include the requirement of playing to win. "You have had quite an evening... quite a night for yourself," he tells Martha, "and you can't just cut it off whenever you've got enough blood in your mouth. We are going on, and I'm going to have at you, and... I want you to get yourself a little alert. (*Slaps her lightly with his free hand.*) I want a little life in you, baby" (p. 208). The "blood in your mouth" to which George refers, recalls the "blood, carnage and all" which he previously described as being to Martha's taste. It also ties in with the "Gatling Gun" image with which Martha described herself. It is with her mouth – her words – that Martha draws blood and creates "butchery." Now George

promises to "have at" her and he spurs her on like a coach
before a major-league match, goading her into anger, preparing
her for the final round to be played "to the death":

GEORGE: I want you on your feet and slugging, sweetheart, because
    I'm going to knock you around, and I want you up for it. ... now,
    we're going to play this one to the death.
MARTHA: (*She paces, actually looks a bit like a fighter*) I'm ready for you.
    (pp. 208–9)

"On your feet and slugging" is, of course, boxing jargon, as is
"knock you around." Flexing and pacing, our fighters are
again ready to enter the verbal ring.

In 1968, the Swiss playwright Friedrich Dürrenmatt wrote and
staged an adaptation of August Strindberg's *The Dance of Death*,
which he called *Play Strindberg*. Using much of Strindberg's
original dialogue, though pared down and deflated, Dürrenmatt rearranged Strindberg's two acts into twelve short
"rounds." Each round opens with one of the three characters
– husband, wife, or guest – announcing the number of the
round and its title. Then a gong is heard and the scene begins.
This literal presentation of marital strife as a twelve-round
boxing match makes the implicit apparent. Dürrenmatt
transposes a literary battle "to the death" into a transparent
and highly theatrical metaphor.

   Dürrenmatt's concept is not foreign to Strindberg's play, as
we will later see. The essence of both plays is warfare; but
Strindberg explores the motivation behind the battles, while
Dürrenmatt is interested only in the tactics. Dürrrenmatt has
bared the bones of Strindberg's play in order to expose its
essence, and to comment on that essence. His play is, we might
say, a metacommunication on *The Dance of Death*. What
interests me at this point, however, is not the relationship
between *Play Strindberg* and *The Dance of Death*, but that
between *Play Strindberg* and *Who's Afraid of Virginia Woolf?*.
Dürrenmatt's main critical strategy is structural. The division
into twelve rounds does more than literally represent marriage
as a boxing match: it also focuses attention on the mechanism

of obsession, analyzes each dramatic confrontation, isolates and studies every climax. In *The Dance of Death*, games and playing are loosely laced into the hallucinatory dialogue. The "game" has no separate reality. It is not discussed or named by the characters, and Strindberg allows for little metacommunication. Alice and Edgar are trapped within the failed game of marriage. The rules need not be elaborated in the play, since they pre-exist in the audience.

Dürrenmatt takes the opposite approach by separating the game from its enactment. Audience and characters are explicitly shown the rules, boundaries, and score of the cruel game. The use of a boxing-ring also tells us that the game being played is a spectator sport, in need of an audience. Kurt, like Nick and Honey, plays that audience while also modifying the game itself through his presence. All of this is explicit in Dürrenmatt's version of Strindberg's play: in *The Dance of Death* it is only implicit.

The result of Dürrenmatt's reshaping of *The Dance of Death* is to emphasize the mechanism, the rules of the "collaborative conflict," rather than its psychological motivation. *Play Strindberg* is an analytic play. The characters are at one remove from their roles in the Brechtian tradition: they *play* at being Alice, Edgar, or Kurt to the sound of the game's gong. At the end of each round they revert to being actors or characters *aware* of the game they sometimes play. This ploy inhibits emotional identification in actor and audience, and keeps the metaphoric game structure at the forefront of our attention.

Albee certainly does not go as far as Dürrenmatt. George and Martha differ from Strindberg's Alice and Edgar in that they are aware of their games, are capable of discussing, even naming them, and move consciously from one round to the next. They also differ from Dürrenmatt's Alice and Edgar in that they have internalized their communication games and do not need an outside (author-)imposed structure, which would remove the game from their control. Albee retains Strindberg's realism and intensity; but he has George and Martha comment on their games and thus turn them into theatrical events. Analytic distance and psychological realism coexist, the game and its enactment are held in a "delicate balance," a painful, perverse balance which George decides to destroy through the expulsion of illusion, the destruction of the son-game, and the banishment of the language which nourished them.

Most critics agree that the theme of *Who's Afraid of Virginia Woolf?* centers on Truth and Illusion, truth being rather scarce until illusion, in the form of the fictive son, is expelled from their lives.[19] "When George murders their fictive son," writes June Schlueter, "he just as certainly murders the fictive portion of his and Martha's identities" and thereby demonstrates the relationship between reality and illusion.[20] Although there is general agreement on the centrality of the son-myth to the play's theme, few critics draw the connection between the theme of illusion, its manifestation in the son-myth, and their joint dependence and rootedness in the play's language.

   In Act III verbal realism begins to disintegrate as the focus shifts from communication through language to the recreation of reality *by* language. It is interesting that Watzlawick *et al.* who devote a section to the analysis of the son-myth as a "homeostatic mechanism" which functions as a stable symmetrical coalition between George and Martha, choose to ignore the means through which the son-myth is destroyed: namely, the incantatory recitation of the Catholic Mass for the Dead. They do, however, point out the important distinction between the "son" and the "son-game" or "son-myth," a distinction of which both George and Martha are aware. As Watzlawick *et al.* put it, "While the son is imaginary, their interaction about him is not, and the nature of this interaction, then, becomes the fruitful question."[21] It is only when the son is being discussed that the interaction grows serious. As long as the game is in question, a mocking self-irony characterizes their tone. In Act I, Martha's indiscreet slip about the existence of a son leads to the following double-edged dialogue in which son and son-game are simultaneously discussed:

GEORGE: (*Too formal*) Martha? When is our son coming home?
MARTHA: Never mind.
GEORGE: No, no...I want to know...you brought it out into the
   open. When is he coming home, Martha?
MARTHA: I said never mind. I'm sorry I brought it up.

GEORGE: Him up...not it. You brought *him* up. Well, more or less. When's the little bugger going to appear, hunh? I mean isn't tomorrow meant to be his birthday, or something? ...

MARTHA: I DON'T WANT TO TALK ABOUT IT!

GEORGE: I'll bet you don't. (*To Honey and Nick*) Martha does not want to talk about it...him. Martha is sorry she brought it up...him. (pp. 69–70)

The "little bugger" phrase – repeatedly used – is one of a row of parodic terms through which George, and Albee, mock the platitudes of parenthood and draw attention to the son's fictive status. George also calls his creation a "blond-eyed, blue-haired" boy (p. 72), "the apple of our eye...the sprout" (p. 83), a "comfort, a bean bag" (p. 98), and a "baby-poo" (p. 216). These obviously mocking terms undercut Nick and Honey's – and the audience's – expectations of parental rhetoric and evoke, quite clearly, the "bumble of joy" in *The American Dream*. Mommy and Daddy, like George and Martha, "couldn't have a bumble" of their own, and so they bought one which gave "no satisfaction." George and Martha's son, that perfect product of a parent's imagination – "so beautiful, so wise," as Martha puts it (p. 222) – has much in common with the "American Dream" character who replaces Mommy and Daddy's unsatisfactory first child. "Well, I'm a type," the beautiful young man admits and, in a list of clichés, describes his looks as "clean-cut, midwest farm boy type, almost insultingly good-looking in a typically American way." But he knows that he is only an appearance with no inherent reality: "...I let people love me...I accept the syntax around me, for while I know I cannot relate...I know I must be related to."[22] This absurd manifestation of platitudinal desires and emotional sterility is also evoked by George shortly before the exorcism when, carrying "flores para los muertos," he pretends to mistake the good-looking Nick for his and Martha's son. "Sonny! You've come home for your birthday!" Martha corrects his mock-error:

MARTHA: Ha, ha, ha, HA! That's the houseboy, for God's sake.

GEORGE: Really? That's not our own little sonny-Jim? Our own little all-American something-or-other? (p. 196)

As with the "American Dream" figure, their absent son exists only in so far as he is related *to*. Both characters are propositions, syntactic constructs, elaborated platitudes. The difference is one of idiom: while the "American Dream" figure exists physically, the absurdity of the context renders him a metaphor. George and Martha's son, however, is evoked within a realistic context, thus the climactic revelation that he is a fiction, a verbal illusion, must be prepared in order for the son to attain symbolic meaning.

Bringing Up Baby, or the "exorcism," is thus preceded by a series of dialogues which overtly focus on the theme of Truth and Illusion – and which seek the link between them and the language which constructs them. George and Marth's revelations in the first two acts were questionable and ambivalent; neither Nick nor the audience knew how much to believe, where fiction ended and fact began. But here, just before the climactic expulsion of illusion, the question of veracity and verification is urgently posed by George and Martha themselves. "You always deal in appearances?" (p. 190) Martha asks Nick at one point. Is George really the only man who ever made Martha happy? Did he really once sail past Majorca and see the moon go down, "thought about it for a little... considered it, you know what I mean?... and then, POP, came up again. Just like that" (p. 199)? Is Nick Martha's lover or only a "houseboy"?

GEORGE: Look! I know the game! You don't make it in the sack, you're a houseboy.
NICK: I AM NOT A HOUSEBOY!
GEORGE: No? Well then, you must have made it in the sack. Yes?...
MARTHA: (*Pleading*) Truth and illusion, George; you don't know the difference.
GEORGE: No; but we must carry on as though we did. (pp. 202–4)

The climactic dissection of "illusion" occurs within a layered and evocative image; one which locates illusion within the language which propagates it. The image is suggested by Honey who, apologetically holding up the bottle of brandy she has been drinking, admits "I peel labels." George extends Honey's meaning of the word "label" to cover all false tags, the names which conceal, the words which distort, the "appear-

ances" which hide truth. Like Honey, he too will peel the label
– of his paternity – to expose the fiction beneath:

> GEORGE: We all peel labels, sweetie; and when you get through the
> skin, all three layers, through the muscle, slosh aside the organs
> (*An aside to Nick*) them which is still sloshable (*Back to Honey*) and
> get down to bone…When you get down to bone, you haven't
> got all the way, yet. There's something inside the bone…the
> marrow…and that's what you gotta get at. (*A strange smile at
> Martha*)
> HONEY: Oh! I see.
> GEORGE: The marrow. But bones are pretty resilient, especially in
> the young. Now, take our son… (pp. 212–13)

And with this the final game of Bringing Up Baby begins.

Bringing Up Baby differs from all of the previous games. It
consists of two parallel verbal activities, recitations of pre-
existing litanies, and is played exclusively between George and
Martha. Nick and Honey are reduced to passive spectators
whose shocked reactions reflect those of the audience but do not
modify the game itself. Moreover, unlike the previous games,
Bringing Up Baby is not spontaneous. It has the rehearsed air
of a ritual recitation, and the interlocking of the two litanies is
clearly planned and directed. Martha is reluctant to expose the
"real" child to strangers, but, Albee tells us in a stage
direction, once George has forced her to "play," Martha
speaks "By rote; a kind of almost-tearful recitation" (p. 216).
George literally "prompts" Martha to enact her role:

> GEORGE: All right, Martha; your recitation, please.
> MARTHA: (*From far away*) What, George?
> GEORGE: (*Prompting*) "Our son…"
> MARTHA: All right. Our son… (p. 217)

Martha's "recitation" recreates the life history of an almost
mythic boy. The terms in which she portrays him differ
strongly from the gutsy and vulgar vocabulary we have come
to associate with her. This son is described in terms of heroic
perfection, a "sun" child – "Beautiful; wise; perfect."

> MARTHA: And his eyes were green…green with…if you peered so
> deep into them…so deep…bronze…bronze parentheses around
> the irises…such green eyes!

GEORGE: ...blue, green, brown...
MARTHA: ...and he loved the sun!...He was tan before and after everyone...and in the sun his hair...became...fleece.
GEORGE: (*Echoing her*)...fleece...
MARTHA: ...beautiful, beautiful boy. (p. 220)

At this point, with the mythic fleece, the bronze and the sun all evoked, George begins his parallel litany:

MARTHA: ...beautiful, beautiful boy.
GEORGE: Absolve, Domine, animas omnium fidelium defunctorum ab omni vinculo delictorum.
MARTHA: ...and school...and summer camp...and sledding...and swimming...
GEORGE: Et gratia tua illis succurrente, mereantur evadere judicium ultionis. ... (p. 220–1)

The Catholic Mass for the Dead is an ironic counterpoint to the son's life history. As Martha recreates her son in the only form in which he ever lived – in language – George, using the same means, performs his death. Normally, the Mass *follows* a death. Its purpose is to give meaning and symbolic finality to physical demise. Here, the Mass, through its potency as verbal reality, *accomplishes* the death. An alternate verbal reality, fraught with symbolic and traditional values, is chosen by George as the weapon through which to combat and destroy the "life" to which he and Martha have given verbal birth. Like Priest and Confessor, George and Martha continue their separate, opposed litanies and end with overlapping stanzas: George intoning with terrible finality the *Dies Irae*, Martha completing the biography of "OUR SON." The section ends in a demotic restatement of that which has just been ritually enacted. George proclaims simply: "Martha... (*long pause*)...our son is...dead."

Within the world of the play, this death-through-pronouncement must be accepted as a *real* and effective act. It alters the plot and changes the characters' behavior and view of themselves. Martha, for all her rage, finally accepts both the death of the son and of the son-game, and redefines the relationship between herself and George. George's murder-through-pronouncement does not contain the fantastic elements of, for example, the Professor's murder of his student through the ritual repetition of the word "knife" in Ionesco's *The Lesson*, but George's verbal act is just as irreversible and accomplishes a psychic transformation which results in a reformed interpersonal relationship.

The last section of *Who's Afraid of Virginia Woolf?*, in which George and Martha are alone, without guests, without illusions, consists entirely of simple, one-line dialogue. Albee's stage direction reads: "This whole last section very softly, very slowly," a rhythm sharply contrasting with what preceded.

MARTHA: (*Pause*) I'm cold.
GEORGE: It's late.
MARTHA: Yes.
GEORGE: (*Long silence*) It will be better.
MARTHA: (*Long silence*) I don't...know. ...
MARTHA: Just...us?
GEORGE: Yes.
MARTHA: I don't suppose, maybe, we could...
GEORGE: No, Martha.
MARTHA: Yes. No.
GEORGE: Are you all right?
MARTHA: Yes. No. (pp. 240–1)

Albee's intention in this final dialogue is surely to present "authentic" speech, cleansed of games of invective, of subversive wit. The language of illusion, the frenetic battles, the "blood and carnage," have been "exorcised" along with the fictive son. The son who was "born" and "raised" in verbal cruelty can only "die" when the language which created and defined him also dies. George's Mass for the Dead induces a double death: it kills the illusion, along with the instrument of that illusion.

EXPANDING THE CONTEXT: STRINDBERG AND JARRY

Citing Strindberg's influence on *Who's Afraid of Virginia Woolf?* is a critical commonplace: few critics can disregard the obvious surface parallels between Albee's unhappy couple and Strindberg's mutual mutilators. Strindberg has come to define the "cultural tradition" for *Who's Afraid of Virginia Woolf?*, as has Ionesco for *The American Dream*, or Genet for *The Zoo Story*.[23]

Indeed, in characterization, in plot action, even in the recurrence of certain themes, George and Martha can easily be seen as modern relatives of Strindberg's couples. Like Alice and the Captain in *The Dance of Death* they enact the game/reality of failed marriage and mutual recrimination; like Laura and Adolf in *The Father* they plot and fence for power over each other and over their child; like the Baron and Baroness in *The Bond* they lie, contrive, and torture each other; as with Tekla, Gustav, and Adolph in *The Creditors*, shifting coalitions are manipulated to extract the greatest amount of pain and humiliation. Martha seems deceptively like Strindberg's emasculating harridans, especially Laura and Alice; while George shares a certain weakness with Strindberg's males. All of the couples are locked in a struggle in which, as Adolf says, "one of us must go under" (*The Father*, p. 41). Moreover, the similarities go beyond the "warring couple" idiom. Thematically, sado-eroticism, spiritual cannibalism, cultural/biological antagonism and the will-to-power are common to both authors. Children are always pawns fought over by possessive parents, and often lead to the play's climax. Death or psychic annihilation occur again and again.

The Dance of Death (1901), like Albee's play, consists of a series of games, fights, power manoeuvers, and shifting alliances between Alice and Edgar, miserably married for twenty-five years, and Kurt, a spectator and participant in one night of their marital struggle. Like George and Martha, Alice and Edgar expose and disgrace each other, using their spectator/guest as a backboard against which to bounce off mutual acrimony, past failures, and accusations of parental betrayal. As in *Who's Afraid of Virginia Woolf?*, it is difficult to know who is lying and when; and, as in Albee's play, *The Dance of Death* ends with a tentative reconciliation between the couple after their guest has left. Although the parallels are clear, the Strindbergian model is only externally relevant to *Who's Afraid of Virginia Woolf?* C. W. E. Bigsby rightly warns us that "It is surely...a mistake to regard *Who's Afraid of Virginia Woolf?* as simply a modern version of Strindberg's *The Dance of Death*...The influence is there; the voice is Albee's."[24] This "voice" not only distinguishes Albee's play, it transforms it into something quite different from the Strindbergian model which it adapts. A comparison of two superficially similar passages may help to gauge the differences in their style and language.

ALICE: ...the last time I waltzed wasn't yesterday.
THE CAPTAIN: Could you do it still?
ALICE: Still?
THE CAPTAIN: Ye-es. You're a bit past dancing, same as I am.
ALICE: I'm ten years younger than you.
THE CAPTAIN: Then we're the same age – for the lady always has to be ten years younger.
ALICE: How dare you! You're an old man, and I'm in my prime. (*The Dance of Death*, p. 132)[25]

GEORGE: It's that habit you have...chewing your ice cubes...like a cocker spaniel. You'll crack your big teeth.
MARTHA: THEY'RE MY BIG TEETH!
GEORGE: Some of them...some of them.
MARTHA: I've got more teeth than you've got.
GEORGE: Two more.
MARTHA: Well, two more's a lot more.
GEORGE: I suppose it is. I suppose it's pretty remarkable...considering how old you are.
MARTHA: YOU CUT THAT OUT! (*Pause*) You're not so young yourself.
GEORGE: (*With boyish pleasure...a chant*) I'm six years younger than you are...I always have been and I always will be.
MARTHA: (*Glumly*) Well...you're going bald.
GEORGE: So are you. (*Pause...they both laugh*) (*Who's Afraid of Virginia Woolf?*, pp. 14–15)

The above passages show how two different plays deal with the same subject: age difference. Strindberg presents the subject in a straightforward style. His language translates information or emotion; it is concise, precise, and rather explicit. Strindberg tends to allow his characters to express their psychological states through rational and analytic language. Elsewhere, for example, Alice explains that "we really are the most unhappy people in the world" (p. 146), or Edgar rationalizes that "people were so vindictive that I became vindictive too[...]" (p. 181). There is nothing extraordinary in their mode of expression; indeed, the "nightmarish atmosphere" which some critics note in *The Dance of Death*[26] is a cumulative feeling. It is the things said which are horrifying, not the way they are said. "Boozer, boaster, liar! Curses on you!" Alice at one point says to Edgar, to which he replies: "This is a bottomless pit" (p. 164). Compare this with George and Martha's way of cursing:

GEORGE: Monstre!
MARTHA: Cochon!
GEORGE: Bête!
MARTHA: Canaille!
GEORGE: Putain! (p. 101)

The surprising use of French swearwords, their richness and variety, does more than merely translate aggression into language. Albee's characters wound through wit, hyperbole, the turn of a phrase – the way they speak is wounding, not only what is said. When George describes Martha as "the slashing, braying residue that called itself MOTHER" he is doing more than accusing her (as Alice does Edgar) of "set[ting] them [the children] against me" (p. 147). His lines cannot be reduced to their factual content without losing the very marrow of which George and Martha's relationship consists. George and Martha play roles similar to those of Alice and Edgar, but the shifting chain of incidents which are the heart of Strindberg's drama are transformed by Albee into verbal moves. Strindberg's language reveals; Albee's demonstrates, enacts. This is succinctly captured in Dürrenmatt's adaptation of *The Dance of Death*. In his opening Note to *Play Strindberg* Dürrenmatt writes that "By eliminating the literary side of Strindberg, his dramatic vision becomes more sharply focused."[27] That is, Strindberg's couple do not need language to practise their mutual tortures. Dürrenmatt's play loses neither in intensity nor in demonic strength through the expulsion of much of Strindberg's dialogue, and was, in fact, highly popular and successful. If the same exercise were attempted on *Who's Afraid of Virginia Woolf?*, not only would the flavor and wit of the play suffer, its very substance would be lost. George and Martha struggle *within* language, not merely through it.

Although *The Dance of Death* has structural affinities with *Who's Afraid of Virginia Woolf?*, *The Father* is closer in theme and spirit. Written in 1887 as a naturalistic play influenced by the theories of Emile Zola, *The Father* takes place in a bourgeois living-room and traces the animosity between a long-married and unhappy couple. Unlike *The Dance of Death*, *The Father* contains a clear and dramatic plot: the struggle of Captain Adolf and his wife Laura over control of their only daughter, Bertha. This struggle is a conflict of wills which results, in Strindberg's term, in a *Själamod* – a soul murder, or psychic murder.[28] *The Father* is an obsessive, nightmarish play. Although realistic in detail, its compressed form and thematic monomania work against realism. Robert Brustein goes so far as to suggest that *The Father* is set "less in a bourgeois household than an African jungle, where two wild animals, eyeing each other's jugular, mercilessly claw at each other until one of them falls."[29]

Like *The Dance of Death*, *The Father* is largely lacking in humor or wit. The language, however, is less straightforward and expository. Strindberg relies heavily on innuendo, on allusions, on whispered insinuations, on the nuance of words. The Captain's apoplectic insanity and death – his soul-murder – result directly from Laura's insinuations as to his paternity. This biological problem, the impossibility (in 1887) of scientifically establishing a father's "chromosomological partnership" (to quote George), is the center of the play's plot. The obsessive need to possess the child, and the murder of the parent through "loss" of the child, are the themes which link *The Father* to *Who's Afraid of Virginia Woolf?*.

LAURA: [...] a mother is closer to her child – more so since it has been discovered that no one can be absolutely certain who is the father of a child.
THE CAPTAIN: What bearing has that on this case?
LAURA: You don't know whether you are Bertha's father!
THE CAPTAIN: Don't I?
LAURA: How can you know what no one else knows?
THE CAPTAIN: Are you joking?
LAURA: No – I am simply employing your teachings. Besides, how do you know that I have not been unfaithful to you? (p. 25)

The Captain's reaction to this is a feverish doubt which eats into his reason and finally leads him to beg for the word which would release him from his mental torture. "I plead with you, as a wounded man pleads for his final death blow, to tell me everything. [...] All I ask of you is that you show compassion, as to one who is sick. I lay down all authority and I ask for mercy – ask that you let me live!" (p. 39).

This same subject occurs in *Who's Afraid of Virginia Woolf?* in parodic form. Martha, like Laura, questions George's paternity. But George's reaction is not to appeal to rationality or compassion, in which he has little faith, but to employ superior rhetoric. He "rises to the occasion" and triumphs over Martha through verbal imagination.

MARTHA: George's biggest problem about the little...ha, ha, ha, HA!...about our son, about our great big son, is that deep down in the private-most pit of his gut, he's not completely sure it's his own kid.

GEORGE: (*Deeply serious*) My God, you're a wicked woman.

MARTHA: And I've told you a million times, baby...I wouldn't conceive with anyone but you...you know that, baby.

GEORGE: A deeply wicked person. ...Martha's lying. I want you to know that, right now. Martha's lying. (*Martha laughs*) There are very few things in this world that I *am* sure of...national boundaries, the level of the ocean, political allegiances, practical morality...none of these would I stake my stick on any more...but the one thing in this whole sinking world that I am sure of is my partnership, my chromosomological partnership in the...creation of our...blond-eyed, blue-haired...son.

HONEY: Oh, I'm so glad!

MARTHA: That was a very pretty speech, George.

GEORGE: Thank you, Martha.

MARTHA: You rose to the occasion...good. Real good. (pp. 71–2)

Martha admits defeat when she praises George's "pretty speech." After all, the question of George's paternity is a literary one. Since his son has no biological reality, George need not grapple with scientific doubts, with chromosomes, as must the Captain. Martha's insinuation has no objective correlative. Still, George's "deeply serious" reaction to her accusation is sincere, since their shared fiction *is* their reality. The son that they have been inventing for twenty-one years is their mutual, albeit literary, creation. Thus, George's absurdly phrased "chromosomological partnership," his striking description of their son as "blond-eyed, blue-haired," his unshakeable faith in this unreal "partnership," confirm George's paternity in the idiom most fitting his creation: verbal mastery.

Another theme common to both *The Father* and *Who's Afraid of Virginia Woolf?* is "murder-through-pronouncement" – although one is realistic and psychologically motivated, while the other is a rhetorical ploy which banishes a verbal fiction. Laura's trickling of doubt, her whisper-campaign against the Captain, leads to his death. Her brother, the Pastor, leaves us no doubt as to Laura's guilt: "Let me look at your hand! Not a sign of blood to betray you – not a trace of insidious poison! An innocent murder that cannot be reached by the law..." (p. 45). *The Father* ends in the triumph of evil. Laura has brought insanity and death to the Captain by killing the father in him, by casting doubt on his paternity. *Who's Afraid of Virginia Woolf?* inverts this ending. It ends in the triumph of truth and the return of sanity. George saves Martha and himself by proclaiming the death of their fictive son and thus killing the illusions within them.

Albee shares Strindberg's intensity and moral seriousness, his surface realism and certain recurrent themes. Strindberg supplies an inspirational frame for Albee's play; but that which is of specific interest in *Who's Afraid of Virginia Woolf?* breaks out of the psychological Strindbergian model, travesties his seriousness, and suggests an opposed and very different source.

Alfred Jarry's name is not usually invoked in connection with Albee. Albee has not, to my knowledge, mentioned him as an inspiration, nor is it obvious that *King Ubu* (*Ubu Roi*, 1896) had any direct influence on *Who's Afraid of Virginia Woolf?*. Still, I would like to use Jarry's play as an alternate – or complementary – model to Strindberg: the model for an *anti*-realistic farce of marital brawling, full of exhilarating obscenities and infantile vulgarity. *King Ubu*, as opposed to, for example, *The Dance of Death*, is a play which does not take its own themes seriously. Jarry seems more interested in the forms of imagination than in the suffering of the soul. Nor do George and Martha have very much in common with Mother and

Father Ubu, at least on the level of plot or characterization. I will, however, try to suggest that as with Jarry's explosive language, with its self-reflective and perverse aspects, Albee, too, uses language to critique the conventional and banal, and as an implicit challenge to the realistic model so often associated with Strindberg.

Ubu is a grotesque parody of an heroic king whose essence is his excess. A degenerated and infantile Macbeth-figure of gross appetite and no dignity, he murders and curses his way to power. Ubu is a mixture of offensiveness and vitality: while his cowardice and vulgarity repel us, his energy and inventiveness act as attractive and joyous foils. As with George and Martha, the audience is caught between revulsion for the unaesthetic excesses and admiration for the unconventional brilliance. These contradictory impulses are also felt in Ubu's language, which became both scandal and legend through its vulgarity and playful ingenuity. Like its main character, *King Ubu*'s language is convention-breaking, embarrassing, and titillating. The famous opening "Merdre!" ("Shitr"), exclaimed to the flourish of a toilet-brush, is only the first of a list of suggestive oaths and original verbal inventions.[30]

This language, more than any other aspect of the play which Jarry himself directed in 1896, turned the opening performance into a tumultuous riot. The play that made Jarry and the Théâtre de l'Oeuvre famous had only two performances, and was not revived until twelve years later, a year after Jarry's death.[31] Jarry's language was an open affront to its audience. It was meant to shock and provoke, to force a re-evaluation of the norms and conventions of the theater, and of the bourgeois morality which underlies it.

Similarly, the shocked reactions to Albee's "filthy play," which one reviewer compared to a "sewer overflowing,"[32] derived largely from the barbed abusiveness of his dialogue, the savagery and excess which became the play's most characteristic features. Like Jarry's, Albee's language is *subversive*: it subverts the generic expectations of salon realism and of psychological analysis. Albee sets up a conventional situation: unhappy married couple; places it in a conventional location:

middle-class living-room; and then bombards the audience with what was considered "filth" and "depravity."[33] So finely crafted as almost to make of the language artifice, Albee's dialogue, like Jarry's, is all on the surface. Passages are more quotable than revealing, and verbal imagination is often preferred to psychological verisimilitude.

Both Jarry and Albee invest abundant energy in being offensive, and, in both, this offensiveness goes beyond the exigency of plot and becomes an end in itself. Jarry's language, for example, is not only scatological, it is also gratuitous. Early in the play, Mother Ubu prepares a dinner for Ubu and his henchmen. The menu, rich and varied, is also unusually repulsive (even in translation):

MOTHER UBU: Polish soup, roast ram, veal, chicken, chopped dog's liver, turkey's ass, charlotte russe...
FATHER UBU: Hey, that's plenty, I should think. You mean there's more?
MOTHER UBU: (*continuing*) Frozen pudding, salad, fruits, dessert, boiled beef, Jerusalem artichokes, cauliflower à la shitr.[34]

When Ubu later asks Captain Bordure whether he has had a good meal, Bordure answers: "Very good, sir, except for the shitr," to which Ubu replies, "Oh, come now, the shitr wasn't bad at all" (pp. 9–10). This irrelevant vulgarity is one of the play's staples. In one of Jarry's funniest scenes, Mother Ubu stumbles upon her cowardly husband, on the run from his enemies, sleeping in a cave. She tries to hide her identity by pretending to be a supernatural apparition, the archangel Gabriel. The conversation between them is a collection of infantile abuse which has little to do with the plot of that scene and everything to do with the gratuitous and joyous invention of vulgar wit.

MOTHER UBU: We were saying, Mr. Ubu, that you are a big fat fellow.
FATHER UBU: Very fat, that's true.
MOTHER UBU: Shut up, Goddammit!
FATHER UBU: Oh my! Angels aren't supposed to curse!
MOTHER UBU: (*aside*) Shitr! (*Continuing*) You are married, Mr. Ubu?
FATHER UBU: Absolutely. To the Queen of Witches.

MOTHER UBU: What you mean to say is that she is a charming woman.

FATHER UBU: A perfect horror. She has claws all over her; you don't know where to grab her.

MOTHER UBU: ...Mr. Ubu, your wife is adorable and delicious; she doesn't have a single fault...She doesn't drink!

FATHER UBU: Only since I've taken the key to the cellar away from her. Before that, she was drunk by seven in the morning and perfumed herself with brandy. Now that she perfumes herself with heliotrope, she doesn't smell so bad any more. Not that I care about that. But now I'm the only one that can get drunk!

MOTHER UBU: Stupid idiot!...That's all a bunch of lies – you've got a model wife, and you're a monster.

FATHER UBU: That's all a bunch of truth. My wife's a slut, and you're a sausage. (pp. 47–8)

The subjects discussed – the wife's looks, her drinking, her virtue – are all familiar from Strindberg. But here the point of the accusations is the crude wit which they allow, not the character revelation which they afford. Compare Ubu's description of his wife's drinking habit with the following conversation between George and Martha:

GEORGE: ...back when I was courting Martha, she'd order the damnedest things! You wouldn't believe it! We'd go into a bar...you know, a *bar*...a whiskey, beer, and bourbon *bar*...and what she'd do would be, she'd screw up her face, think real hard, and come up with ...brandy Alexanders, crème de cacao frappés, gimlets, flaming punch bowls...seven-layer liqueur things...

MARTHA: Hey, where's my rubbing alcohol?

GEORGE: (*Returning to the portable bar*) But the years have brought to Martha a sense of essentials...the knowledge that cream is for coffee, lime juice for pies...and alcohol (*Brings Martha her drink*) pure and simple...here you are, angel...for the pure and simple. (p. 24)

Here too, the turn of phrase and witty evocation are far more important than the veracity of this history, or the character exposition offered.

Ubu is more buffoon than man. Dim and thick-skulled, he gives very little appearance of having any self-awareness, any critical faculty. Unlike George and Martha, the Ubus have no "mind," no psychology. They are the incarnation of oafish vulgarity (Father Ubu) and crafty greed (Mother Ubu), unnuanced, unaware. Their language is not a conscious form of protest, a determined slap at conventionality; like Mommy and Daddy of Albee's *The American Dream*, the Ubus are flat vehicles who speak for their author and in his distinctive voice. The target of this language is not in the world of the play, but in the world of the audience. Verbal offensiveness and playful subversion are directed against the hypocritical conventions of stage and society, conventions through which, Jarry seems to imply, the stupid and greedy "Ubus" of this world cover up *their* base desires and motives.

George and Martha are, of course, far more complex characters, with a distinct psychology and abundant self-awareness. Yet a similar subversive verbal excess – although more sophisticated and polished – is part of their characterization. Their sharp wit is usually played off against the overconventional and dull Nick and Honey, who rarely react or seem to grasp the humor. Indeed, their deadpan silence when confronted with George's irrelevant verbal exercises or Martha's puns is one sign that these excesses are outside the bounds of the play's normal "communication." It is also a sign that "normal" communication – if Nick and Honey can be taken to represent some norm[35] – is being critiqued and challenged: verbal imagination set alongside verbal conventionality. In the first conversation between George and Nick, for example, George renders Nick speechless when he confronts him, for no reason, with his declension "Good, better, best bested" (p. 32). Later, during a discussion of the dangers of biology, George suddenly and inexplicably proclaims that: "I am a Doctor. AB...MA...Ph.D...ABMAPHID! Abmaphid has been variously described as a wasting disease of the frontal lobes, and as a wonder drug. It is actually both" (p. 37). Again Nick does not react. Throughout this section George seems to be carrying on two conversations: one, a conventional, if aggressive, chit-chat with Nick; the other, a mad-cap, bitter, and verbally brilliant monologue with himself.

Another example of seemingly gratuitous offence occurs in

George's second attack on the dangers of biological ex-
perimentation:

GEORGE: ...I am unalterably opposed to it. I will not give up
   Berlin!...
HONEY: I don't see what Berlin has to *do* with anything.
GEORGE: There is a saloon in West Berlin where the barstools are five
   feet high. And the earth...the floor...is so...far...below you. I
   will not give up things like that. No...I won't. I will fight you,
   young man...one hand on my scrotum, to be sure...but with my
   free hand I will battle you to the death.
MARTHA: (*Mocking, laughing*) Bravo!...
NICK: (*Angry*) Oh for God's sake!
HONEY: (*Shocked*) OH!
GEORGE: The most profound indication of a social malignancy...no
   sense of humor. None of the monoliths could take a joke. Read
   history. (pp. 67–8)

Nick and Honey cannot relate to these outbursts of irrelevant
imagination, just as they do not react when George tells Martha
to show Honey where they keep the "...euphemism" (p.
29), or when Martha accepts George's gift of flowers with the
words: "Pansies! Rosemary! Violence! My wedding bouquet!"
(p. 196). In each of these examples, the conventional context is
purposely strained. The most outrageous example of a realistic
frame being threatened from within occurs when George tells
Martha the news of their son's road accident. Martha, shattered,
weeping, demands to see the fateful telegram, to which George
replies: "I ate it." Nick and Honey react with horror at
George's seeming callousness; they see only the conventional
context and expect the usual rhetoric of grief. The tension
between apparent realism and a parallel travesty of realistic
expectations is lost on them. But this tension, with its implicit
critique of the placid and banal, is obviously uppermost among
Albee's goals and is, perhaps, most succinctly rendered in one
of the play's few non-verbal "actions." In Act I, Martha tells
Nick and Honey the embarrassing and silly story of how she
once accidentally knocked George out in a mock boxing match.
While Martha is explaining that "it was an *accident*...a real
goddamn accident," George silently takes a short-barrelled

shotgun from behind his back "and calmly aims it at the back
of Martha's head. Honey screams...rises. Nick rises, and
simultaneously Martha turns her head to face George. George
pulls the trigger" (p. 57). This highly dramatic and violent
moment, which promises to confirm the sadistic, realistic genre
of the play, is then exploded and turned into farcical comedy
as George shouts "POW!!!" and "a large red and yellow
Chinese parasol" blossoms forth from the barrel of the gun.
The juxtaposition of cruelty and farce, of aggression set off by
imagination, is meant to startle and perhaps alienate. Like the
play itself, the image manifests both Strindbergian intensity
and Jarry's *jeu*, and in the gap between the two opposing
contexts resides a challenge to the audience and its own
conventional expectations.

A wonderful example of shared verbal eccentricity occurs in
the play's only section of straightforward name-calling. In Act
II, George and Martha exchange seemingly conventional
abuse – except that the words are in French: "Monstre!-
/Cochon!/Bête!/Canaille!/Putain!" It should be noted that
this exchange erupts with total suddenness, and ends just as
unexpectedly. The use of French is unmotivated and unexplained, the vituperation is not expanded beyond this
stylized, rather elegant explosion, and, although Nick witnesses
this dialogue, he is not shown to have any reaction. It is as
though this section, as well as some of the other examples given,
occur outside of the realistic framework of the play altogether,
or on a parallel level. The French curses might have been taken
straight from Jarry – at least in spirit – or, more probably, from
Beckett's *Waiting for Godot*. Didi and Gogo, like George and
Martha, pass their time by playing a series of aggressive and
sad games. At one point they decide to play at mutual abuse:

VLADIMIR: Moron!
ESTRAGON: That's the idea, let's abuse each other...
VLADIMIR: Moron!
ESTRAGON: Vermin!
VLADIMIR: Abortion!
ESTRAGON: Morpion!
VLADIMIR: Sewer-rat!

ESTRAGON: Curate!
VLADIMIR: Cretin!
ESTRAGON: (*With finality*): Crritic!
VLADIMIR: Oh![36]

Like Albee and Jarry, Beckett assumes the audience within his dialogue ("Crritic!") and uses vituperation in a non-realistic and self-reflective manner. While George and Martha's aggression is real, the form it takes is often not. Their wit and inventiveness, their sudden switches of tone and idiom seem purposely to force our critical attention to the language. The intruding wit threatens to crack the realistic frame of the Strindbergian marital drama, and within this crack we can perceive an attack on the frame itself and on its conventions, which we so often uncritically accept.

Ernest Lehman's screen adaptation of Albee's play (1966; director: Mike Nichols) avoids the risks of annoying or alienating its audience. While largely loyal to the original, Lehman's script is clearly geared toward a psychological, realistic rendering of this unhappy marriage (aided by a naturalistic set and Method acting); one which does not strain genre expectations. Lehman adds very little to Albee's text, but he does cut; and the sections he chooses to delete are most instructive. Almost none of the passages quoted above – the "rubbing alcohol," "Abmaphid," "I won't give up Berlin," Martha's puns, the French abuse – appear in the film. Moreover, most of the direct discussions of language – the "hacking" and "flagellation" images, Martha's use of "abstruse" and her admonition "Don't you tell me words," the gangle/gaggle section, Nick's threat to George that "I'll play in your language," and others – have been expunged in the screenplay. This does not impair the story: in fact it probably strengthens it. Everything extraneous to the psychological interest, everything which cannot be realistically motivated, is omitted; and what remains is a model Strindbergian marital battle.[37] The subversive, self-reflective language and sharp wit which undercut and question that same surface realism – have been removed. The play remains, but Albee's "voice" has been modulated, and with it his critique of "reality" and of the language through which we, unthinkingly, construct and confine it.

Ten years after *Who's Afraid of Virginia Woolf?* opened on Broadway, Sam Shepard's *The Tooth of Crime* had its first American production, far from Broadway, at Princeton University's McCarter Theater (1972). Despite certain similarities, Shepard's rock singers, Hoss and Crow – who do vocal battle "head to head till one's dead" – are distanced from Albee's warring couple by more than a mere decade: a generation, a cultural ravine, a re-imaging of America posit Shepard light-years from Albee's surface salon realism.

Considered by many to be Shepard's best play, *The Tooth of Crime* is set in a sci-fi futuristic present on the far side of the American Dream. Part Western, part rock-and-roll fantasy, it is wholly American in its concerns with frontier roots, success ethics, identity, and the hard-rock images of a narcissistic pop industry turned into cultural myth. On a bare stage adorned only by "an evil-looking black chair...something like an Egyptian Pharaoh's throne" (p. 3), the aging king, Hoss, a rock-star/gunslinger past his prime, awaits his fall. High on the charts but threatened by younger contenders, Hoss is fighting to protect his "turf" and reach "gold." Like the aging Elvis Presley, Hoss lives in seclusion surrounded by a coterie of advisors and protectors. Star-Man, his astrologer and strategist, and Becky, his personal manager who "landed" him when he was no more than a "mad dog," a "sideways killer," have molded, shaped, and sharpened him "down to perfection" (pp. 10–11). They now advise him not to go out "for a kill" against invading Gypsy Markers, young warriors out to dethrone him. Hoss is on the inside, he is a player controlled by the "code." Going to war would force him to "change class" and lose "solo rights." He would be thrown out of the "the game" and turned into "a gang man. A punk":

STAR-MAN: The wrong move'll throw you back a year or more... The charts are moving too fast. Every week there's a new star... You

want something durable, something lasting. How're you gonna
cop an immortal shot if you give up soloing and go into gang
war? They'll rip you up in a night. Sure you'll have a few
moments of global glow, maybe even an interplanetary flash. But
it won't last, Hoss, it won't last. (p. 8)

Thus, within the first pages of the play the dramatic conflict is
set up; but in terms so foreign and disorienting that the
audience can only immerse itself in the jargon and try to follow
what Hoss calls "the flash." It is not the last time in this play
that the audience will be forced to work its way into a foreign
discourse.

The Tooth of Crime is "A Play with Music in Two Acts." The
music for its seven songs was written by Shepard himself, yet
Shepard insists in his stage directions to the opening song that:
"The words of the song should be understood so the band has
to back off on volume when [Hoss] starts singing" (p. 3). This
instruction is indicated a number of times in the play. Despite
an abundance of physical action – song performances, gun
play, a scene in which Hoss stabs a stuffed dummy who bleeds,
the threatening physicality of the young invader, Crow – and
despite the abundance of music in the play: Shepard repeatedly emphasizes the importance of the words. *The Tooth of
Crime* "started with language," Shepard told an interviewer,
"it started with hearing a certain sound which is coming from
the voice of this character, Hoss... the whole kind of world that
he was involved in, came from this voice."[38] Shepard's
reluctance to allow Richard Schechner and his experimental
Performance Group to stage the play (in 1973) stemmed from
his fear that under Schechner's direction "the play will become
over-physicalized and the language will fall into the background,"[39] – which did in fact occur. *The Tooth of Crime* is a
play about language, power, and identity; and as in Handke's
Kaspar, Ionesco's *The Lesson,* Havel's *The Memorandum,* or
Albee's *Who's Afraid of Virginia Woolf?* the power of words
functions both as thematic center and overt subject within the
play.

Hoss opens the play by singing the prologue, "The Way Things

Are." Dressed in "black leather rocker gear with silver studs," holding a microphone and looking "mean," Hoss sings the song as a metatheatrical warning to the audience that they are about to see an illusion, a possible construct of reality, "A livin' talkin' show of the way things seem";

> You may think every picture you see is a true history
> of the way things used to be or the way things are
> …ain't it a drag to know you just don't know
> you just don't know
> So here's another illusion to add to your confusion
> Of the way things are…
> So here's another sleep-walkin' dream
> A livin' talkin' show of the way things seem… (p. 4)

The audience is assured that the following tentative "picture" of reality can offer neither clarity nor truth. Hoss himself, who will remain on stage throughout the play, almost never leaving until he is carried off at the end, having shot himself in the head, will learn during the play that the way things seem is not at all the way they are, and perhaps never is. Hoss is the "hero" of the play, a declining hero like the one described in the prologue song: "All the heroes is dyin' like flies they say it's a sign a' the times." Act I is in many ways an expository act, setting up the plot conflict, introducing us to Hoss, and easing the audience into a jargon of the "world" which his voice evokes. In Act II the landscape shifts and is derealized. Visual metaphors organize the action; Crow, the young invader, moves to center stage; and the battle of discourses, the refereed language-match fought between king and usurper, father and son, past and present – becomes the major plot action.

Set entirely on that almost bare stage, the first act proceeds through a number of dialogues, interactions between Hoss and his coterie, Hoss and himself. There is no plot other than a tense anticipation of the Gypsy Marker who was "sussed" by Eyes, and is now on his way to rub Hoss out. "They're all lookin' to put you under," Becky tells Hoss; "You're the main trigger. The word's out" (p.19). Despite the soothing prophecies of Galactic Jack, the super top-40 chart reader, that "We got the power. We got the game… The crown sticks where it fits and right now it looks about your size" (p. 17), Hoss has "got a feeling," a premonition that his time is up.

HOSS: They've got time on their side. Can't you see that? The youth's goin' to 'em. The kids are flocking to Gypsy Kills. It's a market opening up, Jack. I got a feeling. I know they're on their way in and we're going out. We're gettin' old, Jack.

GALACTIC JACK: You just got the buggered blues, man. You been talkin' to the wrong visions. You gotta get a head set. Put yer ears on straight. Zoot yerself down, boy. These Gypsies is committin' suicide. (p. 16–17)

Hoss lives in a world controlled by Game Keepers, Refs, and critics. Success means accumulating "points" according to a strategy plotted by the "charts" in keeping with a network of "codes." Transgression can induce penalties, or even ejection from the "game." Hoss was once a true Marker – "born to kill," who made it to the top by allowing himself to be molded to play inside the "game." But now he's slipping in the charts and losing points. Mojo Root Force has deviously "knocked over" his mark, Vegas – "the big one," and he is not even allowed to retaliate. "You can't go against the code," Becky warns him, "Once a Marker strikes and sets up colors, that's his turf. You can't strike claimed turf. They'll throw you out of the game" (p. 8). Hoss is being primed to reach "gold," which can only be done within the game. "The course is clear," Galactic Jack assures him; "Maybe a few Gypsy Killers comin' into the picture but... [s]ome polls don't even mention their kills for fear of the Keepers comin' down on 'em" (p. 16).

The Gypsy Killers really have Hoss worried. "There's power there. Full blown," he warns. The Gypsies are renegades, outsiders who reject the code and whose originality and courage have generated "a whole underground movement." Gypsies don't play by the rules, "They're into slaughter straight off. Not a clean kill in the bunch" (p. 17). But they have courage and are free from the outside control of Keepers and critics. When Hoss learns that he is being marked by a Gypsy renegade, he decides to fight back and "live outside the fucking law altogether. Outside the whole shot;"

CHEYENNE: So it's back to the rumble?... What about the Keepers?

HOSS: Fuck them, too. We'll take 'em all on...
CHEYENNE: What about our reputation? We worked hard to get where we are. I'm not ready to throw that away. I want a taste a' that gold.
HOSS: I'm surrounded by assholes! Can't you see what's happened to us? We ain't Markers no more. We ain't even Rockers. We're punk chumps cowering under the Keepers and the Refs and the critics and the public eye. We ain't free no more! Goddamnit! We ain't flyin' in the eye of contempt. We've become respectable and safe. Soft, mushy, chewable ass-lickers. What's happened to our killer heart? What's happened to our blind fucking courage!...We were warriors once.
CHEYENNE: That was a long time ago. (pp. 20–2)

What are we to make of this vocabulary of violence – warriors, killers, gangs, invaders, rumble, slaughter, turf, marks, trigger, shot? As can be seen from these examples, *The Tooth of Crime* seethes with contained violence. Its terminology evokes Mafia takeovers and gangster brutality; its visual images emit a lurking sense of menace. The stage is described as "evil-looking," Hoss is said to look "mean," Crow's very presence exudes violence and contempt. The stage itself is filled with weapons of slaughter. Directly after the prologue song, Becky brings Hoss a black velvet cloth containing a variety of revolvers, pistols, derringers, rifles, and shotguns. Later, Hoss practises for battle with the invader by knifing a stuffed dummy. The knives and guns remain visibly strewn on stage throughout the play. These violent visual and verbal contexts, together with the heavy rock music and threats of imminent battle, intimate real violence to come. And yet, as in Pinter's *The Birthday Party*, when the assault begins, with the combatants in place and battle being done – it is *verbal* assault that is offered, rather than the physical violence we have been led to expect.

Act I is spent planning war strategies. Becky suggests fighting the invader with "shivs" (knives), waiting him out and "gettin' him before he gets you." All are worried, both because Hoss has not used a "blade" for over ten years, and because the methods of these young killers are different from what Hoss used to know:

HOSS: ...Things have changed that much. They don't even apprentice no more. Just mark for the big one. No respect no more... There's no sense of tradition in the game no more... It's just back to how it was. Rolling night clubs, strip joints. Bustin' up poker games. Zip guns in the junk yard. Rock fights, dirt clods, bustin' windows. Vandals, juvies, *West Side Story.* (p. 24)

Crow doesn't appear until Act II, but his presence is felt much earlier. It is against the backdrop of his difference from Hoss – his youth, courage, freedom, lack of respect and tradition – that Hoss unfolds and questions his own values. "Doc, what do you think about Gypsy kills. Do you think it's ethical?" Hoss wonders (p. 25). Hoss is troubled by the lack of values that such a challenge of youth against established stars seems to imply: "They don't even apprentice no more." While waiting for Crow, Hoss and Becky reminisce about the "old times" and sing snatches of well-known "old" songs, all evoking the sound and spirit of America of the fifties. This recognizable past, and a more distant and mythic past of cowboys and the West, are then contrasted with the present which Crow represents, and of which Hoss knows very little:

BECKY: Do you know what it's like out there, outside the game? You wouldn't recognize it... The streets are controlled by the packs. They got it locked up. The packs are controlled by the gangs. The gangs and the Low Riders. They're controlled by cross syndicates. The next step is the Keepers.
HOSS: What about the country? Ain't there any farmers left, ranches, cowboys, open space. Nobody just livin' their life?
BECKY: You ain't playin' with a full deck, Hoss. All that's gone. That's old time boogie. (pp. 28–9)

It is these two worlds – the world of "ranches, cowboys, open space," on the one hand, and the world of the packs and gangs, on the other; of historical memory and nostalgia for the past as compared with futuristic jargon and an unmemoried faith in "now," of age versus youth – which will finally come to do battle through Hoss and Crow.

The first concrete detail we hear about Crow is the car he drives. Car jargon appears throughout the play alongside the gangster, cowboy, business, music, and invented jargons which

Shepard melds and hammers into the particular idiom of the play.[40] Car talk is one more disorienting and intimidating code, and functions as a shorthand for describing the personality and potency of characters. Hoss's dangerous Maserati, "greased like a bullet" (p. 5), is the first (and last) subject discussed in the play. Little Willard, a player from the "old school," with whom Hoss wants to team up against the young invaders, used to drive a Galaxie:

CHEYENNE: East Coast. Drove a Galaxie. Into Remington over and unders.
HOSS: Yeah. He's changed his style now. Got himself a Lotus Formula 2 and a Baretta.
CHEYENNE: Sounds mean.
HOSS: He is, man. And I trust him. (p. 21)

When Crow is spotted heading their way, Hoss's first question is "What's he drivin'?"

CHEYENNE: You won't believe this. A '58 black Impala fuel injected, bored and stroked, full blown Vet underneath.
HOSS: I'm gonna like this dude. OK let him through. (p. 31)

Hoss is both scared and intrigued by this Gypsy. "His style is copping my patterns... He's got a presence. Maybe even star quality. His movements have an aura... I mean nobody rides a '58 Impala to do battle with a star Marker" (p. 34). Hoss decides to "Jam a little before the big kill," to "Find his tuning" and see if they are "in the same stream" (p. 34). Thus, even before Crow appears, Hoss tries to pick up his "sound" and learn his voice.

The age difference between Crow and Hoss is of great importance in the play. Crow is youth and virility which must inevitably inherit the place of age. The transient nature of power, one of the play's central themes, is given most directly in this age difference. From the moment Crow's style (car) has been ascertained, a transition section ensues in which the mythic imagery of the aging king/warrior, or the father who will give way to the son, becomes dominant. Hoss, doped up by Doc in preparation for the battle, rebels against what he has become, and against the cyclic inevitability of the struggle which awaits him.

HOSS: Look at me now. Impotent. Can't strike a kill unless the charts are right. Stuck in my image. Stuck in a mansion. Waiting. Waiting for a kid who's probably just like me. Just like I was then. A young blood. And I gotta off him. I gotta roll him or he'll roll me. We're fightin' ourselves...He's my brother and I gotta kill him. He's gotta kill me. (p. 36)

Left alone on stage Hoss, tired, sits on his throne and speaks with himself in two voices, his own and the voice of his father. He admits to his father that he feels lost, trapped and unsure. No longer a true Marker, he has become the "establishment"; "They're all countin' on me. The bookies, the agents, the Keepers. I'm a fucking industry. I even affect the stocks and bonds." With this admission, and the father's council that "You're just a man, Hoss. Just a man" (p. 38), Hoss is ready for the showdown of his manhood with the young contender. Hoss sleeps on stage before the final *agon*, while "a huge shadow of Crow is cast across the upstage wall behind Hoss" (p. 39). To this image is added the voice of Crow who sings his introductory song: "Poison." Thus, Crow's entrance is anticipated through shadow, voice, and Hoss's intimations of his power.

Shepard has said of the character of Crow that he came "from a yearning toward violence. A totally lethal human with no way or reason for tracing how he got that way. He just appeared. He spit words that became his weapons...He speaks in an unheard-of tongue."[41] Crow opens Act II. Our first experience of him is physical, through his style; he wears "highheeled green rock-and-roll boots...a shark tooth earring, a silver swastika hanging from his neck and a black eye-patch covering the left eye." Swinging a chain from hand to hand he "chews a stick of gum with violent chomps" and "exudes violent arrogance" (p. 41). Like the young heir-apparent trying out the throne, Crow sits on Hoss's chair and "chews gum at the audience." With Crow's first sentence it becomes clear that a new language has entered the play. If the audience was disoriented in Act I by the sci-fi terminology and gangster, car, and Western jargons, Crow's language proves even more impenetrable and disruptive. Crow's language is so private that, in comparison, Hoss sounds tame and old-fashioned – which, as we will see, he actually is. With Crow, language is forefronted and becomes an explicit subject discussed by the characters. From the start, Crow's vocabulary, like his clothing and movements, is characterized by its overtly violent imagery.

HOSS: My sleuth tells me you're drivin' a '58 Impala with a Vet underneath.

CROW: Razor, Leathers. Very razor.

HOSS: Did you rest up?

CROW: Got the molar chomps. Eyes stitched. You can vision what's sittin'. Very razor to cop z's sussin' me to be on the far end of the spectrum...

HOSS: You wanna drink or somethin'?

CROW: (*laughs with a cackle*) Lush in sun time gotta smell of lettuce or turn of the century. Sure, Leathers, squeeze on the grape vine one time.

HOSS: White or red?

CROW: Blood. (p. 42)

Crow's dangerous words (razor, chomps, stitched, blood) and the opacity of his diction disconcert Hoss who asks: "Can't you back the language up, man? I'm too old to follow the flash." Crow answers with a verbal challenge: "Choose an argot, Leathers. Singles or LP's. 45, 78, 33⅓" (p. 44).

The audience of *The Tooth of Crime* is not allowed to remain passive. It is provoked and annoyed in much the same way as is the audience of *Kaspar*, *Glengarry Glen Ross*, or *The Memorandum*: it is forced to assimilate a foreign verbal code, a discourse outside of its experience which frustrates its need to construct meaning. Shepard has commented on the redundancy of physically involving the audience in *The Tooth of Crime*, as Richard Schechner did in his Performance Group production of the play. In an interview, Shepard objected to Schechner's removal of the boundaries between stage and audience, saying: "There's a whole myth... that in order for the audience to be actively participating in the event that they're watching they have to be physically sloshed into something, which isn't true at all. An audience can sit in chairs and be watching something in front of them, and can be actively participating."[42] The language, which Shepard insists be clear and audible throughout, achieves the physical contact and involvement on its own.

This extremely verbal play contains two sets of languages, both synthetic constructs unfamiliar and disorientating to the audience. From the start, the language can only be intuitively grasped as the strange terms – charts, marker, Gypsy, Keepers, codes, killer, etc. – and a collage of jargon styles slowly integrate into plot and gain in referentiality. Meaning is not given analytically, it is established through experience of the world of the play. But, unlike any of the other plays discussed, once the audience has grown more secure in the play's discourse, it is *re*-subjected and again verbally assaulted and disorientated with the appearance of Crow. Again the world of the play grows opaque, again the audience loses its bearings and must relearn how to construct meaning. The audience's insecurity and difficulty, the alienation induced by the aggression of incomprehensible language and seemingly random codes, produces an emotional correlative to the play's theme, clearly articulated in Act II, of shifting and tentative discourses, of a loss of tradition and life-sustaining roots. As Don Shewey writes: "(T)he amazing – and disturbing – thing about *The Tooth of Crime* is that Shepard flips through [...] modern jargons and topical references without settling on any one, theatricalizing through sheer language the kind of dislocation he's dramatizing."[43]

This dislocation becomes acutely obvious during the first dialogue of Act II as Crow continues to speak his "unheard-of tongue" and to sit on Hoss's throne while Hoss tries, with difficulty, to learn about the outside world from which he is so isolated. Crow clearly has the upper hand until he slips and speaks a "normal" sentence:

CROW: We're star marked and playing intergalactic modes. Some travel past earthbound and score on Venus, Neptune, Mars.
HOSS: How do you get to fucking Neptune in a '58 Impala!
CROW: How did you get to earth in a Maserati?
HOSS: There! Why'd you slip just then? Why'd you suddenly talk like a person? (p. 46)

With this, Hoss regains his strength and throws Crow "the fuck outa' my chair!!"

Crow only rarely slips out of his language, or slips at all. As opposed to Hoss, we learn nothing about Crow during the play; he has no history, no inner conflicts, no psychology. Crow is given to us only through his style and speech. He is all surface. Hoss falters and seeks answers; but Crow betrays neither emotion nor doubts. "There ain't no Gods or saviors," he sings (p. 49) recalling, perhaps, Ted Hughes's nihilistic anti-hero of the same name of whom Hughes wrote: "God went on sleeping / Crow went on laughing."[44] Crow's strength seems to stem from an almost seamless unity of style, language, and moral coldness. "Gypsy King," Hoss asks, "where's your true heart." His is the real contemporary voice, the invading discourse which will replace the "sound" of a previous period. As we soon see, Crow is not only dangerous and cold, but also brilliant and seductive, and during the ensuing "style match," as Hoss calls it (p. 46), Crow's verbal opacity shifts into transparent, but deadly, verbal assault.

It is Hoss who chooses the weapon of their battle-to-the-death, and his choice of language as the means of battle is of great significance. Although other options are offered – "shivs," pistols, a car race – and although the guns and knives deployed in Act I imply a physical battle, Hoss refuses the easy route. "There's no Marker on the planet can outkill me with no kinda' weapon or machine" (p. 52).

CROW: I can't cipher why you wanna play this course, Leathers. It's
      a long way from shivs.
HOSS: Just to prove I ain't outside.
CROW: To me or you? (p. 51)

The meaning is clear: words are the real inside game, a power beyond steel or pistols. To own the language, the discourse, is to really rule.

Act II is organized around the metaphor of a wrestling or boxing match. As in Dürrenmatt's *Play Strindberg*, the visual dimension of the competition – the presence of a referee, the division of the action into "rounds," the discussions of rules and

codes – objectifies the plot and forefronts its essentially com-
petitive and aggressive nature. But Dürrenmatt abstracts the
underlying action in Strindberg's play from its verbose surface,
discarding most of the language; while Shepard intensifies the
language itself and only structures it theatrically into the form
of a wrestling match. This use is similar to the wrestling
metaphors in *Who's Afraid of Virginia Woolf?*, which underscore
the aggression and potency of its weapon, language. As in all
"wrestling" matches, success is gauged by the efficiency and
skill with which harm is inflicted on the opponent, as far as the
rules allow. Here, however, the punches and blows are verbally
delivered. It is not the body of the opponent, but the
formulation of his being, his history, talent, and spiritual
substance, which are the objects of attack. Just as George
roughs Martha up verbally before their final game of "Bringing
Up Baby" in order to ensure a worthy opponent, Hoss
introduces their match through threats which employ the
language of physical violence. "I'm gonna have fun skinnin'
you," Hoss says; "I'm gonna leave you paralyzed alive.
Amputated from the neck down" (pp. 51–2). Thus begins the
battle, a battle to be fought "head to head till one's dead."

The role of the referee in the verbal match is similar to that
of Nick and Honey in *Who's Afraid of Virginia Woolf?*, or Kurt
in *The Dance of Death*: he modifies the game and objectifies it,
while also affording an outside vantage point through which
the audience can test the results of the struggle. But unlike
Kurt, or Nick and Honey, this referee (called "Ref") has no
identity other than his sports function. He is a comic-strip
figure "dressed just like an NBA ref, with black pants, striped
shirt, sneakers, a whistle, baseball cap" (p. 50). Before the
match starts he sets up a huge scoreboard with the letters "H"
and "C" written on top, does some yoga positions and runs in
place. These effects physically evoke the sports arena, but at the
same time strain and parody the realistic/ritualistic context of
the struggle. This strain will be broadened into real incongruity
during Round 1 when all of Hoss's retinue come on stage
dressed as cheerleaders with pom-poms and "Victory" signs,
and do a silent routine. Their antics, which go so far as to
"bend over bare assed" at the audience, hobbling and giggling,

create a radical opposition to the highly charged, even emotional narratives of the two fighters. Throughout the battle Shepard undercuts the verbal struggle through fatuous visuals, thereby enhancing the "game" aspect, enforcing objectivity, and deterring audience identification with either of the two opponents. He also keeps the sporting aspect of the match at the forefront by interrupting the contestants' texts with comments on the rules of the game itself. At one point the Ref blows his whistle, stops the fight, and using professional jargon warns the opponents: "No clinches. This ain't a wrestlin' match...Just keep daylight between ya'" (p. 61).

Shepard begins the match by overtly identifying physical assault with verbal assault. The Ref tells the opponents to "...come out swingin'...No bear hugs, rabbit punches, body pins, or holdin' on. If a man goes down, we give him five and that's it. After that you can kick the shit out of him." A bell rings and the music starts, "a lurking evil sound." The stage instructions then tell us that Hoss and Crow pick up their microphones, an action which is later compared with the holding of a knife (p. 57), and "begin their *assaults* just talking the words in rhythmic patterns...Their voices build so that sometimes they sing the words or shout. *The words remain as intelligible as possible*, like a sort of talking opera" (p. 52–3, my emphases).

Round 1 has Crow on the offensive. His language moves into a new idiom, a poetic diction of rhythmic and repetitive cadences in which he evokes the traditional rock motif of the young loser, "the runt," "the shame kid." Crow develops a seething and violent narrative around (assumedly) Hoss's shameful and loveless past, the adolescence of a battered sissy, "the kid with a lisp. The dumb kid. The loser. The runt. The mutt. The shame kid."

CROW: Catch ya' outa' breath by the railroad track...Catch ya' with yer pants down. Whip ya' with a belt. Whup ya' up one side and down to the other. Whup ya' all night long...Leave ya' bleedin' and cryin'. Leave ya cryin' for Ma. All through the night. All through the night long. Shame on the kid. Little dumb kid with a lisp in his mouth. (p. 53)

Hoss protests that all of this is untrue, but Crow continues, now positing images of the masturbating boy "Comin' in a wet dream... Naked on a pillow. Naked in a bedroom. Naked in a bathroom. Beatin' meat to the face in a mirror. Beatin' it raw. Beatin' till the blood come..." He invokes a scared and cowardly boy – "Lonely in a bedroom. Dyin' for attention" – who seeks success through petty crime and winds up in prison "doin' time time" (p. 54). The assault reaches a violent crescendo with Crow's description of the boy "in the slammer" who "does his schoolin'" through pain and humiliation.

CROW: ...Storin' up his hate cells... Gotta pay his dues back... Finally gets his big chance and sucks the warden's dinger... I'll take away your time. Just gimme some head, boy. Just get down on your knees. Gimme some blow, boy. I'll give ya' back the key. I'll give ya' back the key, boy! Just get down on my thing, boy! Just get down! Get on down! Get on down! Get down! Get down! Get down! Come on! (p. 55)

With this, the bell rings and Crow falls exhausted into his corner.

Hoss barely get a blow in during this round and Ref marks Crow the winner. Crow's power results not only from his vile and shameful images, but from his hypnotic rhythm, the hard cut of his phrases, the insistent repetitions and spaceless diction which deter any interruption or countering. Bruce Powe writes on the musicality of this section that "The repetition of words and sounds, of perfect and imperfect rhymes, makes the passage formulaic, like a song... The syntax... is expressive; the diction is orally associative; the rushing rhythm, the accelerando, is accented at the end." The hard, cutting words, Powe notes, "exist in the characters' mouths like savage, affective things. Characters hurtle the words... they project them, perform them. Employed in this way, words are *dangerous*. They have power precisely because they are alive as sound."[45] All Hoss can do is protest against Crow's "flash," his lack of heart, claiming Crow's attack to be unfair and all lies. "He was pickin' at a past that ain't even there. Fantasy marks... How can you give points to a liar?" The Ref answers: "I don't. I give 'em to the winner" (p. 56). The Ref is not interested in whether Crow's text is true, but in whether it is a *winning* text, powerful and convincing. In this "style match" truth is irrelevant, and Hoss's appeal to old-fashioned values such as "heart" and "honest pool" are dismissed. Hoss is left "smokin'" and incapable of countering.

Leonard Wilcox, in his article "Modernism vs. Postmodernism: Shepard's *The Tooth of Crime* and the Discourses of Popular Culture," suggests that Crow accomplishes Hoss's degradation by rewriting his identity in terms of a discourse foreign to Hoss's experience. Hoss's history is reconstituted as a Deleuzean text of "poisonous foods and encased excrements," a schizoid language of ungrounded desire which Gilles Deleuze describes as one pole of postmodern language.[46] According to Wilcox:

> Crow's ferocious assault on Hoss appropriates the discursive and textual territory of the fifties – Hoss's territory – and turns it against him in a ritual of degradation. This Crow does by re-reading the basic themes of the fifties – the master code of existentialism and the preoccupation with alienation – in terms of powerlessness...Crow's rabid language consumes and devours: it appropriates Hoss's energy and "cops his patterns"; it usurps his very history and re-reads it in terms of fear, sexual frustration, and regressive masturbatory activity...Moreover, Crow's pop intertextuality implies a postmodern challenge to essentialist notions of originary voice and consciousness as center of meaning. Thus when Hoss replies in Round Two, defending origins, presence, and the idea of an authentic identity, the verbal battle begins to take on the dimensions of a battle between modernism and postmodernism.[47]

Indeed, Hoss attempts a new strategy for Round 2: he insists they play without music, microphone, or any other mediation, and "strip this down to what's necessary."

HOSS: What'sa matter, Crowbait? Afraid to do it naked? Drop the echo stick and square me off.
CROW: You should be past roots on this scale, Leathers. Very retrograde. (p. 57)

Hoss now takes the initiative and begins talking roots "like an ancient delta blues singer." His narrative is very different from Crow's: rather than attack his opponent's past, which is and remains a void, he attacks Crow's lack of past: his rootlessness.

"Growing physically older," Hoss becomes "a menacing ancient spirit. Like a voodoo man" (p. 57–8) and inflicts a magic incantation on Crow by becoming the physical and verbal incarnation of the origins of American rock music. Hoss's language here is a collage of styles drawn from the sources of Jazz and Blues music. His diction imitates the black man's South as he evokes the birth of the blues, music born of the black slave's "moan," music as emancipation, "somethin' inside that no boss man could touch." Hoss attacks Crow with tradition and essence, "you miss the origins, milk face." But Crow remains indifferent to Hoss's narrative and rejects the demands of history: "I'm in a different time," he counters, "Bring it up to now":

HOSS: You'd like a free ride on a black man's back.
CROW: I got no guilt to conjure! Fence me with the present... (p. 59)

Ref interrupts Hoss's attack to call the round a draw. "Somethin's funny. Somethin's outa' whack here...I can't make heads or tails outa' this" (p. 60). What Ref objects to is Hoss's claim to authenticity, to an originary and integral voice – a claim which Crow will demolish in the next round. Hoss, who in Act I admits to having been created by Becky and the industry, who admits his own impotence and confusion and even tells Becky: "Ya' know, you'd be OK, Becky, if you had a self. So would I" (p. 37), poses in Round 2 as the spirit of the past, the incarnation of origins. It is this pose, and through it Hoss's very identity, which become the objects of Crow's counterattack in the final round of the battle, the round which will determine who is to reign as king.

In Round 3 the physical reality of the sports ring returns to center stage as Crow jumps into action, "dancing like Muhammad Ali." Hoss, who from the start of the round is on the defensive, uses the rules of the match itself as a tactic to counter Crow's wild text. Thus, the jargon of physical battle coexists with the brutality of verbal assault. Ironically, it is only when the Ref finally names Crow as winner of the round, and thus of the match, that the play's only act of real physical violence occurs: Hoss shoots and kills the Ref.

As in Round 1, from the moment Crow begins his narrative – his diction musical, seductive – Hoss becomes incapable of creative response. Crow's rhythmic and flowing patterns threaten to hypnotize Hoss who says, as much to himself as to Crow, "...this time I stay solid. You ain't suckin' me into jive rhythms. I got my own. I got my patterns. Original. I'm my own man. Original. I stand solid." But it is precisely Hoss's originality, twice declared, which Crow questions in a voice and style which repulse refutation.

CROW: So ya' wanna be a rocker. Study the moves. Jerry Lee Lewis. Buy some blue suede shoes. Move yer head like Rod Stewart. Put yer ass in a grind. Talkin' sock it to it, get the image in line. Get the image in line, boy. The fantasy rhyme. It's all over the streets and you can't buy the time. You can't buy the bebop. You can't buy the slide. Got the fantasy blues and no place to hide. (p. 61)

Crow presents Hoss as derivative and inauthentic, "Collectin' the South. Collectin' the blues." Hoss, Crow claims, has no voice of his own, no inner reality. He only practises an "image"; is no more than a collage of pop voice – "Tries trainin' his voice to sound like a frog. Sound like a Dylan, sound like a Jagger" (p. 62) – an erector set of movements and gestures taken from the "real" stars (real in the double sense of authentic, and actual names of singers the audience would recognize). Crow now achieves the winning move by attacking Hoss's manhood, connecting his artistic impotence with sexual failure: "Still gets a hard on, but can't get it up." Crow describes Hoss as an impotent chameleon, dressed in the fashion of the day ("Wearin' a shag now, looks like a fag now"), torn asunder through trying to accommodate his synthetic image with a belief in originality and authentic voice.

CROW: Can't get it together for all of his tryin'. Can't get it together for fear that he's dyin'. Fear that he's crackin' busted in two. Busted in three parts. Busted in four. Busted and dyin' and cryin' for more. Busted and bleedin' all over the floor. All bleedin' and wasted and tryin' to score. (p. 62)

Thus, Hoss's identity is reduced to an amalgam of fashion and cultural codes, no more than an expression of his times.

Crow never makes a claim for his own originality. He rejects Hoss's appeal to roots by denying the relevance of roots: "I'm in a different time." He knows that he is all surface, no more than an image of his own times. Shepard's Hoss and Crow are poet/warriors who act and gain power through language – as Shepard said of Crow: "He spit words that became his weapons." But there is a sense, articulated here by Crow, in which their language and style precede and control them. They are only capable of creating within the verbal style and norms of the age they represent, or embody. Both characters are locked within the world of their separate "sounds," conditioned and determined by their separate discourses. Hoss, after losing the style-match, will try to adjust to the new ruling discourse – which Crow represents – to move into the new style; but he will inevitably fail. "It ain't me!" he comes to realize, and chooses to go out, by his own hand, "in the old style."

The killing of the Ref places Hoss outside of the game. No longer a player, he becomes, like Crow, a Gypsy, outside the law, dependent on himself. It is interesting that Hoss does not kill Crow. With the gun still in his hand Hoss says "I should cut you in half right now. I shoulda' slit yer throat soon's you came through the door." Instead, rather than kill him, Hoss offers Crow his "turf" – 'Anything. It's all yours" – if Crow will teach him, "Just help me into the style" (pp. 63–4). With this request Hoss admits not only his own defeat, but the defeat of the values, language and style he embodied.

HOSS: How did this happen?... Everything was going so good. I had everything at my fingertips. Now I'm outa' control. I'm pulled and pushed around from one image to another. Nothin' takes a solid form. Nothin' sure and final. Where do I stand! Where the fuck do I stand! (p. 65)

Crow's verbal attacks have destroyed Hoss's identity, his "image," and his own weapon: words. He is left without any existential certitudes – "Nothin' takes a solid form" – in a crisis of *angst*, and begging to be reconstituted in the new ruling style, the discourse of power. Thus, discourse itself moves to center stage. The last part of the play will portray a cruel act of failed transference as the heartless young victor tries to reconstruct the vanquished king in his own visual and vocal image.

In describing Crow, Shepard has claimed that he "doesn't 'mean' anything. He's simply following his most savage instincts."[48] But Crow's power is more than just the working out of personal "instincts." Crow is not so much a character as the embodiment of an idea. Wilcox identifies his power with the amoral postmodern discourse which he embodies, a discourse of alienation and "heartlessness." Crow does not develop during the play and the audience experiences him in the same way as Hoss does: from the outside. His dangerous outfit, his arrogant walk, the gum-chewing, and especially his cold, disorienting jargon – his "unheard-of tongue" – are the only clues to his identity; *are* his identity. Crow remains cold and unmoved from first to last. He never betrays emotion and, finally, it is his "heartlessness" which comes to define him. "OK Gypsy King, where's your true heart," Hoss asks in anticipation, even before Crow arrives; "Let's get down. You talk a good story. You got the true flash but where's your heart. That's the whole secret...There ain't no heart to a Gypsy. Just bone" (p. 32). One of the Ref's jobs during the match is to count points "scored and lost on deviation from the neutral field state," i.e. the state of emotional neutrality. "I'd say you already broke the mercury in round one," (p. 50) Crow tells Hoss even before the match begins. Hoss's weakness, and humanity, are repeatedly shown through his emotional reactions to Crow's narrative. He is "sucked into" Crow's "jive," manipulated by the way Crow recreates him in words. "You can't do that!" Hoss tells him when Crow reinvents his history as a tale of shame and humiliation. "History don't cut it. History's in the pocket" (pp. 54–5). But history is not "in the pocket"; it is not a closed, written text. Crow proves that it, like personal identity, can be rewritten, is in fact reinvented with each style of retelling. Crow's relentless, spaceless attack on Hoss's past, and on his manhood, is aimed at emotional effect. Since truth is always tentative, and thus irrelevant, refutation becomes impossible. The Ref calls Crow's verbal moves "Good clean body punches. Nice left jab. Straight from the shoulder. Had you rocked on your heels" (p. 56). It is the *effect* of Crow's attack, not its essence, which counts: and the effect is to force Hoss's deviation from the "neutral field state." Crow, however, remains unaffected throughout. He rejects appeals to his conscience or guilt, never argues with the Ref, is immune to slurs, taunts, or threats. "The image is my survival kit," he later tells Hoss, and it is all that we ever get to know of him.

Crow's discourse is closed, spaceless, manipulative – can both destroy and reconstitute identity. Its rhythm, as well as its use of collected jargons, has much in common with the language attacks of Goldberg and McCann in Pinter's *The Birthday Party.* There, too, verbal gangsterism takes the form of relentless, hypnotic speech tirades in which the jargon of power destroys an "outsider" – one outside of the ruling discourse. Goldberg and McCann's accusations against their victim, Stanley, are hyperbolic and irrational, show a disregard for truth, and recreate reality in their own verbal mold. Like Crow, Goldberg and McCann seek emotional effect and make Stanley deviate from the "neutral field state" – to the point of losing his capacity for speech – while they themselves remain unemotional and cool. Moreover, like Crow, Goldberg and McCann try to recreate their victim in their own image through the very language which has destroyed him. But while Pinter's gangsters seem to succeed in their reconstruction, Crow fails.

With the Ref's murder, Hoss puts himself into Crow's control and begs to be recreated in Crow's image. What ensues is an attempted reconstruction of identity through the surface images of style. Crow's lessons, like his own image, all concentrate on external, material functions: Hoss's eyes (the look), his walk, and his body movements. "We gotta break yer patterns down, Leather...Re-program the tapes...Shake off the image" (pp. 68–9). Although Hoss protests that he's not "a fuckin' machine," Crow's lessons are given in computer terminology. "Start with a clean screen," Crow advises as he attempts to

produce a *tabula rasa*, a "blank" on which he can imprint his
own style. Crow puts Hoss through a number of exercises whose
goal is to make him cold and pitiless. "Get mean. There's too
much pity, man. Too much empathy...Too much searchin'.
I got no answers...Just kill with the eyes" (p. 66). He teaches
Hoss to reset his body movements using terms which are both
violent and unnatural, and which parallel the effect he seeks to
attain. "Spit out yer teeth. Ear pulls. Nose pulls...Tighten yer
ass. Tighten one cheek and loosen the other. Play off yer thighs
to yer calves. Get it all talkin' a language" (p. 68). Crow's
lessons imply that the essence of the ruling style resides in its
"language" of disjunctive form, and that style *is* identity, not
an outcome of identity.

At the climax of Hoss's re-education he tries to visualize
himself in Crow's image. Concentrating, Hoss begins to pick up
a vision of himself which is "just like me only younger. More
dangerous...No doubt. No fear..." At this point a double
process takes place on stage. In a long monologue, Hoss
describes the new "me" whom he has conjured up, whom he
is inventing (for the audience, who do not see this "vision")
through the terms of the description itself. Using clipped,
incantatory phrases, Hoss creates a new identity. But the
descriptions are all platitudes, pasteboard concepts of heroic
manhood:

HOSS: Mean and tough and cool. Untouchable...True to his heart.
   True to his voice. Everything's whole and unshakeable...He
   knows his own fate. Beyond doubt. True courage in every
   move...Knows where he stands. Lives by a code. His own
   code...Speaks the truth without trying. Can't do anything
   false...Died a million deaths...Holds no grudge. No blame. No
   guilt...Passed beyond tears. Beyond ache for the world. Pitiless.
   Indifferent and riding a state of grace. (p. 71)

Parallel to this oracular litany of heroic attributes, four men –
Cheyenne, Star-Man, Doc, and Galactic Jack – appear on
stage "in a tight group" wearing white tuxedos with pink
carnations in their lapels. In perfect "choreographed movements like the old *a capella* bands," they slowly begin to sing

"harmony notes." That is: while Hoss is rejecting his old, humanist identity and trying to construct a new, cold and pitiless "me," the audience watches and hears an old-fashioned "barbershop quartet" singing a sweet, harmonic melody. The quartet's fancy party dress, its synchronized movements, melodic tune, and cohesive group pose are all diametrically opposed to the identity Hoss is trying to put on "like a suit a' clothes" (p. 71). They belong to a past in which harmony of movement and voice were prized above "mean and tough and cool." It is as though the singers emanate from Hoss's own past, as though, despite his effort to change and adapt to Crow's present, the only sounds he can produce are bound up with past tradition. Thus, the "old" Hoss is given in a visual cliché of harmony, while the "new" Hoss is being formed through verbal clichés of power. As a result, Hoss cries out, in the middle of his monologue: "It ain't me! IT AIN'T ME! IT AIN'T ME!!" With this recognition that the identity he has been imaging is not, and cannot be, his own, Hoss collapses.

The quartet of singers, with their old-fashioned harmony, function here very much as do the duplicate Kaspars at the end of Handke's play. There, the duplicate figures disrupt Kaspar's cascading platitudes of order through their chaotic, elemental noises which seem to emerge from the inner, real Kaspar. They thereby incite Kaspar to rebel against the Prompters' coercive normative language, and to embrace his own death. Here, the same process occurs: but in the opposite direction. Shepard's four singers offer harmony, melody, and community in opposition to the disjunctive raw surfaces of the new approaching Hoss. The result: they induce Hoss's rejection of *his* "Prompter" and lead, ultimately, to his suicide.

Implicit in this double image of harmony and disjunction is an opposition of two worlds, or two modes of expression and experience. Wilcox identifies this opposition in terms of modernism/postmodernism. Shepard is certainly dramatizing a process of displacement, or replacement; the language and ethos of Hoss, as presented in Act I, are replaced by the style and power of Crow. But the cycle of change does not end here.

By the end of the play it is clear that Crow, too, is only temporary, and his power tentative. Cheyenne, looking at Hoss's dead body, calls him a "true Marker" who "came the long route. Not like you. He earned his style." Crow counters that Hoss had outlived his time and his "power" was "goin' backwards," no longer relevant. "Now the power shifts and sits till a bigger wind blows," Crow predicts. "Not in my life run but one to come. And all the ones after that. Changin' hands like a snake dance to heaven." Crow understands that he will only control the "power" until a different wind, a new style, another ruling discourse comes to replace him. "Not in my life run" implies that the "bigger wind" is not a question of a more talented or meaner Gypsy, but of a Marker from a future generation, perhaps, "and all the ones after that," all of whom will again embody the cultural codes, the style, the discourse of their age. Crow sees himself as a representative of the present, as embodying the ruling idiom which is always tentative, shifting, curling and shedding its skin each season "like a snake dance to heaven." "This is my time, Cowboy," Crow says in one of the last lines of the play, "and I'm runnin' it up the middle" (p. 75).

Hoss is defeated because he is the past, clearly identified as such by his memories, references, values, and age. He has lost the "power" because the power has changed and he can no longer change with it. This "power" is given by Shepard in terms of, and through, style and language, or more broadly, cultural discourse. "You're a master adapter. A visionary adapter" (p. 73), Hoss says bitterly, conceding his defeat as a failure to "adapt," to imbibe and become the style and language of the day. But Hoss's defeat involves an additional layer, an additional set of images.

As I previously indicated, Hoss is portrayed not only as a rock-star but also as a gunslinger, a cowboy who claims "The West is mine" (p. 20). The West obsesses Shepard in many of his plays. His first produced play was titled *Cowboys*; others contain Western characters bearing names such as Slim (*Cowboy Mouth*),

Dodge (*Buried Child*), Cody (*Geography of a Horse Dreamer*; this is the real name of Buffalo Bill, also discussed in *The Tooth of Crime*), or Cisco and The Kid (*The Unseen Hand*). Through characterization, desert landscapes, historical references, and language, Shepard repeatedly invokes one of the constituting myths of the American psyche, a myth whose images have funded American popular culture but whose roots and ethos, he seems to say, have failed to sustain American society.

Hoss is specifically associated with images of this mythic West. Crow immediately recognizes him as such and from the first calls him "Leathers," conjuring up the leather chaps worn by the cowboy or cattle ranchers. The names Hoss and Cheyenne obviously evoke horses, cowboys, Indians. In his song "Cold Killer" Hoss sings of the "snakes in my pockets," his "silver studs," "black kid gloves," fast "cold gun," "whip-lash magic and a rattlesnake tongue" (p. 13). Becky calls Hoss's impatience "buck fever" (p. 11), and warns him to "carry your gun wherever you go" (p. 28). Hoss's memories of the world "outside the game," the world that Becky says has so changed, include "farmers...ranches, cowboys, open space," all of which Becky calls "old time boogie" (p. 29). These and other references identify Hoss with the cowboy and the West. But one passage in the play specifically connects this mythic past, or rather its failure, with the "power" which shifts and is lost to Hoss.

There is only one section between Hoss and Crow in which Crow shows any weakness and feels he is "losing the match." Before the referee arrives, the two opponents spar and grapple verbally, trying to feel each other out. Suddenly, Hoss switches from his own voice into "a kind of cowboy-Western image." "A pup like you," he says, "Up in Utah we'd use yer kind fer skunk bait and throw away the skunk":

CROW: Throwin' to snake-eyes now, Leathers.
HOSS: So you gambled your measly grubstake for a showdown with the champ. Ain't that pathetic. I said that before and I'll say it again. Pathetic.
(*Crow is getting nervous. He feels he's losing the match*)...

We'd drag you through the street for a nickel. Naw. Wouldn't even waste the horse. Just break yer legs and leave ya' fer dog meat.

CROW: That's about all you'll get outa' second. Better shift it now, Leathers. (p. 47)

With that suggestion Hoss shifts into a 1920s gangster style and, Shepard tells us, "Crow begins to feel more confident now that he's got Hoss to switch" (p. 48). Why this sudden fear on Crow's part? Is there some power inherent in the style of the West which threatens him? It does seem that the voice of the West carries an authority and potency which, were Hoss its authentic speaker, might endanger the power of the present that Crow wields. But Hoss is easily manoeuvered out of that voice precisely because he is not its authentic spokesman, because the West is, in the world of this play, but one more "style," an image as easily shed as worn. Thus, the cowboy imagery and terminology which lace through the play are shown to be as impotent and transient as Hoss himself. These appeals to roots and source do not evoke a "True West" (as Shepard titled another of his plays), and consequently question the authenticity, or relevance, of the myth itself.

Another "myth," it seems, has taken its place. Hoss was, after all, molded by the "industry," groomed and guided by Becky and the Charts. Now Crow will inherit the same fate: for above them both lurks the reality of the ultimate image-makers, the purveyors of success. "I just hope you never see yourself from the outside," Hoss says to Crow just before his suicide; "Just a flash of what you're really like":

CROW: Like you?
HOSS: Like me...Yeah. You win all right. All this. Body and soul. All this invisible gold. All this collection of torture. It's all yours. (p. 73)

With Hoss's suicide "in the old style," Becky immediately shifts her loyalty to Crow. "I had a feeling you'd take him," she says. Crow accepts Becky as rightfully his, but fires the aging Cheyenne whom he calls "Cowboy," thus identifying him with Hoss. In the last gesture of the play, Cheyenne throws the keys to Hoss's Maserati at Crow's feet; and Crow bends to retrieve them. Thus, a world is not destroyed by Hoss's death. It continues in the same Maserati, with the same desire for success, controlled by the same "industry," affecting the same stocks and bonds. In the absence of any underlying cultural voice or overriding historical discourse, all that remains is the "snake dance" of shifting styles which will be molded, in succession, into the coinage of success. "You're the winner and I'm the loser," Hoss says to Crow; but although the voice and style have been modulated, the game remains the same.

CHAPTER 6

Conclusion

The title of Handke's second full-length play, *The Ride Across Lake Constance*, refers to a nineteenth-century ballad by the poet Gustav Schwab, *The Rider and Lake Constance*. This ballad tells of a horseman who rode across the seemingly frozen Lake Constance only to learn, on reaching the other side, that the ice he had taken for solid was less than an inch thick. Hearing this, he drops dead from fright. In Handke's play this image comes to denote the "thin ice" of rationality, the abyss which, without our knowing it, lurks beneath the sign-systems we take to be solid and real. Botho Strauss interprets the analogy quite bluntly:

The ride parallels the functioning of our grammar, of our system of co-ordinating perception and meaning, and of our linguistic and sentient powers of reason; it is only a provisional, permeable order, which, particularly when, as in Handke's play, *it becomes conscious of its own existence*, is threatened by...schizophrenia and madness.[1]

It is the unconscious nature of our assumptions about language which is here the important point; the madness which threatens – like Kaspar's "madness" once he rejects the coercive speech order of the Prompters – may be preferable to the tyranny of pre-ordered consciousness. The attempt to make the hidden dangers of our unexamined assumptions explicit, to expose the "thin ice" of convention, is one of the common denominators among all these plays.

This perspective, shared by so many postwar plays, betrays an implicit anxiety concerning modern man's capacity to fashion his/her own fate in the face of pervasive exposure to,

224

and manipulation by, language. Verbal proliferation is found in the accelerating propagation of speech-coins and slogans by the electronic media, advanced technology, and the press; in the ease with which propaganda, commercial and political, invades every home; in the growing bureaucratization of society, producing endless compartmentalization and specialized jargon. The hallmarks of this invasion, speed and mechanical agglomeration, are most sharply caught by Ionesco's manic word-torrents in *The Bald Soprano* and *The Lesson*, and by Havel's mechanical repetitions of official jargon, as though a machine were jammed into "replay," in *The Garden Party*. The speed with which new jargon and cliché are produced in the process, and the opaque, anonymous, traditionless nature of this verbal flood, are perhaps responsible for the "nausea" which many of the dramatists I discuss experienced when faced with the need to mold public speech into private expression.

It is interesting, and probably more than coincidental, that almost all the authors studied here wrote their language-oriented plays early in their careers. Most of them later develop in other directions, some totally abandoning a language-oriented dramaturgy, others metamorphosing these concerns into broader social critiques. It seems likely that one reason for this has to do with a young playwright's early confrontation with the medium of his craft, language, and finding the words so tainted by the ubiquitous slogans and platitudes of commercial and political propaganda, so apt to form automatic verbal chains tacked together "like the sections of a prefabricated hen-house," as Orwell put it,[2] that the resistance of language to personal meaning became painfully apparent. This is attested to by, for example, Ionesco's language-inflicted vertigo and nausea, his awareness that words "had gone mad" which led to the writing of his first play.[3] Pinter experienced, and describes, a similar language-nausea:

Such a weight of words confronts us day in, day out, words spoken in contexts such as this, words written by me and by others, the bulk of it stale and dead terminology; ideas endlessly repeated and permutated, become platitudinous, trite, meaningless. Given this nausea, it's very easy to be overcome by it and step back into paralysis. I imagine most writers know something of this paralysis. But if it is possible to confront this nausea, to follow it to its hilt, then it is possible to say something has occurred, that something has been achieved.[4]

What Pinter achieves by "confronting" his nausea is an indictment of its source. Handke goes so far as to *recommend* nausea as an appropriate response to language manipulation: "One should learn to be nauseated by language, as the hero of Sartre's *Nausea* is by things. At least that would be a beginning of consciousness."[5] In his radio-play *All That Fall* (1956), Beckett, in a lighter vein, writes of his own nausea, of the "excruciating" feeling which results from "overhearing" the way language speaks *us*:

MRS. ROONEY: No, no. I am agog, tell me all, then we shall press on and never pause, never pause, till we come safe to haven. (*Pause*)
MR. ROONEY: Never pause … safe to haven … Do you know, Maddy, sometimes one would think you were struggling with a dead language.
MRS. ROONEY: Yes indeed, Dan, I know full well what you mean. I often have that feeling, it is unspeakably excruciating.
MR. ROONEY: I confess I have it sometimes myself, when I happen to overhear what I am saying.[6]

But can one really portray language, and its dangers, *through* language? Such a procedure can lead to a certain abstractness, and courts the danger of circularity. Using language to critique language – as Wittgenstein was well aware, and herein lies one of his main criticisms of Mauthner[7] – can be self-defeating. The inevitable regression which results from this is, however, to an extent minimized by the adoption of dramatic devices through which language is *objectified*. Handke's bodiless Prompters, who represent social norms and speech-dictates (*Kaspar*); Pinter's "organization men," who are a medium for socially endorsed values and idioms (*The Birthday Party*); Havel's dehumanized dogma-machine, Pludek, who finally becomes identical with the jargon he spouts (*The Garden Party*); Kroetz's or Bond's uncommented, realistic replay of a speech-world wrought merely from platitutdes and quotes – act as dramatic objects through which the action of language is both tested and exemplified.

Moreover, these "objectified" representatives of language help to locate the sources of language perversion within a broader social context, and point to the inevitable link between language and values, between speech options and morality. The Prompters, Ionesco's Professor, Goldberg and McCann, Pludek, all speak for, and in the voice of, a ruling social or political discourse. On the other hand, the characters of Kroetz, Bond, and to an extent Mamet, personify the moral and physical debasement of the socially disenfranchised, those denied, or in any case lacking, "owned" language or speech options. But the struggle in these plays is not only with language, it is also *for* language – for the possession of language. The language-battles between Martha and George (*Who's Afraid of Virginia Woolf?*) or Hoss and Crow (*The Tooth of Crime*) implicitly equate reality with the discourse which defines it. Power struggles are carried out not through, but within language. And the ground against which these struggles take place is the verbal and gestural conventions found in the world of the audience.

Language aggression is not only demonstrated and discussed in these plays, it is also practised upon the audience. The audience is drawn into the text and subjected through language in ways parallel to the sufferings of the characters. Handke wrote the paradigmatic play of such audience torture in *Offending the Audience*, in which the habits and docility of the audience become the material of the drama and the object of the actors' abuse. But audience abuse through verbal manipulation is also apparent in the intermission text of *Kaspar*, in the irritating and opaque verbal torture scenes of *The Birthday Party*, in the inscrutable jargon, or verbal inventions, in *The Memorandum*, *Glengarry Glen Ross*, or *The Tooth of Crime*. These devices purposely alienate and frustrate the audience and thus set up a relationship of antagonism between it and the language. But the audience is not only victimized and antagonized; it is also cast in the role of accomplice. For it is through the consciousness of the audience that the torture of the characters becomes possible and meaningful. Kaspar is taught our grammatical structures and dictums of order; Stanley (*The Birthday Party*) is attacked with clichés, truisms, and consumer banalities lifted from the world of the audience; the hopeless fatuities of Kroetz's characters implicate the verbally superior audience who alone understands what the characters cannot begin to say, and whose verbal superiority, like that of Handke's tycoon Quitt, becomes the ground against which the characters' poverty is measured. These plays demand the audience's active participation in decoding the systems which determine *it* no less than the characters on stage. If the power of language can destroy, then the audience both shares in that power and is itself in its thrall. It is perhaps in the gap between the audience's superiority to the characters and its resemblance to them, that understanding and awareness of the dangers of language manipulation and domination reside.

Notes

1 INTRODUCTION

1 Jean Vannier, "Langages de L'Avant-Garde," *Théâtre Populaire* 18 (May 1956), pp. 30–9; "A Theatre of Language," trans. Leonard C. Pronko, *Tulane Drama Review* 7(3) (Spring 1963), pp. 180–6. The following is quoted from the English translation, pp. 181–2.

2 Martin Esslin, *The Theatre of the Absurd*, revised edn. (Harmondsworth, Middlesex: Penguin Books, 1968), pp. 389–400.

3 Eugène Ionesco, as quoted by Richard Schechner in 'The Inner and the Outer Reality," *Tulane Drama Review* 7(3) (Spring 1963), p. 92.

4 Erich Heller, *The Ironic German: A Study of Thomas Mann* (London: Secker and Warburg, 1958), p. 22.

5 W. B. Yeats, *Explorations* (London: Macmillan, 1962), p. 167.

6 Hugo von Hofmannsthal, "The Letter of Lord Chandos," in *Selected Prose*, trans. M. Hottinger and T. and J. Stern (New York: Pantheon Books, 1952), pp. 131 and 135.

7 Hugo von Hofmannsthal, *The Difficult Man*, trans. Willa Carter in *Selected Plays and Libretti*, ed. Michael Hamburger, Bollingen Series XXXIII, Vol. 3 (New York: Pantheon Books, 1963), p. 759.

8 Ludwig Wittgenstein, *Philosophical Investigations*, trans. and ed. G.E.M. Anscombe (New York: Macmillan, 1953), p. 47e.

9 See Terry Eagleton, *Literary Theory: An Introduction* (Oxford: Basil Blackwell, 1983), p. 112.

10 Jonathan Culler, *Structuralist Poetics* (Ithaca: Cornell University Press, 1975), p. 28.

2 LANGUAGE TORTURE

1 Martin Heidegger, *Der Satz vom Grund* (Pfullingen: S. Neske, 1957), p. 161; my translation.

2 Peter Handke, *Kaspar*, in *Kaspar and Other Plays*, trans. Michael Roloff (New York: Farrar, Straus and Giroux, 1969), p. 59.

3 *Ibid.*, p. 59.

4 *Ibid.*, p. 59. Roloff translates "den Helden" as "the Protagonist"; I think "Hero" is better here.

5 *Ibid.*, p. 60. Roloff has deleted the words "other than their own" in his translation. They appear in the German original: *Kaspar* (Frankfurt-am-Main: Suhrkamp, 1967), p. 8.

6 Peter Handke, as quoted by Artur Joseph in "Nauseated by Language: From an Interview with Peter Handke," trans. E. B. Ashton, *The Drama Review* 15(1) (Fall 1970), pp. 56–61; p. 58.

7 *Ibid.*, p. 61.

8 Richard Gilman, *The Making of Modern Drama* (New York: Farrar, Straus and Giroux, 1974), pp. 270–1.

9 Joseph interview, p. 61.

10 Eugène Ionesco, *Notes and Counter Notes*, trans. Donald Watson (New York: Grove Press, 1964), p. 179.

11 Joseph interview, p. 57.

12 Peter Handke, "Note on *Offending the Audience and Self-Accusation*," in *Kaspar and Other Plays*, unnumbered page.

13 Peter Handke, *Ich bin ein Bewohner des Elfenbeinturms* (Frankfurt-am-Main: Suhrkamp, 1972), p. 20; my translation.

14 Hofmannsthal, "The Letter of Lord Chandos," pp. 134–5.

15 Karl Kraus, *Beim Wort genommen* (Munich: Kösel Verlag, 1955).

16 Wittgenstein, *Philosophical Investigations*, p. 47e.

17 Joseph interview, p. 57.

18 Gilman, *The Making of Modern Drama*, p. 288.

19 See William Barrett, *The Illusion of Technique* (New York: Doubleday, 1978), especially Part I, on Wittgenstein.

20 Ludwig Wittgenstein, *Tranctatus Logico-Philosophicus*, bi-lingual edition, translator not given (London: Kegan Paul, Trench, Trubner and Co., 1922; rpt. 1947), section 5.6, p. 149.

21 Quotations from *Kaspar* will be followed parenthetically by the number of the section to which they refer, unless otherwise noted.

22 This is how Kaspar Hauser's sentence is transcribed by A. Ritter von Feuerbach, *Kaspar Hauser, Beispiel eines Verbrechens am Seelenleben des Menschen* (Ansbach: J. M. Dollfuss, 1832). For a more recent historical study of Kaspar Hauser see F. Merkenschlager and K. Saller, *Kaspar Hauser, ein zeitloses Problem* (Nuremberg: Spindler, 1966).

23 See R. D. Theisz, "Kaspar Hauser im zwanzigsten Jahrhundert. Der Aussenseiter und die Gesellschaft," *German Quarterly* 49(2) (March 1976), pp. 168–80. Theisz studies the Kaspar Hauser motif in twentieth-century literature, especially Jakob Was-

sermann's novel *Kaspar Hauser oder die Trägheit des Herzens* (1908);
Georg Trakl's poem "Kaspar Hauser Lied" (1913); Hans Arp's
poem "Kaspar ist tot" (1920); and Handke's play *Kaspar*.
Handke himself prefaces his play with Ernst Jandl's "concrete"
poem "16 Jahr," which refers to the lisping, astounded Kaspar
Hauser when he first appears in society at the age of sixteen.

24 Joseph interview, p. 60.
25 *Ibid.*, p. 60.
26 See Wolfram Buddecke and Jörg Hienger, "Jemand lernt
   sprechen: Sprachkritik bei Peter Handke," *Neue Sammlung* 11(6)
   (1971), pp. 556–8.
27 Joseph interview, p. 61.
28 Roland Barthes, *The Pleasure of the Text*, trans. Richard Miller
   (New York: Hill and Wang, 1975), p. 50.
29 Benjamin Lee Whorf, *Language, Thought, and Reality* (Cambridge,
   Mass.: MIT Press, 1956), p. 258.
30 *Ibid.*, p. 156; my emphasis.
31 Peter Handke, *Hörspiel*, no. 1, in *Wind und Meer, Vier Hörspiele*
   (Frankfurt-am-Main: Suhrkamp, 1970), pp. 93–4; my translation.
32 Wittgenstein, *Tractatus*, section 4.01, p. 63.
33 *Ibid.*, sections 2.131 and 2.16, pp. 39 and 40.
34 *Ibid.*, section 4.116, pp. 77 and 79.
35 See Barrett, *The Illusion of Technique*, pp. 34–6, on "picture
   theory" and "mirroring." An excellent reading of the implications and sources of Wittgenstein's "picture" theory and his
   critique of language is offered by Allan Janik and Stephen
   Toulmin in *Wittgenstein's Vienna* (New York: Simon and Schuster,
   1973); see especially pp. 182–90.
36 Whorf, *Language, Thought, and Reality*, p. 148.
37 *Ibid.*, pp. 213–14; Whorf's emphasis.
38 *Ibid.*, p. 221.
39 Roland Barthes, "Inaugural Lecture, Collège de France," trans.
   Richard Howard, in Susan Sontag, ed., *A Barthes Reader* (New
   York: Hill and Wang, 1982), pp. 460–1.
40 Whorf, *Language, Thought, and Reality*, p. 212.
41 In *Die Innenwelt der Aussenwelt der Innenwelt* (Frankfurt-am-Main:
   Suhrkamp, 1969), pp. 96–7; my translation.
42 These are, with a slight variation, the last words spoken by
   Elisabeth before she dies in Ödön von Horváth's *Glaube Liebe
   Hoffnung (Faith, Hope, and Charity*, 1936).
43 Nicholas Hern, *Peter Handke: Theatre and Anti-Theatre* (London:
   Oswald Wolff, 1971), p. 67.
44 Joseph interview, p. 61.

45 Suhrkamp first published *Kaspar* in 1967 with this last sentence in the text. It was deleted in subsequent printings.

46 Culler, *Structuralist Poetics*, p. 29; my emphasis.

47 Claude Lévi-Strauss, *La Pensée sauvage* (Paris: Plon, 1962), p. 326; quoted and trans. by Culler, *Structuralist Poetics*, p. 28.

48 Joseph interview, p. 61.

49 See Michel Foucault, *Madness and Civilization*, trans. Richard Howard (New York: Pantheon, 1965) for an expansion of this idea.

50 *Kaspar*, p. 8 of the German (Suhrkamp) edition; p. 60 of Roloff trans., but Roloff leaves out the last clause of the sentence.

51 Wittgenstein, *Tractatus*, section 6.54, p. 189.

52 Handke's suggestions for this text (section 59) are very precise, even though he writes that "The text might be as follows."

53 In Joseph interview, p. 58, Handke says: "If the theatre makes us aware that there are functions of man's power over man that we didn't know about, functions that we accept by force of habit; if these functions suddenly strike us as man-made, as not at all nature-given [...] then the theatre can be a moral institution [...]."

54 Barthes, "Inaugural Lecture," p. 461.

55 Peter Handke, "Beschreibungsimpotenz, zur Tagung der Gruppe '47 in USA," first published in *konkret* (June 1966). Also appears in *Elfenbeinturms*, p. 34; my translation.

56 Whorf, *Language, Thought, and Reality*, p. 156.

57 Handke, *Elfenbeinturms*, p. 30; my translation.

58 Fritz Mauthner, *Beiträge zu einer Kritik der Sprache*, 3rd edn. (Leipzig, 1923; rpt. Hildesheim: Georg Olms, 1967), Vol. 1, pp. 39ff.

59 George Orwell, *Nineteen Eighty-Four* (New York: Harcourt, Brace and Co., Inc.; Signet Classic, 1949), p. 46.

3 GAGGED BY LANGUAGE

1 Esslin's original edition (1961) did not include Havel, since Havel only wrote his first play in 1963.

2 Martin Esslin, *The Theatre of the Absurd*, revised and enlarged 1968 edn. p. 396.

3 See *Ibid.*, chapter 7, "The Significance of the Absurd," for further details.

4 See *Ibid.*, chapter 6, "The Tradition of the Absurd," for further details.

5 J. S. Doubrovsky, "Ionesco and the Comic of Absurdity," *Yale French Studies* 23 (1959), p. 8.

6 Eugène Ionesco. *The Lesson*, trans. Donald Watson, in *Rhinoceros, The Chairs, The Lesson* (Harmondsworth, Middlesex: Penguin Books, 1962), pp. 183–4. Subsequent page references will appear parenthetically within the text and will refer to this edition.

7 Henri Bergson, "Laughter," translator not given, in Wylie Sypher, ed., *Comedy* (New York: Doubleday Anchor, 1956), p. 79.

8 Richard N. Coe, *Eugène Ionesco* (New York: Grove Press, 1961; revised edn. 1970), p. 37.

9 Claude Bonnefoy, *Conversations with Eugène Ionesco*, trans. Jan Dawson (New York: Holt, Rinehart and Winston, 1970), p. 110.

10 *Ibid.*, p. 107.

11 Ronald Hayman, *Eugène Ionesco* (New York: Frederick Ungar, 1976). p. 32.

12 Esslin, *The Theatre of the Absurd*, p. 143.

13 Cornelia Berning, *Vom "Abstammungsnachweis" zum "Zuchtwart": Vokabular des Nationalsozialismus* (Berlin: Walter de Gruyter and Co., 1964), p. 7.

14 *Ibid.*, p. 33.

15 Bonnefoy, *Conversations*, p. 113.

16 Dolf Sternberger, "Vorbemerkung 1967," in Dolf Sternberger, Gerhard Storz, and Wilhelm E. Süskind, *Aus dem Wörterbuch des Unmenschen*, 3rd edn. (Hamburg: Classen Verlag, 1968), p. 12.

17 Eugène Ionesco, *Jack, or the Submission*, trans. Donald M. Allan, in *Four Plays* (New York: Grove Press, 1958), p. 86.

18 *Ibid.*, p. 84.

19 Eugène Ionesco, *Le Roi se meurt*, in *Théâtre IV* (Paris: Gallimard, 1963), p. 43; my translation.

20 Bonnefoy, *Conversations*, p. 111.

21 Harold Pinter, *The Birthday Party*, in *The Birthday Party and The Room* (New York: Grove Press, 1968), revised edn., p. 23. Three versions of this play appeared: 1959, 1960, 1965. I use the 1965 text throughout. Subsequent page references will appear parenthetically within the text and will refer to this edition.

22 Richard Schechner, "Puzzling Pinter," *Tulane Drama Review* 11(2) (Winter 1966), pp. 177–8.

23 Raymond Williams, *Drama from Ibsen to Brecht* (Harmondsworth, Middlesex: Penguin Books, 1968), p. 372.

24 John Russell Brown, *Theatre Language* (London: Allen Lane, Penguin Press, 1972), p. 39.

25 Martin Esslin, *The Peopled Wound: The Plays of Harold Pinter* (London: Methuen and Co., 1970), p. 78.

26 Austin E. Quigley, *The Pinter Problem* (Princeton, New Jersey: Princeton University Press, 1975), p. 64.

27 Harold Pinter, *The Caretaker* (London: Methuen and Co., 1960), p. 36.
28 Harold Pinter, *The Homecoming* (New York: Grove Press, 1966), p. 51.
29 G. L. Evans, *The Language of Modern Drama* (New Jersey: Dent, 1977), p. 171.
30 Orwell, *Nineteen Eighty-Four*, p. 220.
31 *Ibid.*, p. 211.
32 Peter Handke, *Kaspar*, trans. Michael Roloff, p. 97
33 *Ibid.*, pp. 100–1.
34 Schechner, "Puzzling Pinter," p. 177.
35 Harold Pinter, *The Dwarfs*, in *Three Plays* (New York: Grove Press, 1961), p. 97. Subsequent page references will appear parenthetically within the text and will refer to this edition.
36 Austin E. Quigley, "*The Dwarfs*: A Study in Linguistic Dwarfism," *Modern Drama* 17(4) (December 1974), p. 414.
37 *Ibid.*, p. 417.
38 *Ibid.*, p. 417, my emphases.
39 Milan Kundera has been living in Paris since the early seventies. He is best known for his novels, although he has also written plays, most notably *Jacques and His Master* (first version, 1971). Pavel Kohout, whose play *Poor Murderer* was staged in New York in 1981, lives in Vienna. Other less known Czech playwrights still living in Czechoslovakia, who shared Havel's fate of official "invisibility" in their own country, are Ivan Klíma and Milan Uhde. See Marketa Goetz-Stankiewicz, "Introduction" to *Drama Contemporary: Czechoslovakia* (New York: Performing Arts Journal Publications, 1985), pp. 13–16.
40 See Marketa Goetz-Stankiewicz, "Ethics at the Crossroads: The Czech 'Dissident Writer' as Dramatic Character," *Modern Drama* 27(1) (March 1984), pp. 112–23, for a discussion of how these two careers have merged in his trilogy: *Audience* (1975), *Vernissage* (1975), and *Protest* (1978).
41 Jan Grossman, "A Preface to Havel," translator not given, *Tulane Drama Review* 11(3) (Spring 1967), p. 118.
42 *Ibid.*, p. 119.
43 Quoted in J. M. Burian, "Post-War Drama in Czechoslovakia," *Educational Theatre Journal* 25(3) (October 1973), pp. 299–317; p. 311.
44 Václav Havel, *The Garden Party*, trans. and adapted by Vera Blackwell (London: Jonathan Cape, 1969; the Czech original appeared in 1964), pp. 10–11. This is the only English translation of the play available. It does not always read very well; Blackwell

seems to prefer literal to literary translation. Subsequent page references will appear parenthetically within the text and will refer to this edition.

45 Karl Popper, *Unended Quest* (La Salle, Illinois: Open Court Pub. Co., 1974), p. 42.
46 See Paul I. Trensky, *Czech Drama Since World War II* (New York: Columbia Slavic Studies, 1978), p. 108.
47 *Ibid.*, p. 113.
48 Fredric Jameson, *Marxism and Form* (Princeton, New Jersey: Princeton University Press, 1971; first Princeton paperback edn., 1974), p. 53.
49 *Ibid.*, p. 53.
50 Václav Havel, "On Dialectical Metaphysics," trans. Michal Schonberg, *Modern Drama* 23(1) (March 1980), pp. 6–12; p. 7.
51 *Ibid.*, p. 8.
52 Václav Havel, *The Memorandum*, trans. and adapted by Vera Blackwell (London: Jonathan Cape, 1967; the Czech edition appeared in 1966). See my comment in note 44; the same applies here. Subsequent page references will appear parenthetically within the text and will refer to this edition.
53 Orwell, *Nineteen Eighty-Four*, p. 46.
54 *Ibid.*, p. 246.
55 Martin Esslin, *Reflections: Essays on Modern Theatre* (New York: Doubleday and Co., 1961; Anchor Books edn., 1971), p. 138.
56 Václav Havel, "Acceptance Speech" for the Peace Prize of the German Booksellers Association, trans. A. G. Brain. Published in the *New York Review of Books*, 18 January 1990, p. 8.
57 Mandelstam's poem, in Robert Lowell's adaptation, appears in George Steiner, *Extraterritorial* (New York: Atheneum, 1976), pp. 151–2.
58 *Ibid.*, p. 152
59 Orwell, *Nineteen Eighty-Four*, p. 210.
60 George Orwell, "Politics and the English Language, in *A Collection of Essays* (New York: Doubleday Anchor, 1954), p. 170.
61 Herbert Marcuse, "The Closing of the Universe of Discourse," in *One-Dimensional Man* (Boston: Beacon Press, 1964), p. 87.
62 *Ibid.*, pp. 90–1; my emphasis.
63 Orwell, "Politics and the English Language," p. 165.
64 *Ibid.*, p. 172.
65 Marcuse, "The Closing of the Universe," p. 85.
66 Sternberger, "Vorbemerkung 1967," pp. 11–12.
67 Eugène Ionesco, *Notes and Counter Notes*, trans. Donald Watson (New York: Grove Press, 1964), p. 92.

68 *Ibid.*, p. 66.
69 Hannah Arendt, *On Violence* (New York: Harcourt, Brace and World, 1970), pp. 38–9.
70 Marcuse, "The Closing of the Universe," p. 88.
71 Susan Sontag, in her "Introduction" to *A Barthes Reader*, p. xxxi.
72 Roland Barthes, "Inaugural Lecture," p. 461.
73 *Ibid.*, p. 460.
74 Bernard-Henri Lévy, *Barbarism with a Human Face*, trans. George Holoch (New York: Harper Colophon, 1979), p. 32. Lévy quotes from Oswald Spengler's *The Decline of the West*.
75 Lévy, no longer quoting Spengler, pp. 32 and 34; Lévy's emphasis.
76 *Ibid.*, pp. 146–7.

4   LANGUAGE AS A PRISON

1 Peter Handke, *They Are Dying Out*, trans. Michael Roloff in collaboration with Karl Weber (London: Eyre Methuen, 1974), p. 38.
2 *Ibid.*, pp. 38–9.
3 Marieluise Fleisser, "Alle meine Söhne. Über Martin Sperr, Rainer Werner Fassbinder und Franz Xaver Kroetz," in Günther Rühle, ed., *Materialien zum Leben und Schreiben der Marieluise Fleisser* (Frankfurt-am-Main: Suhrkamp, 1973), p. 410; my translation.
4 Franz Xaver Kroetz, "Liegt die Dummheit auf der Hand?" in *Weitere Aussichten...* (Cologne: Kieperheuer and Witsch, 1976), p. 525.
5 Kroetz, *Weitere Aussichten...*, p. 605.
6 All of these early plays can be found in Franz Xaver Kroetz, *Gesammelte Stücke* (Frankfurt-am-Main: Suhrkamp, 1972). Subsequent references to these plays will appear parenthetically within the text, by act and scene numbers. All translations are my own unless otherwise noted. Full English translations of *Farmyard* and *Michi's Blood* can be found in Franz Xaver Kroetz, *Farmyard and Four Plays* (New York: Urizen Books, 1976).
7 See Harald Burger and Peter von Matt, "Dramatischer Dialog und restringiertes Sprechen. F. X. Kroetz in linguistischer und literaturwissenschaftlicher Sicht," *Zeitschrift für Germanistische Linguistik* 2(3) (1974). This excellent and detailed article provides a careful socio-linguistic analysis of Kroetz, applied mainly to his play *Oberösterreich* (1972), but is equally useful for Kroetz's earlier work.

8 Wilhelm von Humboldt, *Linguistic Variability and Intellectual Development*, trans. G. C. Buck and F. A. Raven (Philadelphia: University of Pennsylvania Press, 1971), p. 39.

9 See Burger and von Matt, "Dramatischer Dialog," pp. 272–4.

10 *Ibid.*, p. 281.

11 The following is drawn from Basil Bernstein, "Elaborated and Restricted Codes: Their Social Origins and Some Consequences," in *The Ethnography of Communication*, ed. J. J. Gumperz and Dell Hymes, a Monograph issue of the series *American Anthropologist* 66(6), part 2 (March 1964).

12 Burger and von Matt, "Dramatischer Dialog," suggest that Kroetz's dialogues are "almost didactic illustrations of a clear socio-linguistic concept [...] as exemplary and significant as any sociolinguist could desire," p. 270; my translation.

13 "Preface" to *Heimarbeit*, when first published in *Drei Stücke* (Frankfurt-am-Main: Suhrkamp, 1971), p. 6. In the *Gesammelte Stücke* this Preface has been removed.

14 Kroetz, "Horváth von heute für heute," in *Weitere Aussichten...*, p. 520; my translations.

15 Richard Gilman, 'Introduction' to Kroetz, *Farmyard and Four Plays*, p. 14.

16 Burger and von Matt, "Dramatischer Dialog," p. 291.

17 See Christopher Innes, "Edward Bond's Political Spectrum," *Modern Drama* 25(2) (June 1982), pp. 189–206; pp. 196–7, in which Innes compares Bond and Kroetz in terms of their political use of speechlessness.

18 Herbert Kretzmer, "Saved," in Geoffrey Morgan, ed., *Contemporary Theatre* (London: Magazine Editions, 1968), p. 45.

19 Edward Bond, "Author's Preface" to *Lear*, in *Plays: Two* (London: Eyre Methuen, revised edn. 1978), p. 3.

20 Edward Bond, *Saved*, in *Plays: One* (London: Eyre Methuen, revised edn. 1977), p. 71. Subsequent scene references will appear parenthetically within the text and will refer to this edition.

21 *Ibid.*, "Author's Note" to *Saved*, p. 49.

22 Martin Esslin, "Edward Bond's Three Plays," in *Brief Chronicles* (London: Temple Smith, 1970), p. 175.

23 See William Babula, "Scene Thirteen of Bond's *Saved*," *Modern Drama* 15(3) (September 1972), pp. 147–9, for a discussion of this scene and its sexual overtones.

24 Edward Bond, *The Pope's Wedding*, in *Plays: One*. Subsequent scene references will appear parenthetically within the text and will refer to this edition.

25 John Worthen, "Endings and Beginnings: Edward Bond and the

Shock of Recognition," *Educational Theatre Journal* 27(4) (1975), pp. 466–79; p. 469.

26 Walter Kerr, "Language Alone Isn't Drama," *The New York Times*, Sunday, 6 March 1977, section D, p. 3.

27 Clive Barnes, "Skilled *American Buffalo*," *The New York Times*, 17 February 1977, p. 50.

28 David Mamet, *American Buffalo* (New York: Grove press, 1976). Subsequent page references will appear parenthetically within the text and will refer to this edition.

29 Bernstein, "Elaborated and Restricted Codes," p. 59.

30 Quoted by C. W. E. Bigsby, in his monograph: *David Mamet*, Contemporary Writers series (London: Methuen, 1985), p. 19.

31 Bigsby, *David Mamet*, p. 67.

32 Mamet, in an interview with Richard Gottlieb, *The New York Times*, 15 January 1978, section D, p. 4.

33 Robert Storey, "The Making of David Mamet," *The Hollins Critic* 16 (October 1979), p. 2.

34 Bigsby, *David Mamet*, p. 17.

35 David Mamet, *Glengarry Glen Ross* (London: Methuen, 1984). Subsequent page references will appear parenthetically within the text and will refer to this edition.

36 Marcuse, "The Closing of the Universe," p. 88. See my discussion of this in chapter 3, above.

37 "Author's Note" to *Glengarry Glen Ross*, p. 1.

38 Bigsby, *David Mamet*, p. 123.

39 Whorf, *Language, Thought, and Reality*, pp. 256–8.

5 WRESTLING WITH LANGUAGE

1 This remark by a member of the Pulitzer Prize full committee is quoted in Wendell V. Harris, "Morality, Absurdity, and Albee," *Southwest Review* (Summer 1964), p. 249.

2 See Michael E. Rutenberg, *Edward Albee: Playwright in Protest* (New York: Avon Books, 1969), p. 93.

3 Sam Shepard, *The Tooth of Crime*, in *The Tooth of Crime and Geography of a Horse Dreamer* (New York: Grove Press, 1974), p. 49. Subsequent page references will appear parenthetically within the text and will refer to this edition.

4 Ruby Cohn, *Currents in Contemporary Drama* (Bloomington: Indiana University Press, 1969), chapter 2: "Dialogue of Cruelty." Cohn applies this category to a group of plays which, she claims, are influenced by Strindberg's use of verbal cruelty.

5 Edward Albee, *Who's Afraid of Virginia Woolf?* (New York: Pocket

Books, Cardinal Edition, 1962), p. 92. Subsequent page references will appear parenthetically within the text and will refer to this edition.

6 August Strindberg, *The Father*, trans. Arvid Paulson, in *Seven Plays by August Strindberg* (New York: Bantam Books, 1960), p. 36. Subsequent page references will appear parenthetically within the text and will refer to this edition.

7 See Roger Shattuck, *The Banquet Years* (New York: Vintage Books, Random House, 1955; revised edn., 1968), pp. 206–11, for a description of reactions to *Ubu Roi*'s first performance.

8 See C. W. E. Bigsby, *Albee* (Edinburgh: Oliver and Boyd, 1969), pp. 47–9, for an expanded treatment of New Carthage, Spengler, and St. Augustine.

9 *Ibid.*, p. 38.

10 P. Watzlawick, J. H. Beavin, D. D. Jackson, *Pragmatics of Human Communication: A Study of Interactional Patterns, Pathologies, and Paradoxes* (New York: W. W. Norton and Co., 1967), chapter 5, "A Communicational Approach to the Play *Who's Afraid of Virginia Woolf?*"

11 *Ibid.*, p. 150.

12 *Ibid.*, p. 153.

13 See e.g. Eric Berne, *Games People Play* (New York: Grove Press, 1964).

14 Watzlawick *et al.*, *Pragmatics*, pp. 157, 160, and 182 respectively.

15 *Ibid.*, pp. 168–9.

16 Edward Albee, *The American Dream*, in *Two Plays by Edward Albee* (New York: Signet Books, 1959), pp. 62, 83, and 95 respectively.

17 Ruby Cohn, *Dialogue in American Drama* (Bloomington: Indiana University Press, 1971), p. 137.

18 See June Schlueter, *Metafictional Characters in Modern Drama* (New York: Columbia University Press, 1979), pp. 86–7; and Ruth Meyer, "Language: Truth and Illusion in *Who's Afraid of Virginia Woolf?*", *Educational Theatre Journal* 20(1) (1968), pp. 60–9; p. 65.

19 The major exponent of a variation of this view is Daniel Macdonald, who in "Truth and Illusion in *Who's Afraid of Virginia Woolf?*", *Renascence* 17 (1964), pp. 63–9, claims the "necessity of illusion" for life.

20 Schlueter, *Metafictional Characters*, p. 82.

21 Watzlawick *et al.*, *Pragmatics*, p. 174.

22 Albee, *American Dream*, pp. 113, 107, and 115 respectively.

23 See Robert Brustein, *Seasons of Discontent* (New York: Simon and Schuster, 1959), pp. 155–6.

24 C. W. E. Bigsby, 'Introduction' to *Edward Albee: A Collection of*

Critical Essays, ed. C. W. E. Bigsby (New Jersey: Prentice-Hall, 1975), p. 9.

25 August Strindberg, *The Dance of Death*, trans. Elizabeth Sprigge, in *Five Plays of Strindberg* (New York: Anchor Books, Doubleday and Co., 1960), p. 132. Subsequent page references will appear parenthetically within the text and will refer to this edition.

26 See e.g. Birgitta Steene, *The Greatest Fire: A Study of August Strindberg* (Southern Illinois University Press, 1973), p. 41.

27 Friedrich Dürrenmatt, *Play Strindberg*, trans. James Kirkup (New York: Grove Press, 1973), p. 7.

28 August Strindberg, "Psychic Murder (Apropos 'Rosmersholm')," trans. Walter Johnson, in *Tulane Drama Review* 13(2) (Winter 1968), pp. 113–18.

29 Robert Brustein, *The Theatre of Revolt* (London: Methuen and Co., 1962), p. 106.

30 For a detailed analysis of verbal inventions, usages, and connotations, see Michel Arrivé's semiotic study, *Les Langages de Jarry* (Paris: Klincksieck, 1972), especially pp. 165-319.

31 The history of this famous event is well known and beautifully retold by Shattuck, *The Banquet Years*, especially pp. 203–10. See also Claude Schumacher, *Alfred Jarry and Guillaume Apollinaire* (London: Macmillan Publishers, 1984), chapter 4.

32 *Catholic Transcript*, 1 January 1963.

33 *New York Mirror*, review (no name given), 15 October 1962.

34 Alfred Jarry, *King Ubu*, trans. M. Benedikt ad G. E. Wellwarth, in *Modern French Theatre: The Avant-Garde, Dada, and Surrealism* (New York: Dutton and Co., 1966), p. 8. Subsequent page references will appear parenthetically within the text and will refer to this edition.

35 Watzlawick *et al.*, *Pragmatics*, claim that "Nick and Honey maintain, to each other, an extremely overconventional style of communication" (p. 151), and contrast them with George and Martha's unconventional style.

36 Samuel Beckett, *Waiting for Godot* (New York: Grove Press, 1954), p. 48b.

37 Not only the verbal dimension is simplified in the film; many of the political references and the history/biology antagonism have been delated. The film was very successful: it received three Academy Awards, and six further Academy Award Nominations.

38 Sam Shepard, Interview with the Editors and Kenneth Chubb, "Metaphors, Mad Dogs and Old Time Cowboys," *Theatre Quarterly* 4(15) (1974), p. 10.

39 Sam Shepard in a letter to Richard Schechner, quoted by

Schechner in "The Writer and The Performance Group: Rehearsing *The Tooth of Crime*," in Bonnie Marranca, ed., *American Dreams: The Imagination of Sam Shepard* (New York: Performing Arts Journal Publications, 1981), p. 167. This article first appeared in *Performance* 5 (March/April 1973).

40 See Andrew K. Kennedy, *Dramatic Dialogue* (Cambridge: Cambridge University Press, 1983), p. 250.

41 Sam Shepard, "Language, Visualization and the Inner Library," in *American Dreams*, p. 217. This article first appeared in *The Drama Review* 21(4) (December 1977), pp. 49–58.

42 Shepard, Interview with the Editors, p. 12.

43 Don Shewey, *Sam Shepard* (New York: Dell Publishing Co., 1985), p. 90.

44 Ted Hughes, "A Childish Prank," in his *Crow* (New York: Harper and Row, 1971), p. 7.

45 Bruce W. Powe, "*The Tooth of Crime*: Sam Shepard's Way with Music," *Modern Drama* 21(1) (March 1981), pp. 13–25; p. 22.

46 Gilles Deleuze, "The Schizophrenic and Language," as cited by Leonard Wilcox, "Modernism vs. Postmodernism: Shepard's *The Tooth of Crime* and the Discourses of Popular Culture," *Modern Drama* 30(4) (December 1987), pp. 560–73; p. 562.

47 Wilcox, "Modernism vs. Postmodernism," pp. 555–6.

48 Shepard, "Language, Visualization and the Inner Library," p. 217.

6 CONCLUSION

1 Botho Strauss, "Versuch, ästhetische und politische Ereignisse zusammenzudenken – neues Theater 1967–70," *Theater heute* 11(10) (October 1970), pp. 61–8; quoted in translation by Nicholas Hern, *Peter Handke: Theatre and Anti-Theatre*, p. 93; my emphasis.

2 Orwell, "Politics and the English Language," p. 165.

3 Ionesco, *Notes and Counter Notes*, p. 179.

4 Harold Pinter, "Writing for the Theatre," *Evergreen Review* 33 (August/September 1964), p. 81. This is a revised version of Pinter's speech at the Seventh National Students' Drama Festival, Bristol, first published in *The Sunday Times*, 4 March 1962, with the title "Between the Lines."

5 Handke in Joseph interview, p. 61.

6 Samuel Beckett, *All That Fall* (London: Faber and Faber, 1957), p. 35.

7 See Janik and Toulmin, *Wittgenstein's Vienna*, pp. 180–3.

Index